PENGU

ENLIGHTENMENT

Osho's unique contribution to the understanding of who we are defies categorization. Mystic and scientist, he is a rebellious spirit whose sole interest is to alert humanity to the urgent need to discover a new way of living. To continue as before is to invite threats to our very survival on this unique and beautiful planet.

His essential point is that only by changing ourselves, one individual at a time, can the outcome of all our 'selves'—our societies, our cultures, our beliefs, our world—also change. The doorway to that change is meditation.

Osho the scientist has experimented and scrutinized all the approaches of the past and examined their effects on the modern human being, and responded to their shortcomings by creating a new starting point for the hyperactive twenty-first-century mind: OSHO Active Meditations™.

Once the agitation of a modern lifetime has started to settle, 'activity' can melt into 'passivity', a key starting point of real meditation. To support this next step, Osho has transformed the ancient 'art of listening' into a subtle contemporary methodology: the OSHO Talks™. Here, words become music, the listener discovers who is listening, and the awareness moves from what is being heard to the individual doing the listening. Magically, as silence arises, what needs to be heard is understood directly, free from the distraction of a mind that can only interrupt and interfere with this delicate process.

These thousands of talks cover everything from the individual quest for meaning to the most urgent social and political issues facing society today. Osho's books are not written but are transcribed from audio and video recordings of extemporaneous talks to international audiences. As he puts it, 'So remember: whatever I am saying is not just for you . . . I am talking also for the future generations.'

Osho has been described by the *Sunday Times* of London as one of the '1000 Makers of the 20th Century', and by American author Tom Robbins as 'the most dangerous man since Jesus Christ'. *Sunday Mid-Day* (India) has selected Osho as one of ten people—along with Gandhi, Nehru and Buddha—who have changed the destiny of India.

About his own work, Osho has said that he is helping to create the conditions for the birth of a new kind of human being. He often characterizes this new human being as 'Zorba the Buddha'—capable both of enjoying the earthy pleasures of a Zorba the Greek and the silent serenity of a Gautama the Buddha.

Running like a thread through all aspects of Osho's talks and meditations is a vision that encompasses both the timeless wisdom of all ages past and the highest potential of today's (and tomorrow's) science and technology.

Osho is known for his revolutionary contribution to the science of inner transformation, with an approach to meditation that acknowledges the accelerated pace of contemporary life. His unique OSHO Active Meditations™ are designed to first release the accumulated stresses of body and mind so that it is then easier to take an experience of stillness and thought-free relaxation into daily life.

Two autobiographical works by the author are available: *Autobiography of a Spiritually Incorrect Mystic*, St Martin's Press, New York (book and e-book), and *Glimpses of a Golden Childhood*, OSHO Media International, Pune, India (book and e-book).

OSHO

ENLIGHTENMENT
THE ONLY REVOLUTION

ON THE GREAT MYSTIC ASHTAVAKRA

PENGUIN

ANANDA

PENGUIN ANANDA
Published by the Penguin Group
Penguin Books India Pvt. Ltd, 7th Floor, Infinity Tower C, DLF Cyber City,
Gurgaon 122 002, Haryana, India
Penguin Group (USA) Inc., 375 Hudson Street, New York, New York 10014, USA
Penguin Group (Canada), 90 Eglinton Avenue East, Suite 700, Toronto,
Ontario, M4P 2Y3, Canada
Penguin Books Ltd, 80 Strand, London WC2R 0RL, England
Penguin Ireland, 25 St Stephen's Green, Dublin 2, Ireland (a division of
Penguin Books Ltd)
Penguin Group (Australia), 707 Collins Street, Melbourne, Victoria 3008, Australia
Penguin Group (NZ), 67 Apollo Drive, Rosedale, Auckland 0632, New Zealand
Penguin Books (South Africa) (Pty) Ltd, Block D, Rosebank Office Park,
181 Jan Smuts Avenue, Parktown North, Johannesburg 2193, South Africa

Penguin Books Ltd, Registered Offices: 80 Strand, London WC2R 0RL, England

Published in Hindi as *Mahagita*, Vol.1, by Osho 1976
First published in Penguin Ananda by Penguin Books India 2016
The material in this book is from a series of talks given by Osho to a live audience.

10 9 8 7 6 5 4 3 2 1

ISBN 9780143426394

For sale in the Indian Subcontinent only

Typeset in Sabon by Manipal Digital Systems, Manipal
Printed at Thomson Press India Ltd, New Delhi

A PENGUIN RANDOM HOUSE COMPANY

Contents

Preface

A BEAUTIFUL STORY—very ancient, of the days when the Upanishads were written—is about a man, a young man. He was tremendously intelligent, but he had a body which was so ugly. One hand was long, one hand was small, one eye was missing—even his legs were not of the same length.

There was a great discussion happening in the court of the king, and the father of the young man, a well-known, learned scholar, had gone to participate. But discussions never come to a conclusion—particularly discussions of scholars, and the so-called learned people. If two enlightened persons meet, discussion never starts. Looking into each other's eyes, the conclusion has happened.

So, it was getting late. The mother of the boy told him, 'You should go and see what is happening, and tell your father the food is ready and getting cold.' He went. He was a strangely crippled man, almost like a camel, or perhaps worse. His name was Ashtavakra. 'Ashtavakra' means he was strangely bent in eight places of his body—the hand was not straight; in the middle there was a bend. He could not keep his head straight because his neck was bent. He was certainly made for some circus, some carnival, some museum.

All the learned people were in the court, and as he entered the court, everybody started laughing—they had never seen such a strange creature. But he was immensely intelligent, and finally became one of the great awakened people of the world—of the same height as Gautam Buddha. They were all laughing and joking about him, and his father felt ashamed. Why has he come here?

Ashtavakra went directly to the king and said, 'It seems you have gathered shoemakers here, *chamars*'—that is the word for people who work on leather—'disperse all these idiots! They can only see my skin, my body. They are blind, they don't have any heart—no love, no compassion—and they are talking about self-knowledge, self-realization. What has the self to do with the body?'

There was great silence, because what he said was absolutely true. And he said, 'I had not come here to see all these shoemakers. I have come just to find my father; my mother is waiting.' The king himself was so impressed, because the boy felt neither ashamed nor shocked. But the statement he made was far more important than the things all these learned people had been discussing. 'I am not my body, and these people can see only the body. If they had any self-knowledge, looking at my body, they would not have laughed. They would have felt the presence of a man who is enlightened.'

The whole conference was dissolved, and the king told Ashtavakra, 'From tomorrow you come and teach me, prepare me. I want to be your disciple.'

In the Ashtavakra Gita, the songs of Ashtavakra are compiled, the statements that he made to the king. Each statement is a diamond, invaluable.

Osho
Reflections on Kahlil Gibran's The Prophet

1

The Pure Truth

Janak asked: Oh lord, how does one attain wisdom? How does liberation happen? And how is non-attachment attained? Please tell me this.

Ashtavakra replied: Oh beloved, if you want liberation then renounce the passions as poison, and take forgiveness, innocence, compassion, contentment and truth as nectar. You are neither earth, nor air, nor fire, nor water, nor ether. To attain liberation, know yourself as the witnessing consciousness of all these.

If you can separate yourself from the physical body and rest in consciousness, then this very moment you will be happy, at peace, and free of bondage.

You are not a Brahmin or other caste, you are not in any of the four stages of life, you are not perceived by the eyes or other senses. Unattached and without form, you are the witness of the whole universe. Know this and be happy.

Oh expansive one, religion and atheism, happiness and misery—all are of the mind, they are not for you. You are not the doer nor the enjoyer. You have always been liberated.

WE ARE EMBARKING on a rare journey. Man has many scriptures, but none are comparable to the Gita of Ashtavakra. Before it the Vedas pale, the Upanishads are a mere whisper. Even the Bhagavadgita does not have the majesty found in the Ashtavakra Samhita—it is simply unparalleled.

The most important thing is that neither society, nor politics, nor any other institution of human life had any influence on the statements of Ashtavakra. There are no other statements anywhere that are so pure, transcendental, and beyond time and space. Perhaps that is why Ashtavakra's Gita, the Ashtavakra Samhita, has not had much impact.

Krishna's Bhagavadgita has been very influential. The first reason is that Krishna's Gita is a synthesis. He is more concerned with synthesis than with truth. The desire for synthesis is so strong that if necessary Krishna doesn't mind sacrificing the truth a little.

Krishna's Gita is a hodgepodge containing everything; hence it appeals to everyone, because there is something in it for everyone. It is difficult to find any tradition whose voice is not found in the Gita. It is difficult to find anyone who does not take solace from the Gita. But for such people, Ashtavakra's Gita will prove very difficult.

Ashtavakra is not a synthesizer; he is a speaker of truth. He has spoken the truth as it is without any ifs and buts. He is not worried about the listener. The listener may understand, or may not understand—he is not concerned with that. This kind of purest statement of truth had not happened before and did not happen after.

People love Krishna's Gita because it is very easy to extract one's own meaning from it. Krishna's Gita is poetic: in it two plus two can equal five, two plus two can also equal three. No such tricks are possible with Ashtavakra. With him, two plus two is exactly four. Ashtavakra's statements are statements of pure mathematics. There isn't the least possibility for poetic licence here. He says things as they are, without any sort of compromise.

Reading Krishna's Gita, a devotee extracts something of which he can make a belief, because Krishna spoke on bhakti, devotion. The karma yogi extracts his belief because Krishna has spoken on karma yoga, the yoga of action. The believer in knowledge finds what he wants because Krishna has spoken on knowledge as well. Somewhere Krishna calls devotion the ultimate, somewhere else he calls knowledge the ultimate, again elsewhere he calls karma yoga the ultimate.

Krishna's statements are very political. He was a politician, a perfect politician. Just to say he was a politician is not right; he was a shrewd politician, a real diplomat. In his statements, he considered and included many things. This is why the Gita suits everyone, why there are thousands of commentaries on the Gita.

No one is concerned with Ashtavakra, because to accept Ashtavakra you are going to have to drop yourself—unconditionally. You cannot bring yourself along. Only if you stay behind can you come near him. With Krishna, you can bring yourself along. With Krishna, there is no need to transform yourself. With Krishna, you can fit with him just as you are.

Hence the founders of each tradition have written commentaries on Krishna's Gita—Shankara, Ramanuja, Nimbaraka, Vallabha—everyone. Each has extracted his own meaning. Krishna has said things in such a way as to allow multiple meanings; hence I call his Gita poetic. You can draw out any meaning you like from a poem.

Krishna's statements are like clouds surrounding you in the rainy season: you see in them whatever you want. Someone may see an elephant's trunk, someone sees the whole body of Ganesha, the elephant god. Someone may not see anything. He will say, 'What nonsense! They are clouds, vapour—how is it you see forms in them?'

In the West, psychoanalysts use the inkblot test: just pour some ink on to blotting paper and ask the person to say what he sees in it. The person looks carefully and sees something or other. There is nothing there, only an ink stain on blotting paper—randomly thrown, not thrown with any design, just poured from the bottle. But the person looking at it finds something or other. What he finds is in his mind, he has projected it.

You must have seen lines made by rain falling on a wall. Sometimes a man's face is seen, sometimes a horse's face is seen. You project on to it what you want to see. In the dark of night, clothes hanging on a line seem like ghosts.

Krishna's Gita is just like this—you will be able to see whatever is in your mind. So Shankara sees knowledge, Ramanuja sees devotion, Tilak sees action—and each returns home in a cheerful mood thinking that what Krishna says is the same as his belief.

Emerson has written that once a neighbour came and borrowed the works of Plato from him. Plato lived two thousand years ago and is one of the world's rare, unique thinkers. Weeks later, Emerson reminded him, 'If you've read the books please return them.' When the neighbour returned them Emerson asked, 'How did you like them?'

The man said, 'This man Plato's thoughts are in complete agreement with mine. I felt many times: how has this man come to know my thoughts?' Plato lived two thousand years earlier and this fellow suspects that Plato has stolen his thoughts!

This kind of suspicion often arises with Krishna too. Centuries have passed and commentaries on Krishna keep on coming. Each century finds its own meaning, each person finds his own meaning. Krishna's Gita is like an inkblot . . . it is the statement of the perfect politician.

You cannot extract any beliefs from Ashtavakra's Gita. Only if you drop yourself as you move into it will Ashtavakra's Gita become clear to you. Ashtavakra's message is crystal clear. You won't be able to add even a small bit of your own interpretation to it. Hence people have not written commentaries on Ashtavakra's Gita. There is no scope for writing a commentary; there is no way to distort or twist it. Your mind has no chance to add anything. Ashtavakra has given such an expression that no one has been able to add or take anything from it, even though centuries have passed. It is not easy to give such a perfect expression. Such skill with words is very difficult to come by.

This is why I say we are starting off on a rare journey.

Politicians have no interest in Ashtavakra. Not Tilak, not Aurobindo, not Gandhi, not Vinoba: none of them has any interest, because with Ashtavakra they cannot go on playing their own games. Tilak's interest was to inspire nationalism. He wanted the whole country to get involved in action—and Krishna's Gita was helpful. Krishna is ready to lend a shoulder to anyone. Whosoever wants to steady themselves on his shoulder and shoot their bullets, Krishna is ready. The shoulder is his, you can take the opportunity to hide behind it. And shooting from behind his shoulder makes even bullets appear significant.

Ashtavakra doesn't allow anyone to even rest their hand on his shoulder. So Gandhi is not interested, Tilak is not interested, Aurobindo, Vinoba have nothing to do with him, because they cannot impose anything. There is no room for politics—Ashtavakra is not a political being.

This is the first thing you need to keep in mind: such crystal clarity, an expression like an open sky with no cloud in sight, you cannot see any forms. Only when you drop all forms, become disidentified with all forms and get connected with the formless, will you be able to comprehend Ashtavakra. If you really want to understand Ashtavakra you will have to descend into the depths of meditation. No commentary, no interpretation will be of any help.

And for meditation, Ashtavakra does not ask us to sit and chant 'Ram, Ram'. He says that anything you do will not be meditation. How can there be meditation when there is a doer? As long as there is doing, there is illusion. As long as the doer is present, the ego is present. Ashtavakra says becoming a witness is meditation. Then the doer disappears; you remain only as watcher, nothing but the observer. When you are nothing but the observer, then only is there darshan, seeing; then only is there meditation, then only is there wisdom.

Before we enter the sutras, it is necessary to understand a few things about Ashtavakra. Not much is known as he was neither a social nor a political man, so no historical record exists. Only a few incidents are known—and they are just wondrous, hardly believable. But if you understand them deeply the significance will be revealed.

The first incident happened before Ashtavakra was born. Nothing is known of what came afterwards, but this is an incident while he was still in the womb. His father, who was a great scholar, would recite the Vedas every day while Ashtavakra listened from the womb. One day a voice came from the womb saying, 'Stop it! This is all nonsense. There is no wisdom whatsoever in this. Mere words—just a collection of words. Is wisdom found in scriptures? Wisdom is within oneself. Is truth found in words? Truth is within oneself.'

Naturally his father was enraged. First of all he was a father and on top of that a scholar. And his son hidden in the womb was saying such things! Not even born yet! He exploded in anger, became engulfed in fire—the father's ego had been hit. And a scholar's ego . . . he was a great pundit, a great debater, knowledgeable in scriptures.

In anger he uttered a curse: when born, the boy would be deformed; his limbs would be bent in eight parts. Hence his name: Ashtavakra means one whose body has eight bends. He was born crippled in eight places hunchbacked like a camel. In a rage his father deformed his son's body.

There are other stories like this . . .

It is said that Buddha was born standing up. His mother was standing under a tree; she gave birth standing and he was born standing up. He didn't fall to the ground but started walking! He took seven paces and on the eighth he stopped and proclaimed the four noble truths. He took just seven steps on earth and proclaimed that life is suffering, that it is possible to be free from suffering, that there is a way to become free of suffering, that there is a state free of suffering—the state of nirvana.

About Lao Tzu, the story is that he was born old, that he was born eighty years old, that he remained in the womb for eighty years. Since he had no desire to do anything, he had no desire to leave the womb. Since he had no wants, he didn't want to come into the world either. When he was born he had white hair, an old man of eighty years!

Zarathustra's story is that he burst out laughing as soon as he was born.

But Ashtavakra has defeated them all. These are all events after birth; Ashtavakra made his full statement before he was even born.

These stories are significant. These stories contain the essence, the essential treasure of the life of these masters.

Buddha's story contains the essence of what he taught his whole life . . . Buddha taught the eightfold path, so he took seven steps and stopped on the eighth. There are eight parts in all; the last step is that of right samadhi, and only in that state of samadhi is the whole truth of life known. So he proclaimed the four noble truths.

Lao Tzu was born old. People live eighty years, still they don't have the understanding Lao Tzu had at birth. Do you see people becoming intelligent just by getting old? Getting old and becoming intelligent are not synonymous. At a ripe old age, hair may only be white because it has been bleached by sun.

Lao Tzu's story simply says that if there is urgency, intensity in one's life, then what might take eighty years can happen in one moment. If one's understanding is intense it can happen in one moment, and without pure intelligence it does not happen even in eighty years.

Zarathustra laughed right at birth. Zarathustra's religion is the only religion in the world that can be called a laughing religion . . . very earthy, a religion of the earth. That is why people of other religions don't see Parsees as being religious. They see them dancing, singing, happy— Zarathustra's religion is a laughing religion, a life-affirming religion, not life-negative. There is no place for renunciation in it. Have you ever seen a Parsee sadhu stark naked, having renounced all, standing in the hot sun, sitting facing a fire like a Hindu sannyasin? No, the Parsee religion has no interest in torturing and causing trouble to the body. Zarathustra's whole message is this: if you can realize godliness through laughing, then why realize it crying? When you can reach the temple dancing, why unnecessarily sow thorns on your path? When you can go with flowers, then why follow ways of pain and misery? It is right, the legend is right, that at birth Zarathustra was laughing.

Don't look for historical facts in these stories. It is not that they happened this way, but there is a very profound meaning in these stories.

You have a seed: when you look at the seed you can find no indication of the flowers that will grow from it. There is not even a clue of what it can be. Will it be a lotus—blossoming in the water but remaining untouched by it, dancing in the rays of the sun? And the sun too may become jealous of its beauty, of its tenderness, of its incomparable glory and grace. Its perfume will fly into the sky. Looking at the seed, this cannot be known. Looking at the seed, one cannot even imagine, cannot even guess. But one day it happens.

So we can think in two ways. We can hold tight to the seed and say, 'What is not visible in the seed cannot happen in the lotus either. It is an illusion, it is a trick, it is a lie.' This is the standpoint of those we call rational, sceptics. They say what is not visible in the seed cannot be present in the flower—something is wrong. Hence a sceptical person cannot believe a Buddha, cannot accept a Mahavira, cannot embrace a Jesus, because he says he already knows them.

When Jesus came to his village he was very surprised—the people of the village didn't bother about him at all. Jesus has said a prophet is never respected in his own country. What is the reason? Why won't the village respect its prophet? The village people have seen him as the son of the carpenter Joseph; saw him carrying wood, saw him planing wood, saw him sawing wood, saw him bathed in sweat, saw him playing and fighting in the streets. The people of the village have known him since childhood, have seen him there as a seed. How is it possible that he suddenly becomes the son of God! No, those who saw the seed cannot accept the flower. They say there must be some fraud, some cheating; this man is a hypocrite.

Buddha returned to his village. And the father . . . what the whole world could see, the father could not see. The world was experiencing an illumination, the news was spreading far and wide, people began coming from distant countries. But when Buddha came back to his home after twelve years, his father said, 'I can still forgive you. Though what you did was wrong, you tormented us, you have certainly done a crime, I have a father's heart—I will forgive you. The doors are open for you. Throw away this begging bowl, remove these monk's clothes. None of this will do here. Come back—this kingdom is yours. I have become old; who is going to look after it? Enough of this childishness, now stop all this playing!'

Buddha said, 'Please look at me. The one who left has not returned. Someone else has come; the one who was born in your house has not come back. Someone else is here; the seed has returned as a flower. Look deeply.'

The father said, 'You are going to teach me? I have known you since the day you were born. Go and deceive others; go and lecture other people and delude them—you cannot deceive me. I repeat, I know you perfectly well—don't try to teach me. I am willing to forgive you.'

Buddha said, 'You say you know me? I didn't even know myself before. Only recently have the rays of light descended and I have come to know myself. Excuse me, but I have to say that the one you saw is not me. Whatever you saw is not me. You saw the outer shell, but did you look inside me? I was born out of you but you did not create me. I came via you as a traveller comes via a certain route, but what do the traveller and the road have to do with each other? Suppose that tomorrow the road says "I know you, your being has come from me", just as you are saying.

'I existed before you. I have been on this journey for many lives. I certainly passed through you, as I have passed through others. Others too have been my father, others too have been my mother. But my being is completely separate.'

It is very difficult, extremely difficult: if you saw the seed you cannot believe the flower is in front of you.

One way of looking is that of the distrustful, the rational, the sceptical. They say, 'We know the seed so this flower is not possible. We know the mud—how can a lotus come from it? It is all false—a dream, an illusion. He must have fallen into a kind of hypnosis. Someone deceived him; some magic, some spell . . .'

This is one way. The other is the way of trust—of the lover, the devotee, of the heart filled with empathy. He sees the flower and from the flower begins travelling backwards. He says, 'When the flower has become so fragrant, when such radiance appears in the flower, when there is such beauty in the flower, when such fresh innocence is seen in the flower, then certainly it must also have been present in the seed—because it is not possible that what is present in the flower was not already in the seed.'

It is not that these stories actually happened. Those who saw flowers bloom in Ashtavakra concluded that what has happened today must have also been present yesterday—it was hidden, screened, behind a veil. What is here in the end must have been present at the beginning also. What is seen at the moment of death must also have been present at the moment of birth; otherwise, how could it arise?

So one way is to look backwards from the flower, and the other way is to look forward from the seed. If you look carefully their essence is the same, their foundation is the same, but what a difference—like between earth and sky! The one who knows the seed says, 'How can what is not in the seed be in the flower?' This is his argument. The one who knows the flower says the same thing. He says, 'What is in the flower should be in the seed too.' They have the same argument. But each has a different way of looking.

It is a great hindrance. I have been asked, 'In your childhood, many people studied with you—in school, in college—but they are not to be seen here.' How can they be? It is a great hindrance for them. They cannot believe what they see, it is tremendously difficult for them. Just yesterday somebody sent me a newspaper from Raipur. Shri Harishankar Parsai has written an article against me. He knows me, he knows me from my college days. He is a leading Hindi satirical writer. I have always respected his writing. In the article he writes, 'There must be something wrong with the atmosphere of Jabalpur. Here only swindlers and charlatans are born—like Osho, Mahesh Yogi and Mundhra.'

He listed three names. I must thank him that at least I am number one on his list! He considers me this worthy. He didn't completely push me out of his mind. It is not that he has completely forgotten me. But his difficulty is natural, clear and simple. I can understand his point. It is impossible—he saw the seed; how can he trust the flower? And those who have seen the flower have difficulty trusting in the seed.

So the life story of all great men can be written from two angles. Those who are against him begin the journey from his childhood, and those who are for him begin the journey from the end and go backwards to childhood. Both are right in a way. But those who start with childhood and move towards the end will miss the truth. Their right approach is suicidal. Those who travel from the end and move backwards are blessed. They will get much with no effort . . . much that those thinking the first, the sceptic's way, will not get.

Now not only am I wrong, but because of me, the very air of Jabalpur is wrong! There must be something wrong in the environment. But I want to tell him that Jabalpur has no power over me, whether the environment is good or bad. I don't have much connection with Jabalpur; I was only there for a few years. Mahesh Yogi was also there a few years; he also has no connection.

Both of us are connected with another place. The people of that place are so sleepy that even now they don't know anything about us. Mahesh Yogi's and my places of birth are very near to each other—both of us were born near Gadarwara. He was born in Chichli, I was born in Kuchwada. If the environment is bad, it must be there. Gadarwara should be suffering for it—or receiving the blessing. Jabalpur should not be dragged into this.

But what arguments the mind creates!

Whoever hears Ashtavakra's story will immediately cry, 'False, impossible!' Of course, those who wrote this story know that no one ever speaks from the womb. They are only saying that what finally appears must have been present in the womb. The voice that later blossomed must have been present in some deep place in the womb; otherwise, from where did it blossom, from where did it come? Do things just come out of the void?

There is a reason behind everything. We may not be able to see it but it must have been present. All these stories indicate this.

The second incident known about Ashtavakra happened when he was twelve years old. Only these two incidents are known. The third is his Ashtavakra Gita, or as some call it, the Ashtavakra Samhita. When Ashtavakra was twelve years old, Janak hosted a huge debating conference. Janak was a king, and he invited the pundits of the whole country to debate on the scriptures. He had one thousand cows placed at the palace gate and had the horns of the cows plated with gold and decorated with jewels. He proclaimed, 'Whoever is victorious, shall take possession of these cows.'

It was a great debate. Ashtavakra's father also participated. As dusk was falling, the message came to Ashtavakra that his father was losing. He had already defeated all the others, but he was about to be defeated by a pundit named Vandin. Receiving this message, Ashtavakra went to the palace.

The assembly was already underway; the debate was in its final stage and the decisive moment was fast approaching. His father's defeat was a complete, foregone conclusion—he was on the very edge of defeat.

The pundits saw Ashtavakra as he entered the royal court. They were all learned scholars. His body was bent and deformed in eight places: he had just to move and everyone would start laughing. His very movement was a laughing matter.

The whole assembly broke into laughter. Ashtavakra also roared with laughter. Janak asked, 'Everyone else is laughing. I can understand why they laugh, but why did you laugh, my son?'

Ashtavakra said, 'I am laughing because truth is being decided in this conference of *chamars*, cobblers.' The man must have been extraordinary. 'What are all these chamars doing here?'

A deep silence fell over the assembly. Chamars? Shoemakers?

The king asked, 'What do you mean?'

Ashtavakra said, 'It is simple and straightforward. They only see skin, they don't see me. It is difficult to find a man more pure and simple than me, but they don't see this; they see a bent and deformed body. They are leather workers, they judge by the skin. Your Majesty, in the curve of a temple is the sky curved? When a pot is smashed, is the sky smashed? The sky is beyond change. My body is twisted, but I am not. Look at the one within. You can't find anything more straight and pure.'

It was a very startling declaration. There must have been pin-drop silence. Janak was impressed, astounded: 'Absolutely right, why have I gathered a crowd of chamars here?' He became repentant, he felt guilty that he too had laughed.

That day, the king couldn't manage to say anything, but the following day, when he was out on his morning ride, he saw Ashtavakra on the way. Janak dismounted from his horse and fell at his feet. The day before, in front of everyone, he couldn't find the courage. Then he had said, 'Why do you laugh, my son?' Ashtavakra was a boy of twelve years, and Janak had considered his age. This day, he didn't notice the age. This day, he got down from his horse and fell at Ashtavakra's feet, spreadeagled in prostration.

He said, 'Please visit the palace, and satisfy my eagerness for the truth. Oh lord, be so gracious as to come to my home. I have understood. I couldn't sleep the whole night. You spoke truly: what depth of understanding have those who recognize only the body? They are debating the being, but attraction and repulsion for the body still arise; hate and attraction still arise. They are looking at death while talking of the deathless. I'm blessed that you came and disturbed me, that you broke my sleep. Please come to the palace.'

Janak had the palace decorated magnificently. He welcomed Ashtavakra and seated him on a golden throne— this twelve-year-old Ashtavakra. Then he put his questions to him. The first sutra is Janak's inquiry. Janak asked and Ashtavakra explained. Beyond this, nothing is known about Ashtavakra. And there is no need to know more, it is more than enough. Diamonds are not many; only pebbles and rocks are so common. A single diamond is enough.

These are two small incidents. One before birth: a voice from the womb with the proclamation, 'What madness have you fallen into? Confused by scriptures . . . by words? Wake up! This is not wisdom, this is all borrowed. It is all snares of the mind, not experience. There isn't the slightest bit of reality in it. How long are you going to delude yourself?'

And the second incident: the pundits in the palace laughing and Ashtavakra's saying that in life there are two ways of seeing—one is to see being and the other is to see skin.

Chamars see skin, the wise see being.

Have you noticed? A shoemaker doesn't look at your face, he sees only your shoes. Actually a shoemaker can know everything about you just by looking at your shoes: what your economic situation is, if you are successful or a failure, what your luck is . . . The condition of the shoes tells him. Your autobiography is written on your shoes—the shoemaker can read it. If the shoes are shiny, if the shoes are clean and new, the shoemaker is happy to meet you. For him, your shoes are the proof of your being. A tailor looks at clothes. Seeing how you dress he understands your situation. All have their own narrow vision. Only one full of his own being sees being. He has no fixed vision. He has only seeing, darshan.

One more small incident—it is not about Ashtavakra but about Ramakrishna and Vivekananda, but Ashtavakra is involved in it. After this we will enter the sutras.

When Vivekananda came to Ramakrishna, his name was still Narendranath—later on Ramakrishna named him Vivekananda. When he came to Ramakrishna, he was extremely argumentative, an atheist, a rationalist. He wanted proof for everything.

There are some things that have no proof—it cannot be helped. There is no proof for godliness. It is, and yet there is no proof. There is no proof for love. It is, and yet there is no proof. There is no proof for beauty. It is, and yet there is no proof.

If I say, 'Look how beautiful these ironwood trees are,' and you say, 'I don't see any beauty—trees are just trees. Prove it!'—it will be difficult. How can one prove they are beautiful? To see beauty you need a sense of beauty—there is no other way. You need eyes—there is no other way.

It is reported that Majnu said, 'To know Laila, you will need the eyes of Majnu.' It is true; to see Laila, there is no other way.

The king of his area called Majnu and said, 'You are mad! I know your Laila—an ordinary girl, jet-black—nothing special. I feel sorry for you, so here are twelve girls from my palace—they are the most beautiful women of the country. You can choose any one you like. Seeing you cry, my heart also cries.'

Majnu looked at them and said, 'There is no Laila among them. They cannot even be compared to Laila, they are not even worth the dust of her feet.'

The king said, 'Majnu, you are mad . . . !'

Majnu said, 'That may be so, but I must tell you one thing: to know Laila, you will need the eyes of Majnu.'

Majnu is right. To see the beauty of trees you need an eye for art—there is no proof. If one wants to know love, one will need the heart of a lover—there is no proof. And godliness is the collective name of all the beauty, all the love and all the truth of this universe. For it an unwavering consciousness is needed, a witnessing is needed . . . where no word remains, no thought remains, no wave arises . . . where no mental dust remains and the mirror of consciousness is perfectly pure. What proof?

Vivekananda told Ramakrishna, 'I want proof. If God exists, then prove it.'

Ramakrishna looked at Vivekananda. This youth had great promise, great potential; much was ready to happen within him. There was a great treasure with which Vivekananda was unacquainted. Ramakrishna looked into, peered into, the past lives of this youth. Vivekananda had come carrying a great treasure, a great treasure of integrity, but it was suppressed under his logic. Seeing this, a cry of anguish and compassion must have risen from Ramakrishna's heart. He said, 'Forget all this. We'll talk about proof and such things later on. I have become a little old, I have difficulty reading; you are young, your eyes are still strong—read from the book lying there.' It was the Ashtavakra Gita. 'Read a little out loud to me.'

It is said that Vivekananda saw nothing wrong in this; this fellow was not requesting anything special. He read three or four sutras and his every cell began trembling. He started to panic and he said, 'I cannot read on.'

Ramakrishna insisted, 'Go ahead and read. What harm can there be in it? How can this book hurt you? You are young, your eyes are still fresh, and I am old, it is hard for me to read. I must hear this book—read it out to me.'

It is said that Vivekananda kept on reading aloud from the book, and disappeared in meditation. Ramakrishna had seen great potential in this youth, Vivekananda, a very promising potential, like that of a bodhisattva who one day or other is destined to become a buddha. Sooner or later, no matter how much he wanders, he approaches buddhahood.

Why did Ramakrishna ask that he read the Ashtavakra Gita out loud to him? Because there is no purer statement of truth.

If these words penetrate you, they will start awakening your sleeping soul. These words will thrill you. These words will fill you with ecstasy. These words will shock you.

With these words, a revolution can take place.

I have not chosen the Ashtavakra Gita just like that. Nor could I have chosen it earlier. I have chosen it after a long wait, after much consideration. There was a time when I talked on Krishna's Gita because there was a crowd around me. For a crowd the Ashtavakra Gita has no meaning. With great effort I have got rid of the crowd.

Now there are a few Vivekanandas here.

Now I want to talk to those who have great potential.

I will work with those few on whom work can bring results. Now I will cut diamonds. This chisel is not to be blunted on pebbles and stones. This is why I have chosen the Ashtavakra Gita: I have chosen it because you are ready.

The first sutra:

Janak asked: Oh lord, how does one attain wisdom? How does liberation happen? And how is non-attachment attained? Please tell me this.

'Tell me, Oh lord. Please explain it to me.' To a boy of twelve, King Janak says, 'Oh lord, Bhagwan. Please explain. Give some understanding to an unknowing person like me. Awaken an ignorant person like me.'

Three questions are asked:

How does one attain wisdom? Naturally, we might wonder, why does he need to ask? There are books filled with these things. Janak also knew this.

What books are filled with is not wisdom. It is simply the dust wisdom leaves behind—ash. When the flame of wisdom burns, ash is left behind. Ash goes on accumulating, and it becomes scripture. The Vedas are ashes; once they were burning coals. Vedic sages burned them in their souls and ash was left behind. Then the ashes were collected, compiled and systematically organized.

It is like people collecting the ashes and bones when a man's body has been burned. They call these 'flowers'.

People are very strange. They never called the man a flower when he was alive, but after burning him, they collect his bones saying that they have collected the flowers. Then they preserve them, keep them in a casket. While the man was living they never respected him as a flower; while he was living they never even looked at him as a flower. When he dies . . . man is insane! They call his bones, his ashes, flowers.

In the same way, when a Buddha is alive you do not listen. When a Mahavira walks among you, you get angry. It seems that this man is destroying your dreams or is interfering with your sleep: 'Is this any time to be woken up? Just as my dreams have started coming true, just as success is entering my life, just as my chances are getting better, as the arrow is hitting the target—now this fellow comes and says everything is meaningless! Just as I win the elections and the way is open to get into power, this great man comes along, and says it is all a dream, it has no meaning, that death will come and take everything. Don't talk like this! When death comes we will see, but don't even bring up such things now.'

But when a Mahavira dies or a Buddha dies we collect all their ashes. We create the Dhammapada, we create the Vedas out of them, and then we offer flowers of worship.

Janak also knew that the scriptures are filled just with information. But he asked, *how does one attain wisdom?* Because no matter how much you know, wisdom is not attained. You can go on gathering more and more knowledge, learn the scriptures by heart, become parrots, memorize each and every sutra, let the complete Vedas be imprinted in your memory—but still there will be no wisdom. *How does one attain wisdom? How does liberation happen?* He asks because what you call wisdom, knowledge, binds you instead—how can this be liberation? Wisdom is that which liberates you. Jesus has said, 'The truth shall make you free.' Wisdom is that which liberates you—this is the criterion of truth. Pundits don't appear to be liberated, they look enslaved. They talk about liberation but they don't look free. They seem to be bound with a thousand fetters.

Have you ever observed: your so-called religious people seem to be more enslaved than you. You may have a little freedom, but your saints are more stuck than you. They are just blind followers of tradition. They cannot move freely, they cannot sit freely, they cannot live freely.

A few days ago a message came to me from some Jaina *sadhvi*s, Jaina nuns, saying they want to meet me, but their disciples do not allow them to come. This is a very strange situation! A sadhvi means one who no longer bothers about society, one who has started a journey into the unknown wilderness, one who has said, 'Now I have no need of either your respect or your honour.' But the nuns and monks say, 'The disciples do not allow us to come.' They say, 'Don't even think of going there. If you go there we will close our doors on you.' What kind of seekers are they? This is just dependency, slavery. This is completely backwards. It means that instead of the sadhvi transforming the disciple, the disciple is transforming the sadhvi.

A friend came and told me that a Jaina sadhvi reads my books, but only in secret. She also tries to listen to my tapes, but again, secretly. And if by chance anyone mentions my name in her presence, she sits there pretending she has never heard of me. Is this liberation?

Janak asked: *How does liberation happen?* 'What is liberation? Explain to me the wisdom which liberates.'

Freedom is man's most important longing. Achieve everything, but if you are still not free, it hurts. Attain everything, but if freedom is not attained, you have not attained anything.

Man wants the open sky, unbounded. This is man's innermost longing, most secret longing—for a space where there are no limits, no barriers. You may call it the longing to become divine or call it the longing for moksha, liberation. In Sanskrit we have chosen the right word, moksha. Such a lovely word does not exist in any other language. There are words like 'heaven', 'paradise', but those words don't have the melody of moksha. Moksha has a unique music. It simply means a freedom so ultimate that it has no barrier; a freedom so pure it is unlimited.

Janak asked: How does liberation happen? And how is non-attachment attained? Oh lord, please tell me this. Ashtavakra must have looked carefully at Janak—because this is the first thing a master does when someone inquires. He observes attentively: from what source is this inquiry arising? Why has the questioner asked something? The master's answer can be significant only if he understands clearly why the question is asked.

Remember, a person who has attained truth—a master—does not answer your question. He answers you.

He doesn't bother much about what you ask; he is more concerned with why you have asked, what is behind the question, the complex hidden in the unconscious—what desire is actually hiding behind the screen of your question.

There are four types of people in the world: the wise, the seeker, the ignorant, the idiot. And there are four types of inquiry. The first inquiry is wordless—the inquiry of the wise, the *gyani,* the one who knows. Actually the inquiry of the wise is not an inquiry at all. He knows nothing is left to be known. He has reached; the mind has become clear, become calm. He has come home, he has come to a state of relaxation.

So a gyani's inquiry is not an inquiry at all. This does not mean that a gyani is not ready to learn. A gyani becomes simple, like a small child—he is always ready to learn. The more you learn, the more the readiness to learn increases. The more you become simple and innocent, the more you open to learning. Winds come and find your doors open. The sun comes and doesn't need to knock on your door. Existence comes and finds you always available.

A gyani does not collect knowledge, he simply has the capacity to know. Understand this well, because it will be useful for you. Gyani simply means one who is open totally to learning, who has no prejudice, who has no buffers against learning, who has no pre-planned system or structure for knowing. A gyani means a *dhyani*, one who is meditative.

Ashtavakra must have observed carefully, looked into Janak and seen this person is not a gyani, he has not attained wisdom; otherwise, his inquiry would be silent, there would be no words in it.

There is an incident in Buddha's life . . .

A fakir came to meet him; a lone ascetic came to see him, a wanderer. He came and said to Buddha, 'I have no words capable of asking, I have no skill to bring what I want to ask into words. You know it already. Understand and say whatever is right for me.' This is the inquiry of one who knows.

Buddha was sitting silently. He didn't say a thing. After a short time it seemed as if something happened! The man had been looking at Buddha, and now his eyes started overflowing with tears. He bowed at Buddha's feet and said, 'Thank you! I am really fortunate—you gave me what I came here for.' He got up and left. His face was radiating an aura of unique splendour. He went dancing.

Buddha's disciples were confused. Ananda asked, '*Bhante*, Bhagwan. It is a mystery. First this man says, "I don't know how to ask, I don't know in which words to ask, I don't even know what I have come to ask. But you know everything. Look at me, say whatever is needed for me." First, this man is a mystery. Is this any way to inquire? If you don't know what to ask, then why ask at all? How can you ask? Incredible!

'But the matter doesn't end here. You were sitting silently, and you went on sitting silently. We have never seen you sit so mute. If someone asks, you answer. Sometimes it happens that someone doesn't ask and still you answer. Your compassion is always flowing. What happened that suddenly you were silent and your eyes closed? And then what alchemy happened that the man began being transformed? We saw him changing. We saw him undergoing a complete transformation. We saw ecstasy coming over him. He has gone dancing, flowing with tears, overwhelmed, ecstatic. He bowed at your feet. His fragrance has touched us too. What has happened? You didn't utter a word; how did he hear? And we are with you for so many days, for years. Is your compassion less towards us? Why don't we receive the grace you gave him?'

But remember, you get as much as you are able to receive.

Buddha said, 'Listen. Horses . . .' He talks to Ananda about horses, because Ananda was a warrior. He was a cousin of Buddha, and from an early age was very fond of horses. He was a rider. He was a famous rider, a great competitor.

'Listen, Ananda,' Buddha said, 'there are four types of horses. One type will not budge an inch even if you whip it—the most worthless of all horses. The more you whip them the more they stubbornly resist. They stand still— as stubborn as a hatha yogi. If you whip them, you only provoke resistance.

'Then there is a second type of horse. If you whip them they move. If you don't whip them they won't move. At least they are better than the first.

'And there is a third type of horse. Just crack the whip— to strike them is not necessary. Just crack the whip, the sound is enough. They are more aristocratic—and better than the second kind.

'Then, Ananda, you must know those horses which run just by seeing the shadow of the whip. You don't even need to crack it. That man was that kind of horse—the shadow was enough.'

Ashtavakra must have looked carefully.

When you come to ask me something, you yourself are a question, more important than what you ask. Sometimes you may also feel that I have answered a question you didn't ask. And perhaps you may even feel I have avoided your question, sidestepped it and answered something else. But for me, your inner need is always more important, what you ask is not important—because you yourself don't really know what you are asking, why you are asking. The answer is being given only for your need; nothing of the answer is decided by your question.

Ashtavakra must have seen that Janak is not a gyani. Is he ignorant then? No, he is not ignorant either . . . because the ignorant person is arrogant, he stands proudly erect. He doesn't even know how to bow down—and this man has bowed at his feet, stretched himself full length at the feet of a twelve-year-old boy. This is impossible for the ignorant. The ignorant thinks he already knows—who is going to explain anything to him? If an ignorant person does ask, he asks just to prove you wrong, because the ignorant presumes he already knows and wants to see whether you know or not. The ignorant person asks to test you.

Ashtavakra must have thought, 'No, Janak's eyes are very clear. Even though he's a king, he asked me, an unknown, unfamiliar boy of twelve years, "Oh lord. Please explain to me . . ." No, he is humble, he is not ignorant. Is he an idiot then? Idiots never ask. Idiots don't have any idea that there are any problems in life.'

There is a similarity between idiots and enlightened ones. For the enlightened ones no problem remains; for idiots no problem has yet arisen. Enlightened ones have gone beyond problems; the idiots have not yet entered them. Idiots are so unconscious, how can they ask questions? Will an idiot ask, 'What is wisdom?' Will an idiot ask, 'What is liberation?' Will an idiot ask, 'What is non-attachment?' Impossible!

And if an idiot does ask, he will ask how to fulfil his passions. If an idiot asks, he will ask how to live here a few more days. Liberation? No, an idiot asks how to make his chains golden, how to inlay his chains with diamonds. If an idiot asks, he will ask such things. Wisdom? An idiot does not imagine that wisdom can exist. He cannot accept even the possibility. He will say, 'What wisdom?' An idiot lives like a beast.

No, Janak is not an idiot either. He is a *mumukshu*, a seeker of truth. The word mumukshu needs to be understood. Mumukshu is the desire for liberation, the desire for moksha.

Still he has not reached liberation—he is not a gyani. He is not standing with his back towards liberation—he is not an idiot. He is not sitting stuck to any traditional ideas about liberation: he is not ignorant either. He is a mumukshu. Mumukshu means that his inquiry is simple and straightforward. It is neither corrupted by idiocy nor twisted by ignorant preconceptions. His inquiry is pure—he asks with an innocent mind.

Ashtavakra replied: Oh beloved, if you want liberation then renounce the passions as poison, and take forgiveness, innocence, compassion, contentment and truth as nectar.

If you want liberation then renounce the passions as poison. The word *vishaya*, passion, is very meaningful. It is derived from *visha*, poison. The meaning of visha is a substance which, if one eats it, one will die. The meaning of vishaya is that which, if we consume it, we die again and again. With passions we die again and again; with food we die again and again; with ambitions, anger, hatred, burning jealousy—consuming these, we go on dying, again and again. We have died again and again because of these.

Up until now, we haven't really known life through living, we have known only death. Our life until now . . . where is the flaming torch of life? There is only the smoke of death. From birth to death we are gradually dying. Are we living? We die every single day. What we call life is a continual process of dying.

We don't know life yet; how can we live? The body goes on weakening every day, strength goes on decreasing every day. Enjoyment and passion go on sucking our energy every day, go on ageing us. Passions and desires are like holes, and our energy, our being, goes on flowing out through them. In the end our pail is empty—this is what we call death.

Have you ever seen: if you throw a bucket full of holes into a well, as long as it is submerged in water it seems to be full. Pull on the rope and lift it out of the water and already it has started emptying. It creates a great commotion. Is this what you call life? Falling streams of water—is this what you call life? And as the bucket draws closer to your hands, it becomes more and more empty. When it reaches your hands it is empty . . . not a single drop of water. This is how our life is.

When a child is not born yet, he seems to be full. Just born, he starts emptying. The first day of birth is the first day of his dying. He starts emptying: one day dead, two days dead, three days dead. What you call your birthday would be better called your death day—it would be nearer the truth. You have been dying for one year and you say a birthday has come. You have been dying for fifty years and you say you have lived for fifty years: 'Let's celebrate my golden anniversary.' But you have been dying for fifty years. Death is drawing nearer and life is receding further and further—the bucket is emptying. Do you base your thinking about life on what is receding or do you base it on what is drawing nearer? What kind of inverted arithmetic is this? We are dying every day, death keeps creeping closer.

Ashtavakra says passions are poisonous, because by indulging them we simply die. We never get any life from them.

Oh beloved, if you want liberation then renounce the passions as poison, and take forgiveness, innocence, compassion, contentment and truth as nectar. Nectar means that which gives life, that which gives immortality, ambrosia—when one has found it, one will never die again.

Then . . . forgiveness . . . Anger is poison; forgiveness is ambrosia.

Innocence . . . Deviousness is poison; simplicity, innocence is nectar.

Compassion . . . Hard-heartedness, cruelty, is poison; kindness, compassion is nectar.

Contentment . . . The worm of discontent goes on eating up everything. The worm of discontent sits in the heart like a cancer. It goes on penetrating into it, it goes on spreading poison. Contentment. Satisfaction with what is, no desire for what is not. What is, is more than enough. That it is, is more than enough. Open your eyes a little and see.

No one need impose contentment upon life. If you look attentively you will find that what you get is always more than what you need. You go on receiving what you want, you have always got what you want. If you wanted unhappiness you got unhappiness. If you wanted happiness you got happiness. If you wanted something wrong you got something wrong. Your desires have shaped your life. Desire is the seed, and life is its harvest.

For life after life you have been getting what you desire. Many times you think you desire one thing but receive something else. Then the error is not in what you desire, you have only chosen a wrong word for what you desire. For example, you want success and get failure. You say you failed because what you wanted was success. But he who desired success has already accepted failure. Within, he has become afraid of failure. Because of failure he desires success. And whenever he wishes for success, the idea of failure comes; the idea of failure goes on becoming stronger. Sometimes he succeeds, but he is certain to spend his journey through life in failure after failure. The mood of failure goes on deepening. It deepens so much that one day it manifests. Then you complain that you wanted success. But in wanting success, you have wished for failure.

Lao Tzu has said, 'Wish for success and you will fail. If you really want success, never wish for it. Then no one can make you a failure.'

You say you wanted respect, but you are getting insults. A person who wants respect has no respect for himself, yet he wants respect from others. He who has no respect for himself wants others to cover it, to hide his lack of respect. This desire for respect is the sign that you feel disrespect for yourself within. You have the feeling that you are nothing. Others should make you into something, should put you on a throne, should raise banners for you, should hoist flags in your name—others should do something! You are a beggar. You have already insulted yourself when you wanted respect. And this insult goes on deepening.

Lao Tzu says, 'No one can insult me because I don't want respect.' This is attaining true respect.

Lao Tzu says, 'No one can defeat me because I have dropped the very idea of winning. How can you defeat me? You can only defeat one who wants to win.' It is a strange fact.

In this world those who do not desire respect receive it. Those who do not want success get it, because those who do not want success already accept that they are successful: what more success do you want? You are already honoured by the being within you; what more do you want? Existence has already given you respect by giving birth to you; who else's respect do you want? Existence has given you enough glory. It gave you life. It has blessed you with eyes—open them and see these green trees, the flowers, the birds. It has given you ears—listen to music, to the splashing of a waterfall. It has given awareness so you can become a buddha; what more do you want? You have already been honoured. Existence has certified you; who are you asking, like a beggar, for a certificate? Those who beg a certificate from you?

It is a very hilarious situation, two beggars face-to-face begging from each other. How can you get anything? Both are beggars. From whom are you asking for respect? Who are you standing in front of? You are insulting yourself this way. And the insult will deepen.

Contentment means: Look at what you have! Open your eyes a little and see what you've already got.

This is an extremely valuable key Ashtavakra is giving. It will slowly become clear to you. Ashtavakra's view is very revolutionary, very unique. His revolution is from the very root.

Take . . . contentment and truth as nectar. Because one who lives in falsehood will go on becoming more false. One who tells lies, lives in lies, will naturally be surrounded by lies. His connection to life will be shattered, his roots will be cut.

Do you want roots in existence? Those roots are possible only through truth. You can be linked to existence only through authenticity and truth. Do you want to be cut off from existence? Then create a smokescreen of lies, make great clouds of lies around you. The more you become false the farther away you will be from existence.

> You are neither earth, nor air, nor fire, nor water, nor ether. To attain liberation, know yourself as the witnessing consciousness of all these.

These statements are so immediate, not even an introduction. Ashtavakra has hardly uttered two sentences and meditation comes in; he begins to talk about samadhi, about deep meditation. One who knows has nothing except samadhi to share. He said two sentences first because if he had immediately started talking about samadhi, perhaps you would have been too startled to understand. But two sentences—and immediately he is talking about samadhi.

Ashtavakra does not even take seven steps. Buddha took seven steps and on the eighth step, samadhi. Ashtavakra brings up samadhi on the very first step.

You are neither earth, nor air, nor fire, nor water, nor ether. Let yourself relax into this truth. *To attain liberation, know yourself as the witnessing consciousness of all these.* The witness is the key. There is no more valuable key than this.

Be the observer. Whatever happens, let it happen. There is no need to interfere with it. The body is composed of earth, air, fire, water and ether. You are the lamp within by which all these—earth, air, fire, water, ether—are illuminated. You are the observer. Go deeply into this.

Know yourself as the witnessing consciousness . . . This is the most important sutra in existence. Be a witness. Wisdom will happen through it. Non-attachment will happen through it. Liberation will happen through it. The questions were three but the answer is one.

If you can separate yourself from the physical body and rest in consciousness, then this very moment you will be happy, at peace and free of bondage.

This very moment . . . ! This is why I say it is a revolution from the very roots. Patanjali is not so courageous as to say, 'This very moment.' Patanjali says, 'Practise discipline within and without. Practise control of breathing, turning inward and yoga postures. Purify. This will take innumerable lives—then enlightenment.'

Mahavira says, 'Practise the five great vows. And when innumerable lives have passed, deconditioning will happen, purification will happen. Then one will cut the bonds of karma.'

Listen to Ashtavakra:

If you can separate yourself from the physical body and rest in consciousness, then this very moment you will be happy, at peace and free of bondage. Right here, right now, this very moment.

If you can separate yourself from the physical body, and rest in consciousness . . . If you begin to see the fact, 'I am not the body, I am not the doer and enjoyer—I am that one hidden within me who sees all. When childhood came it saw childhood, when youth came it saw youth, when old age came it saw old age. Childhood did not stay, so I cannot be childhood. It came and passed, still I am. Youth did not stay, so I cannot be youth. It came and passed, still I am. Old age came, and it is also going, so I cannot be old age. How can I be that which comes and goes? I am always. The one to whom childhood comes, to whom youth comes, to whom old age comes . . . to whom thousands of things have come and gone. I am that one eternal, everlasting.'

Like railway stations they go on changing: childhood, youth, old age, birth. The traveller keeps moving. You never think you have become one with train stations. Coming to Pune station you do not think you are Pune. When you reach Manmad you don't think you are Manmad. You know that Pune has come and gone, Manmad has come and gone. You are a traveller. You are the observer that saw Pune—Pune came and went; who saw Manmad—Manmad came and went. You are the one who sees.

The first thing: separate what is happening from the observer. *Separate yourself from the physical body and rest in consciousness* . . . There is nothing else worth doing.

Just as Lao Tzu's key sutra is surrender, Ashtavakra's key sutra is rest, relaxation. There is nothing to do.

People come to me and ask how to do meditation. The very question they ask is wrong. They ask a wrong question, so I tell them just to do it. What should I do? I tell them, 'Do—something or other has to be done.' You are itching to do something; that itch needs to be satisfied. If it itches, what to do?—it can't be left unscratched. But gradually, just keeping them busy doing, I tire them out. Then they say, 'Relieve us of this. How long are we to go on doing this?' I say, 'I was ready from the beginning, but you needed time to understand. Now relax!'

The ultimate meaning of meditation is rest.

Rest in consciousness . . . He who lets his consciousness stop in relaxation, he who rests only in being . . . There is nothing to do because you already have what you are seeking, because you have never lost what you are seeking. It is not possible to lose it—it is your very nature. You are the divine. *Ana'l haq*—you are truth. What place are you seeking, where are you running to? In search of yourself, where are you running? Stop. Relax. Godliness is not attained by running, because it is hidden inside the runner. Godliness is not attained by doing anything, because it is hidden in the doer. To experience godliness nothing needs to be done—you are it.

Hence Ashtavakra says: *Rest in consciousness* . . . Relax, let yourself unwind. Let go of this tension. Where are you going? There is nowhere to go, there is nowhere to reach . . . *and rest in consciousness*. Then right now . . . *this very moment you will be happy, at peace and free of bondage*. The statement is unique. No other scripture is comparable to it.

> You are not a Brahmin or other caste, you are not in any of the four stages of life, you are not perceived by the eyes or other senses. Unattached and without form, you are the witness of the whole universe. Know this and be happy.

How can a Brahmin write a commentary on this? *You are not a Brahmin or other caste* . . . How can a Hindu take this scripture to heart? His whole religion is based on caste and stages of life. And from the very beginning Ashtavakra is cutting the roots of these beliefs. He says you are not a Brahmin, not a low caste Sudra, not a Kshatriya, a warrior—this is all nonsense. These are all projections.

This is all the play of politics and society. You are simply Brahman, the divine—not a Brahmin, not a Kshatriya, not a Sudra.

You are not a Brahmin or other caste, you are not in any of the four stages of life . . . And you are not a *brahmacharya* student, or a householder, or at the stage before *sannyas—* you are not in any of the four stages of life. You are the observer, the witness who is inside passing through all these situations.

The Hindus cannot claim the Ashtavakra Gita as theirs, the Ashtavakra Gita is everyone's. If there were Mohammedans, Hindus and Christians in Ashtavakra's time, he would have said, 'You are not a Hindu, not a Christian, not a Mohammedan.' Who will build a temple for Ashtavakra? Who will champion his scripture? Who will claim him? Because he is denying everyone. It is a direct declaration of truth.

Unattached and without form, you are the witness of the whole universe. Know this and be happy. Ashtavakra does not say that after you have known this you will become happy. Listen to the statement carefully. Ashtavakra says: *Know this and be happy.*

You are not a Brahmin or other caste, you are not in any of the four stages of life, you are not perceived by the eyes or other senses. Unattached and without form, you are the witness of the whole universe. Know this and be happy. Be happy. Be happy right now. Janak asks, 'How can one be happy? How can liberation happen? How can wisdom happen?'

Ashtavakra says it can happen right now. There is no need to delay it even a single moment. There is no reason to leave it for tomorrow, no need to postpone it. This happening does not occur in the future, it happens now or never. When it happens it happens right now, because there is no time except now. Where is the future? When it comes, it comes as now.

So those who have become enlightened, have become enlightened in the now. Do not leave it for some other time—that is the cunning of the mind. The mind argues, 'How can it happen so fast? You have to get ready first.'

People come to meet me and they say, 'We will take sannyas. We'll take it someday.' Someday! They will never take it. If it is put off, it is put off forever. 'Someday' never comes. If you are going to take it, take it now. There is no other time than now. Life is now, liberation is now. Ignorance is now, knowing is now. Sleep is now, awakening can happen now. Why someday?

It is difficult for the mind; the mind says you will have to make preparations. The mind argues, 'How can anything happen without preparations? When a person wants a certificate from the university, it takes years. For a doctorate it takes twenty to twenty-five years, working year after year, and finally one attains a doctorate. How can it happen right now?'

Ashtavakra knows this. If you want to have a store, you can't open it right now. You will have to collect everything, arrange things, bring the goods, construct the store, attract customers, send out advertising—it will take years. In this world nothing happens right now. It happens in orderly steps, and this is good. Ashtavakra knows this, I know it too.

But there is one phenomenon in this world which takes place right now. It is godliness. Godliness is not your shop, nor your examination hall, nor your university. Godliness does not happen in steps, it has already happened. It is merely a question of opening your eyes. The sun has already emerged. The sun is not waiting for your eyes, saying that until your eyes open he won't come out. The sun is already out. Light is spread all over. His music is resounding day and night. The sound of *aum* is vibrating in all directions. The unstruck music is echoing everywhere. Open your ears! Open your eyes!

How much time does it take to open your eyes? It takes even less time to attain godliness. It takes a moment for the eyelid to blink. The Hindi word for 'moment' means the time it takes to blink an eye. But it does not take even that much time to attain godliness.

You are the witness of the whole universe. Know this and be happy. Be happy right now.

Ashtavakra's religion is not by instalments. It is cash in hand, hard cash.

> Oh expansive one, religion and atheism, happiness and misery—all are of the mind, they are not for you. You are not the doer nor the enjoyer. You have always been liberated.

Enlightenment is our inherent nature. Wisdom is our inner nature. Godliness is our way of being. It is our centre. It is the fragrance of our life, our being.

Ashtavakra says: *Oh expansive one . . .* oh bringer of joy, oh luxurious magnificence . . . *religion and atheism, happiness and misery—all are of the mind*. These are all waves of thought. You have done evil or good, committed sin or done good deeds, built a temple or given alms—all this is of the mind.

You are not the doer nor the enjoyer. You have always been liberated. You are eternally free, you have always been free. Liberation is not a happening which we need to strive for. Liberation has already happened in our being. The whole existence of is made of freedom. Every particle of it, every pore of it is made of liberation. Freedom is the material from which the whole existence is produced. Freedom is its very nature.

This declaration—just understand it and the transformation takes place. There is nothing to do except understand it. If it descends into you, if you listen with your whole mind, it is enough.

I would like to say, 'Enough for today.'

Make a total effort to understand Ashtavakra. In Ashtavakra there is no place for doing. So don't think some method which you can do is going to emerge. Ashtavakra does not suggest anything to do. Listen in repose. Nothing is going to happen by doing.

So don't bring a scratch pad or book to take notes in when a sutra comes. Don't write it down to do later. Doing doesn't work here. Listen with no concern for the future. Just listen. Just sit quietly with me and listen. Listen to me in relaxation. Just listening . . . listening, you can become enlightened.

This is why Mahavira said that a *shravaka* is a seeker who can be enlightened just by listening! A shravaka means one who becomes liberated just by listening. A sadhu means one who cannot become liberated by listening. He is a little less intelligent—he has to practise something. The shadow of the whip is not enough for him. This horse belongs to a slightly lower class: the whip cracks, then it moves a little. Or beat it and it moves a little.

The shadow is enough.

Listen—the shadow of the whip will become apparent.

With Ashtavakra one thing has to be remembered: there is nothing to do. You can listen joyfully. You don't have to extract anything from it to try out later. Whatever happens will happen from listening. Right listening is the key.

This very moment you will be happy, at peace and free of bondage. Be liberated right now. Be enlightened this very moment. Nobody is stopping you, nothing is preventing you. There is no need to budge an inch. Be enlightened right where you are, because you are free already. Awaken and be enlightened.

Unattached and without form, you are the witness of the whole universe. Know this and be happy. Be happy. There is no need to wait a single moment. It is a leap, a quantum leap. With Ashtavakra there are no steps. It is not a gradual evolution but sudden. It can happen this very moment.

Hari-om-tat-sat!

2

Right Here, Right Now

Osho,
    While listening to your discourse yesterday, it felt as
if I was not on this earth, rather I was a small particle
of light in the open and infinite sky. After discourse, an
experience of lightness and emptiness continued and I
wanted to keep wandering in this sky. I do not know what
knowledge, karma and devotion are, but in aloneness I
wish to remain immersed in this state. Still, the feeling
sometimes arises that this may be madness, that this may
be a trick of my ego. Kindly shed light on my path.

We are on this earth, but in fact we cannot be on this earth,
and we are not. We feel it: we are strangers to this earth.
We have made a home in our body, but our body is not our
home.

It is as if someone settles abroad and forgets his
homeland. Suddenly in the market one day he meets
someone who reminds him of home, who speaks his own
language. For a moment the foreign country will vanish and
his homeland will be present.

This is the significance of scriptures. This is the real purpose of the words of the masters. After listening to them, for a moment we are no longer here. We go where we belong. We flow in their music. The situations which had completely involved us vanish, and that which was very far away comes near.

Ashtavakra's words are absolutely unique. Hearing them, it will happen again and again; again and again you will feel you are not on this earth but have become part of the sky—because these words are of the sky. These words come from the homeland, come from that source from which we all come, the source to which we must return. Without going back to it we will never find peace.

Where we are is like an inn, not a home. No matter how much we insist it is a home, still an inn remains an inn. Try to explain it away, to forget it; it makes no difference. The thorn goes on pricking us, the memory keeps on coming. And sometimes, if we happen to encounter such a truth that pulls us like a magnet and would show us another world, then we feel we are not part of this earth.

It is good: 'While listening to your discourse yesterday, it felt as if I was not on this earth.' There is no one who is of this earth. We appear to be of it, we feel as if we are; in reality, we exist in the sky. Our nature is of the sky.

Being means the inner sky.

Body means the earth, the body is made of earth. You are made of sky.

These two have met within you.

You are the horizon where the earth seems to be meeting the sky. But has it ever met it? Far away the horizon appears, sky touching earth. Start walking towards it, expecting to reach it in a minute or two. Continue walking for life after life—you will never reach a place where the sky touches the earth. It is only a mirage.

It always appears that you can touch it a little further on, just a little further.

The horizon does not exist, it only appears to. It is the same inside us as with the outer horizon. Inside no contact ever happens either. How will the being touch the body? How will the mortal meet the immortal? Milk mixes with water—both are of the earth. But how will the being merge with the body? Their basic quality is different. However near they come, they cannot touch. They may be forever near, still they cannot touch, they cannot meet. It is only our assumption, our concept—the horizon exists only as our idea.

If you allow Ashtavakra's statements to penetrate your heart like arrows, they will awaken and remind you. They will arouse that long-forgotten memory. For a moment the sky will open, the clouds will break up, and your life will be filled with sunlight.

It may be difficult—the experience goes against our whole way of life. It will cause discomfort. And you did not disperse the clouds within, these clouds were dispersed by the words of a master—the clouds will gather again. Before you reach home, again the clouds will surround you. You won't drop your habits so quickly. Again the clouds will gather, and you will be more uneasy. You will doubt. Was it not a dream that you saw? Was it not some kind of projection? Was it not a trick of the ego, of the mind? Perhaps you fell into a kind of madness?

Naturally, the weight of your habits is heavy, very old. Darkness is ancient—it doesn't exist, still it is ancient. Whenever rays of sunlight burst in, they are fresh—absolutely new, freshly bathed. You see them for a moment, and again you are lost in darkness. Your darkness has a very long history. When you weigh these two, doubt arises about sunlight but not about darkness. Darkness should be doubted. Instead, sunlight is doubted because its rays are new, and darkness is very old. Darkness is like a tradition coming down from century to century. The rays of light have just arrived—fresh, new. So new, how can they be trusted?

'I felt I was not on this earth.' There is no one who is of this earth. We cannot be of this earth. To think otherwise is our belief, our projection. It seems so, but it is not the truth.

'Rather I felt I was a small particle of light in the open and infinite sky.' This is the beginning, '. . . a small particle of light in the infinite sky.' You will soon feel, 'I am the infinite sky.' This is the start.

Right now we are not ready to be completely absorbed in the infinite sky. And if we feel the flight coming, the storm coming, that winds are carrying us away, still we keep separate and save ourselves. ' . . . a particle of light . . .' You are no longer darkness, you have become a particle of light. But the difference from the sky is still there; the division remains, a gap remains. The ultimate will happen the day you become the sky. The particle of light is also separate. The day you become integrated, one, on that day you will feel 'I am the vast empty sky.'

That's how we express it in language: 'I am an empty sky.' But how is it possible as long as 'I' is there? If 'I' is, then the sky remains separate. When the feeling of empty sky comes, then 'I' will be gone, only the empty sky will remain.

People say, '*Aham Brahmasmi*—I am God, I am Brahman.' But when Brahman is, how can 'I' remain? Only Brahman remains, not I. But there is no other way to express it.

Language is for people who are asleep. Language belongs to those who have settled in a strange country but consider it their homeland.

Silence is for those who know.

Language is for the ignorant.

So as soon as you say anything, just in saying it truth becomes untruth. Aham Brahmasmi—I am Brahman, I am the sky. Say it, and it becomes a lie. Only sky is. But to say, 'Only sky is', is not the whole truth, because 'only' indicates that there must be something more; otherwise, why the emphasis on 'only'? 'Sky is'?—there is difficulty even in saying this because 'is' can become 'is not'.

We say, 'The house is.' Someday it will cease to be—it may fall down, become a ruin. We say, 'The man is.' Someday the man will die. The sky is not like this—sometimes it is and sometimes it is not. The sky always is, so to say 'Sky is' is a repetition. The very nature of the sky is to be. So why repeat 'is'? It is correct to say 'is' for those things which someday cease to exist. A man is. One day he was not, today he is, and tomorrow again he will not be. Our 'is' exists between two 'not's.

The 'is'-ness of the sky was yesterday, is today and will also be tomorrow. What is the meaning of 'is' between two 'is's? 'Is' has meaning between two 'is not's. So to say 'Sky is' is also a repetition. Let us say 'Sky'. But when we say 'sky', when we make a word, even then it is wrong. Just to say 'sky' means there is something which is different from it, separate from it; otherwise, what is the need for a word? If there is only one, there is no need to say one. One is meaningful only when two is, three is, four is—where there are numbers. Why say 'sky'?

This is why wisdom is silent. It is impossible to bring the ultimate wisdom into words.

But we are fortunate that rare individuals like Ashtavakra have made untiring, impossible efforts. As much as it is possible, they have made the effort to bring the fragrance of truth into words. And note: few have been as successful as

Ashtavakra in their attempt. Many have attempted to bring the truth into words—all were defeated. Defeat is certain. But if you look among the defeated, the least defeated is Ashtavakra. He is the most successful. If you listen rightly, you will be reminded of your home.

It is auspicious that you felt you were a particle of light. Prepare to be lost. One day you will feel that the particle of light is also lost, and only sky remains. Then drunkenness will completely overwhelm you. Then you will drown in the wine of truth. Then you will dance. Then you will experience the full taste of nectar.

'After discourse, an experience of lightness and emptiness continued. I wanted to keep wandering in this sky.' Here we make a small mistake. When we have any pleasant experience, we want it again and again. How weak man's mind is. It is full of desires, full of greed; temptations go on arising. It wants to repeat whatever is pleasant. But remember one thing: repetition is already wrong. As soon as you wish 'let it happen again', it can never take place, because the first time it occurred it was not from your desire. It happened by itself, it was not your act.

This is where Ashtavakra puts the whole emphasis: truth happens. It is not an act, it is a happening. It happened to you while listening. What were you doing? Listening means you weren't doing anything. You were sitting feeling empty. You were silent, you were alert, you were awake, you were not asleep. Good! But what were you doing? You were simply a receiver. Your mind was mirror-like—what came before it was reflected, what was said was heard. You were not adding anything to it. If you were adding anything, it would never have happened. You were not making commentaries, you were not saying in your mind, 'Yes, this is right, that is wrong. I agree with it, I disagree. It is according to the scriptures,' or 'It is not.' You were not making logical statements about it. If you had been lost in logic, this happening would never have taken place.

The one who has asked—Swami Om Prakash Saraswati—I know him. His mind is far away from logic, far away from doubts and arguments. Those days are gone. Once he may have made logical arguments, may have raised doubts. Now he has ripened from the experiences of life. Now that childishness is not in the mind. This is why it could happen. He was simply listening, sitting, not doing anything—he just went on sitting and it happened.

It happened the first time without your doing anything. If you want it to happen a second time, this will create a disturbance. Desiring was not the cause of its happening. So when such a rare happening takes place, do not desire. When it happens, accept it joyously. When it doesn't happen, don't complain, do not ask for it. Ask and you will miss. In asking is a demand, an insistence: 'It should happen. It happened once, why doesn't it happen now?'

This occurs every day. When people come here to meditate, in the beginning they are fresh and new. They have no experience, so it happens. This is very surprising. You must comprehend this—it will help you understand Ashtavakra better. This is my daily experience. When people come new and fresh and they have no experience of meditation, it happens. It happens and they are filled with joy—but the very experience creates difficulty. Then expectations begin: what happened today should happen tomorrow; not just happen, but happen stronger. But it doesn't happen again, and they approach me, crying. They say, 'What happened? Have we made some mistake? It happened once, but now it's not.'

'This is your mistake,' I tell them. 'When it first happened you were not expecting anything; now you are. Now the mind is no longer innocent. Your expectation has contaminated it. Now you are not genuine, you are not open—asking has closed the doors. Expectation has arisen, and this expectation spoils everything. Now desire is aroused, greed enters.'

This happens every day. People who have meditated a long time go on trying many methods but drop into meditation only with great difficulty. Their experience becomes a barrier. Sometimes someone just comes, flowing with the vibe . . . he had never even thought about meditation. A friend was coming, so he thought, 'Let's go see what it is.' He came out of curiosity—no desire, no spiritual searching, no efforts towards meditation—he just came. Something was triggered inside when he saw others meditating and he joined them. Then it happened! He was surprised: 'I didn't come for meditation, but meditation happened.' Now the problems start. Now, when he comes again there is expectation. The mind is interested; it must happen again. There is greed, a desire for repetition. The mind has come in and the whole process is disturbed.

It happens only when there is no mind.

Remember, mind is the desire for repetition.

Let the pleasant happen again, let the unpleasant never repeat—this is the mind. The mind chooses: let this happen and that not happen. Let it happen again and again like this, but never like that—this is the mind.

When you begin to flow with life: whatever happens, okay; whatever doesn't, okay. Suffering comes, it is accepted. Suffering comes, there is no resistance. Happiness comes, it is accepted. Happiness comes, there is no excitement. When there is calmness, in both happiness and suffering, an equanimity starts arising. Then happiness and suffering begin to appear very similar—because no choice is left. Now it is out of our hands. What happens, happens.

We go on watching—this is what Ashtavakra calls *sakshi-bhav*, witnessing. And he says if witnessing is attained, everything is attained. Inside, sakshi-bhav awakens the witness, outside it brings equanimity.

Equanimity is the shadow of witnessing.

Or, if you achieve equanimity, witnessing comes. These two go together. They are the two feet or the two wings of the same phenomenon.

'I wanted to keep wandering in this sky.' Be alert. Don't give the mind a chance to destroy the moments of meditation. This same mind has already destroyed your life. It has spoiled all of your relationships. This mind has made your whole life dry like a desert. Where many flowers could have blossomed there are only thorns. Do not bring this mind with you on your inward journey. Say goodbye to it and take your leave. Lovingly bid it farewell. Tell it, 'It is enough. Now I won't demand anything. Whatever happens, I will be awake, I will be watching.'

As soon as you demand, you can no longer be a witness. You become identified as the one who enjoys and suffers. Then meditation vanishes. To be identified means you are saying: 'I am the one who enjoyed this, it made me happy.'

'I do not know what knowledge, karma and devotion are, but in aloneness I wish to remain immersed in this state.' Throw this wish away and you will slip into the same state. Not only in aloneness but in the crowd you will slip into it. Even if you are in the market you will remain immersed. This state has nothing to do with aloneness or the crowd, the market or the temple, the masses or isolation. This state is related to your mind becoming quiet, to its being in equilibrium. This happening will take place wherever there is peace, equanimity. But do not demand it, otherwise the very demanding becomes uneasiness, creates tension.

Ashtavakra says, 'Right here, right now.' A demand is always for tomorrow. It cannot be here and now. The nature of demanding is that it is not in the present. It jumps. Demanding means: 'Let it happen—tomorrow, after an hour, in a moment—let it happen.' A demand cannot be right now. Time is required. It may be very short, but time is required. And the future does not exist. The future means what is not. The present means what is. The present and demanding are not related.

When you are in the present you will find there is no demanding. And then the happening takes place. When there is no wish for it, it will happen abundantly.

Understand this double bind well. Become familiar with every aspect of it. The day you don't demand anything is the day everything will happen. The day you aren't running like a madman after the divine, it will come after you. The day you don't show any eagerness for meditation, when there is no tension within you, that day you will be filled, overflowing with meditation.

Meditation does not come from outside. What is left inside you when you are not tense is called meditation. That which remains when there is no desire within you is called meditation.

It is like a lake: waves arise, then sudden gusts of wind come. The surface of the lake is covered with storm and winds; everything goes topsy-turvy. The moon is in the sky, full; but no reflection is made because the surface is shimmering. How can it be a mirror? The moon's reflection is broken into a thousand pieces—like silver spread over the whole lake, but no image is made.

The lake becomes quiet. Have the waves gone somewhere? Did the waves come from somewhere else? They are from the lake. Now they have gone back to sleep, they have returned to the lake. The lake has regained its stillness. The moon, which was scattered like silver all over the surface of the lake, is now gathered in one place. The image becomes clear.

As soon as there are no waves on the lake of your mind, desiring waves, demanding waves, waves of 'This should be so and that should not be so', when there are no waves on the lake of the mind, then truth is reflected as it is. Then how can the beauty of the moon within you be described? How can its ecstasy be told? A river of ecstasy showers. One meets the inner beloved. Then there is a honeymoon, only then.

But if you desire it, you will miss.

And I know this desire looks completely natural. But this is a great hurdle. So much joy comes in such moments, how can you avoid desiring? It is human. I don't say that you have made a big mistake, unworthy of a human being. It is an absolutely human error. When for a moment the window opens and the vast sky flows into you, when for a moment darkness vanishes and rays of light descend, it is impossible, almost impossible, not to wish for more. But the impossible will have to be learned. Learn it today, learn it tomorrow or learn it the day after, but it will have to be learned. The sooner you learn it the better. Become ready right now and it happens immediately. There is no need to wait even a moment.

'I wish to remain immersed in this state.' This state will come. It has nothing to do with your mind, so leave your mind behind. Whenever it sneaks in, you have to tell it again and again, 'Excuse me, but you have meddled more than enough! You have messed up the world, now don't mess up the divine too. You have spoiled all of life's happiness. Now happiness is coming from the inner depths; at least don't spoil this.'

Remain alert and say goodbye to the mind.

Gradually, increasingly, such moments will be coming.
They will come through your experience. Whenever
mind is not, immediately the window opens again. Again
the stream of heavenly joy flows, again the light descends.
Again you are radiant, intoxicated. Again you drown in
nectar.

When this happens again and again, it will become clear.
You will become skilful at keeping the mind away from you.
When it happens, let it happen. When it does not happen,
wait quietly for it. It will come. That which has come once
will come again and again—just do not wish for it. Do not
come in between at all. Do not create any hindrance.

'Still, the feeling sometimes arises that this may be
madness.' Such feelings will arise in the intellect, because it
cannot believe that bliss is possible. Intellect is absolutely at
home with unhappiness. It has totally accepted unhappiness
because it has given birth to it. Who will not accept their
own offspring? So the intellect says, 'If there is unhappiness,
it is absolutely right. But ultimate happiness? Certainly
there must be some mistake. Does it ever happen? It must
be imagination. You saw a dream, you were lost in some
daydream. You went into hypnosis. Certainly you have gone
mad.' The intellect will often say such things. Don't listen
to it. Don't pay any attention to it. If you give attention to
it, the experiences will stop. Those doors and windows will
never open again.

Remember one thing: bliss is the definition of truth.
Wherever you find joy, know it is the truth. That is
why we have called the divine, *sat-chit-anand*—truth,
consciousness, bliss. Anand is the ultimate definition for it.
Bliss is above even truth, even above consciousness—truth,
consciousness, bliss. Truth is a lower step, consciousness is a
lower step, bliss is ultimate. Wherever bliss flows, wherever
you find ecstasy—don't worry at all, you are near the truth.

It is like someone nearing a garden. The breeze becomes cooler; he begins to hear the singing of birds, he begins to feel a coolness. The garden is not yet visible, yet these signs tell him that he is on the right path, he is nearing the garden. Similarly, as you start approaching truth, springs of bliss well up. The mind begins to cool down, you begin to be in equilibrium, patience begins increasing, happiness increases. An exultation overwhelms you, uncaused. No cause can be found. You haven't won the lottery or made a big business profit, nor been offered a prestigious job. Or it may happen that you lost the job you had, you lost what was in your hands, your business went bankrupt—but there is an uncaused exultation that goes on dancing within, never stopping. The intellect will say, 'Have you gone mad? These are the signs of madness!'

This is a very strange world. Here, only the mad look happy. This is why the intellect says you must have gone mad. Have you ever seen anyone here cheerful and happy besides madmen? There are thousands of reasons to be happy, but still man is not happy. He may have a big palace, wealth, all sorts of comforts; still he is not happy. This world is a world of miserable people, the majority are miserable. So if you begin to laugh without cause here, people will say you are mad. And if you say, 'This laughing comes for no reason, its waves arise within, it just spreads,' people will say, 'Enough! His mind is disturbed.'

But if you pull a long face, look so dejected that seeing your face even ghosts are frightened, then you are fine, then you are okay here—no problem, everything goes smoothly for you. You are a man just like any other man. You are human the way human beings should be. But when you start smiling, start laughing, start humming songs, when you begin dancing by the side of the road, then certainly you have gone mad.

This is the way we have denied God. If he should come here, we would put him away in a madhouse. Perhaps this is why he doesn't come. He is afraid of coming.

Imagine: if you met Krishna on the street, playing on his flute, wearing his peacock feather crown, his yellow silks, his girlfriends dancing all around, what would you do? Run immediately to the police station, reporting, 'There's trouble on the road. What's going on there? That kind of thing is not supposed to happen!' You would throw him in jail.

Bliss has been boycotted.

We have banished joy from our lives. We sit embracing unhappiness. Here, a pessimistic man appears intelligent, a cheerful man appears insane. Our whole criterion is upside down. It is natural: if all of a sudden what you had considered intelligent throughout your life begins disappearing, begins slipping away, if the foundation of your so-called intelligence begins shaking, and suddenly you start seeing joy everywhere, and remember, 'without cause'. This is what insanity means, happy without cause, no cause at all. You are sitting alone and you start smiling. Enough, you've gone mad, because we have seen only mad people sitting like that.

Understand, the insane and the *paramahansa*s, enlightened ones, are a little similar. The insane laugh and are happy; they have lost their intelligence. Paramahansas also laugh and are happy; they have gone beyond intellect. Both laugh—an insane person because he has fallen below, a paramahansa because he has gone beyond intellect. There is this small similarity between the two. The insane and the paramahansa have one thing in common: both have lost the intellect. One has forsaken it consciously, the other in unconsciousness. Hence the difference is vast, as different as earth and sky, and yet there is this similarity. So sometimes you see a paramahansa as a mad person and sometimes a mad person as a paramahansa. Mistakes go on happening.

In the West there are many people locked up in asylums who are not insane. Recently a great revolution has begun there. Some psychologists, notably R.D. Laing and his co-workers, have started a movement. They claim that many in the asylums are not insane. If these people had been born in the East they would have been respected as paramahansas. R.D. Laing does not know that the opposite happens in the East—here many madmen are taken for paramahansas. But to err is human. Here in the East are many madmen who are understood to be paramahansas. These mistakes happen because the boundaries of these two touch. This confusion is natural.

Make it a point that if joy is increasing, there is no need to worry. But joy can increase due to insanity also. Then what is a safe criterion for it? This is the criterion: if your joy is increasing and at the same time you are not causing anybody's unhappiness to increase, then continue untroubled. Your joy should not be dependent on violence towards anyone, on aggression towards anyone, or on making anyone unhappy. Then there is no reason to be afraid of going mad. Even if you are going mad, it is a good sign, it is right. Go into it with no hesitation.

You need to be concerned only when you begin to harm somebody. Nobody is bothered by your dance. But if somebody is sleeping and you play your drum over his head and start dancing? Dance, there's no problem in it. Chant your prayers, that's fine. But if in the middle of the night you set up a mic and start non-stop kirtan singing, then you are really mad—although in India no one would call you mad because you are singing devotional songs. Many madmen do this. They say, 'We are performing a non-stop kirtan—twenty-four hours straight. Whether you sleep or not is your problem. And if you object to our programme, you are irreligious.'

See that your joy is not violent. This is sufficient. Your joy should be your own. Don't disturb anybody else's life with it. Let your flowers bloom, but in blooming, don't let anyone be pricked by its thorns. If you always make sure of this then you are moving in the right direction. When you feel that now others are being disturbed by your behaviour, be careful—you are not moving towards enlightenment but are on the path to insanity.

Nobody is disturbed by Om Prakash. You can proceed without hesitation, fearlessly.

Yesterday I was reading a poem:

All that was beautiful, lovable, desirable;
what was good, refined, new, true and real;
I picked and brought,
presented my offerings.
But what happened?
It all withered where it was placed.
Dried out. Wilted.
Not a thing did he lift a hand to take,
though somewhere it is written he would accept . . .
But what I gave or received,
what I drank or dropped,
what I poured out or spilled,
what I distilled or strained,
intoxication or its fading,
what I gathered, dropped or discarded—
the final account of all this,
I saw that it too fell into the same sacrificial fire,
and at that very moment I felt,
Oh! I am released, I have made it across!
All right, accepted, I have gone mad . . .

Yes, the man makes it across—the mind is a craziness. You may go on offering very select things to the divine, the very best—but nothing will come of it until you offer your head.

Listen again: 'All that was beautiful, lovable, desirable; what was good, refined, new, true and real; I picked and brought, presented my offerings. But what happened? It all withered where it was placed. Dried out. Wilted. Not a thing did he lift a hand to take . . .'

Find the most beautiful and bring it, find the most valuable, offer the Kohinoor diamond—all will pale into insignificance. Pick flowers, lotuses, roses, offer them—all will wilt. Only one thing is accepted here: your head, your ego, your intellect, your mind. These are different names for the same thing. You must offer yourself here.

'And at that very moment I felt, Oh! I am released, I have made it across! All right, accepted, I have gone mad.' Om Prakash, people will tell you the same thing: you have gone mad. Let them say so! Don't worry about what they say. When people call you crazy they are trying to save their own heads, nothing else. When they say you are crazy, they are saying, 'Keep away from us, don't come near us! Don't sing these songs to us, don't bring this laughter to our doors, don't show us your wine-filled eyes, don't bring us this message.' They feel threatened.

They have this same music within. They have a veena lying within them, waiting many lives for someone to caress its strings. But they are afraid, insecure. They have built much and become settled in this phony world. Now they fear being uprooted.

I was in Allahabad, and a man was sitting right in front of me, listening to me. Millions of people have sat before me and listened, but there are very few who have listened with as much feeling as he was listening. Streams of tears were flowing down his face.

Suddenly, he got up in the middle of the lecture and left the hall. I was a little surprised and I asked the organizer what happened. It turned out that the man was very famous—I hadn't known. He was a literary man, a poet, a writer.

The organizer went to his house and inquired. The man told him, 'Forgive me—I was becoming disturbed. After twenty minutes, I thought it is better to run away from here. If I stay a little longer, something or other will happen. This man is already cuckoo—he will drive me mad. I will come, but not now. I will certainly come again, but give me a little time. I could not sleep for two nights, and what he said is echoing in my mind. No, at present I have so much work. Now my children are young, I have a house and family to look after, but I will certainly come. Go and please tell him I shall certainly come—but not now.'

When someone says you are cuckoo, he is only trying to protect himself. By deciding you are mad, he is repressing his attraction. He also has an irrepressible longing within him. Who has not sought the ultimate reality? Who has no thirst for bliss? Who is not longing for truth? Such a person has never existed. Those you call atheists are people who have become frightened. They say, 'No, there is no God,' because if they don't deny him, they will have to seek him.

It is my own experience that there is a deeper desire for truth in an atheist than in a believer. He is afraid of going to a temple, but you are not. You are not afraid because the desire in you is not so strong that it will drive you mad. You go to the temple as if you were going to your shop. You go in and out of the temple but you are not affected at all.

An atheist is a person who knows that if he enters the temple he will not be able to return. If he enters, he will not return the same as he entered. So there is just one escape; he says, 'God does not exist—religion is all hypocrisy.' In this way, he saves himself, persuading himself, 'There is no God, so why go to the temple? There is no God, why get into all this mess? Why meditate? Why pray?'

As I see it, the atheist is inwardly trying to save himself. I have not yet seen a real, authentic atheist. How can man be an atheist? An atheist is a person who tries to live in 'no'. How can anyone live in 'no'? How can anyone live in atheism?

To live, one needs 'yes'.

Do flowers ever bloom in 'no'? 'Yes' is needed. Acceptance is needed. The more acceptance of life, the more flowers bloom in it. But you are afraid flowers will bloom beyond your capacity, that the flowers will be so abundant that you will not be able to contain it.

Last night a young man told me, 'Help! This experience is becoming uncontrollable. I am so elated, it seems I will burst. The ecstasy is too great, I cannot contain it. The vessel of my heart is so small. Help me! It is carrying me away. All my limits are being smashed. And I am afraid that if I flow along with it, there will be no return.'

Losing control—this is the fear. Ego can readily live with unhappiness; control is not lost in unhappiness. No matter how much you weep in misery, you remain the master. Control is lost in joy, the limits are shattered. Limits are never broken in misery. Even in hell limits are never broken. If you fall into hell you remain strong inside. Limits are broken in heaven—there, control is lost. And where control is lost, ego is lost. Where control is lost, the grip of intellect is lost, the power of reasoning is lost.

This is what is happening. Don't be afraid. The moment of being released, of making it across is near. But that has never happened unless the mind accepts its craziness.

I am in search of a tune,
which does not reverberate on lips

but throbs in the veins,
blazing like lava—
for melting.
I am in search of a fire
that my each and every cell melts away
and I am reduced to bare threads;
that someone weaves me into a net so fine
that I become transparent.
I am in search of a fragrance
that, becoming weightless,
I float on the air,
quiver in the soft shower of a light rain.
On the slatey sky of the darkening evening
I want to shine for a while,
I am in search of a vibrant colour . . .

Om Prakash, I have given you this vibrant colour; these orange clothes are the vibrant colour. Go on flowing, transcending limits. Float beyond intellect. Let go of control. Control means the doer—leave control aside. If there is a doer, it can only be existence. Do not compete with existence, do not become its adversary. Don't fight with it. Surrender, flow with its stream. You will float.

Those who drown are carried afloat; those who try to swim are drowned.

The second question:

Osho,
It has always been the observation of seekers that the realization of godliness is a very arduous phenomenon. But enlightened ones like you always emphasize that it can happen right here, right now. Is saying this again and again a provocation? And a method or device to arouse thirst in us?

It is the truth.

It is not a method, not a device.

Your asking this is a method and a device to save yourself. The mind is not ready to accept that godliness can be attained here and now. Why can't it accept it? It can't accept it because if godliness is available here and now and we are not attaining it, then what could be causing this? How can we explain it? If it can be attained here and now, why are we not attaining it? A great uneasiness arises: it can be attained here and now, but we are not attaining. How to explain it? It becomes a great frustration. To relieve the frustration, you say godliness can be achieved but that you need to be worthy.

Intellect always manages to find a way. Whatever complication arises, the mind finds a solution. It says, 'The way has to be sought, worthiness has to be sought, you will have to become purified—then you will attain. And if Ashtavakra says it can be achieved here and now, certainly he must have a reason for it. He says it so we will start making intense effort. But we will have to make efforts.' The mind is very clever.

Ashtavakra's statement is absolutely clear. Godliness can be found here and now, because it is not an achievement, it is your nature. His whole emphasis is simple: You are it. The very idea of attaining is wrong.

When we say godliness can be attained here and now, it simply means it is already attained. Just open your eyes and see!

The very language of attaining is wrong. In attaining it seems that you and existence are separate. You are the seeker and it is the objective to be sought. You are the traveller and it is the destination. No, that it can be attained here and now simply means you are that which you are seeking.

Know thyself.

Open your eyes and see—or close your eyes and see. But see!

It is a matter of insight, not of worthiness.

Worthiness means that even the divine is a business deal. When you go to the market something is sold for a thousand rupees, something for one hundred thousand rupees, something for a million rupees. Everything has its price. Worthiness means that godliness also has its price. Whosoever pays the price by proving his worth will get it. You want to make even godliness a commodity in the market: 'Renounce, do austerities, then you will attain it. Pay the price and you will get it. Where can you get it for free?' You drag the divine into a shop, seal it in a box, stick on a price tag, and put it on the shelf. You say, 'Do this many fasts, that many meditations, this much austerity; stand in the sun, suffer cold and heat, then you will attain it.'

Have you ever thought about what you are saying? You are saying that realizing godliness is related to your doing something. Whatever you do will be your doing, and your doing cannot be greater than you. Your austerity will be yours—as low as you are, as dirty as you are. Your austerity cannot be greater than you. And whatever you attain through your austerity will be limited, finite, because through the finite only the finite can be obtained, not the infinite. Through austerity you will find a projection of your mind, not the divine.

Ashtavakra says the divine already is. It is the one throbbing within you. It is the one breathing within you, it is he who comes as you in your birth, it is he who passes away as you in your death. It is eternally manifesting itself in infinite forms—here as a tree, there as a bird, somewhere else as a person. The divine is! There is nothing else except it.

The recognition of this truth, the remembrance of this truth . . .

I have heard that once an emperor was very upset with his son and sent him into exile. Because he was an emperor's son, the boy didn't know how to do anything. He had never done anything else—he could only beg. When an emperor is no longer an emperor, begging is the only thing he can do.

He began begging. Twenty years passed and he completely forgot—can anyone begging for twenty years remember he is an emperor? Impossible. It is difficult, it would make begging difficult. It is better to forget it. So he forgot; otherwise how could he beg? An emperor and begging! Door to door, holding his begging bowl, standing in front of hotels and restaurants begging, asking for leftovers? An emperor! He had to forget the emperor. It had to be wiped out of his memory. It was finished, that chapter was closed. It was like a dream, like a story he had read long ago or a movie he had once seen. What did it have to do with him?

Twenty years later when the emperor, the father, became old, he became upset—he had only one son and that son would be the ruler. He said to his ministers, 'Go and find him. And wherever he is bring him back. Tell him his father has pardoned him. It is not a question of pardoning or not pardoning—I am dying. Who will look after the kingdom? It is better that it stay in the hands of my own blood rather than go to someone else. However he may be, good or bad, bring him back.'

The ministers found the prince standing in front of a dining hall with his broken bowl, begging for money. He was naked. He had no shoes on his feet. It was mid-afternoon, in the heat of summer, a hot wind blowing. His feet were burning and he was begging for a little money to buy shoes. He had a little change in his bowl.

The chariot came and stopped. The minister got down and fell at his feet—he was the future emperor. As the minister touched his feet, in a flash it happened, it all came back. For twenty years he had not remembered that he was an emperor. Now, to remember he had no need to sit and think, contemplate, do austerities, meditate. No, within one second, not even a second, in a moment the transformation happened.

The man became something else. He was still a beggar, impoverished. He was still naked, he still had no shoes on his feet. He threw away his begging bowl and told the ministers to arrange for his bath and make arrangements for proper clothing. He stepped forward and mounted his chariot. His glory was a sight to see. He was still the same, but his face was majestic, his eyes were shining, there was a splendour all around. He was an emperor. The memory returned. His father had sent the invitation.

It is just like this.

When Ashtavakra says here and now, he is saying the same: however long you have travelled—twenty years, even twenty lives . . . You have been in exile, you have been begging a long time, you have totally forgotten. The memory is sound asleep—it had to be put to sleep. If the memory were not asleep, begging would have been impossible. You wandered from door to door with a begging bowl. Ashtavakra is saying, 'The invitation has arrived. Wake up! You are not a beggar! You are the son of an emperor!'

If someone listens rightly, the happening takes place just by listening. This is the greatness, the glory of the Ashtavakra Gita. There is no insistence on doing anything. Just listen, just let the truth reach your heart. Don't come in the way, just be receptive. Just listen, let the arrow reach your heart. Its impact is enough. The forgetfulness of many, many lives will break open, the memory will come back: you are the divine. Hence he says right here, right now . . .

Don't find excuses. You say that perhaps this is a method, a device, to increase urgency, to increase intensity in people.

This question is from Swami Yoga Chinmaya. In Chinmaya's intellect there is too much effort, striving, asceticism. His understanding is like an ordinary yogi's. Ashtavakra's statements are not for the ordinary yogi. They are for the extraordinary, the intelligent—those who can awaken just by listening. Chinmaya is a bit of a hatha yogi—he moves only after a thorough beating. He cannot move just by seeing the whip, just by seeing the shadow of the whip.

Don't laugh, because most people are just like Chinmaya. Don't think that your laughing proves that you are different than Chinmaya. Chinmaya at least got up the courage to ask—you didn't even ask. This is the only difference. You are just like him. If you haven't become the divine by the time the Ashtavakra Gita discourses are over, then know that there is no difference, you are just like him. But if while listening you wake up and become the divine, then just the shadow of the whip has worked.

'It has always been the observation of seekers that the realization of God is a very arduous phenomenon.' The seeker is off the track from the very beginning. The very meaning of 'seeker' assumes that the divine has to be sought, that he has lost it somewhere. The seeker accepts that he has lost the divine somewhere. What a strange idea. He has lost God? How can you lose him?

People come to me saying they want to seek God. I say, 'All right, seek! But where did you lose him? When?' They say, 'We don't know anything about that.' Look into it first. It may be that you have not lost him at all. Sometimes it happens that your glasses are on your nose and you are searching for them even while looking through them.

Could it not be that the divine is on the tip of your nose and you are searching for it? This is how it is. The seeker is fundamentally mistaken. He has accepted that he has lost the divine, or has not yet found him, that God is somewhere far away and has to be found.

The divine is never found by seeking. By searching and searching one learns that there is nothing in seeking. While searching, one day the very seeking drops away.

As soon as the seeking drops the divine is found.

Buddha sought for six years, he searched totally. Where can you find a greater seeker than him? Wherever he heard that someone had attained knowledge, he went there. He put his head at their feet. He did whatever the gurus, the teachers, told him. Even the teachers tired of him. Teachers never tire of students who don't follow their instructions. They are never tired of them because they can always say, 'You are not following instructions. That's why nothing is happening. What can we do?' A teacher is relaxed when you don't obey him—he can always say that you didn't obey. If you had obeyed it would have happened.

But with Buddha the teachers were in trouble. Buddha did whatever the gurus said. Buddha always managed to do even more than they said. Finally the gurus, exasperated, told him, 'Look, go somewhere else. Whatever we have to say, we have said.' Buddha said, 'But nothing has happened through it.' They said, 'Nothing has happened to us either. We cannot hide it from you. Just go somewhere else.'

Faced with such an authentic man, even the gurus could not be deceptive. After searching intensely in every direction, at last, Buddha saw that seeking is futile, the divine is not found by seeking. The world already had no meaning for him; spirituality also became meaningless. Worldly pleasures had no meaning for him. The day he left the palace, all had become meaningless for him. Yoga also became meaningless. Nothing left in pleasure, nothing left in yoga. What to do now? Now there was nothing left to be done—it was no longer possible to be a doer.

Understand this situation correctly. Neither worldly pleasure nor yoga remains, neither the world nor heaven. There is no space left for the doer. If there is something to do, the doer can remain. Nothing was left to do, and that very night it happened.

That evening, sitting under the bodhi tree, there was nothing to do. Buddha was thrown into confusion. When he renounced the world, he grabbed hold of yoga: when he renounced indulging, he jumped into spiritualism. There was something to do—the mind remained busy. Now the mind had no space. The mind-bird began fluttering—no space! The mind needs space. The ego needs the nourishment of doing, it needs duties. If there is something to do, the ego can survive. There was nothing left to do. Think about it a little. A deep indifference was born in him—what Ashtavakra calls non-attachment.

A yogi is not detached, because a yogi seeks new pleasure—a yogi seeks spiritual pleasure. He is not indifferent, he still has the desire to enjoy. He couldn't find it in the world, so he searches for it in the divine—but the search continues. It is not found here, so he looks there. It is not found outside, so he looks inside. But the search continues. Neither the hedonist nor the yogi is indifferent to pleasure. Yes, they search differently for pleasure. One goes inside, one goes outside, but they both go somewhere.

That night there was nowhere for Buddha to go, neither inside nor outside. Just imagine that night, bring it to life. Feel how that night must have been. For the first time he attained rest, as Ashtavakra says—the rest in consciousness, out of which one attains the truth. That day relaxation happened.

As long as there is something to do, effort continues. As long as there is something to do, tension continues. Now there was no question of tension. The body was completely exhausted, the mind was completely exhausted. Buddha collapsed under that tree and fell asleep. At dawn when his eyes opened, they opened the way everyone's eyes should open. At dawn when he opened his eyes, those eyes opened for the first time. Those eyes that had been closed for centuries opened.

At dawn when he opened his eyes, the last star of the morning was fading. He watched as the last star disappeared outside. Outside, the last morning star dissolved—inside, the last trace of the mind also disappeared. There was nothing, no one left inside. There was absolute silence, a void, a great void, space.

It is said that Buddha remained sitting that way for seven days—like a statue, without the slightest movement. They say the gods became worried and descended from heaven. Brahma, creator of the universe, descended and fell at the feet of Buddha saying, 'Please speak! Such a phenomenon occurs only once in centuries, and that too with great difficulty. Please say something. We are eager to hear what has happened!'

Hindus are very angry that in Buddhist stories Brahma is made to fall at the feet of Buddha. But the story is perfectly right . . . because gods may be living in heaven but they don't live beyond the sky. Today the phenomenon has happened that an individual has gone beyond desire. Now there is no one higher than Buddha. Buddhahood is the ultimate. Even gods are lower. They still have the desire for heaven and heavenly pleasures.

That is why there are stories that Indra's throne begins to shake when he hears that some competitor is coming, some sage is going deep in meditation. Indra becomes nervous, his throne starts shaking. It is the same story with the throne in Delhi. Call it Indra's throne or Indira's, it is the same, there is no great difference. A challenger is coming: competition, anxiety, fear . . .

Buddha attained by non-doing. What happened in Buddha's life must have happened in Ashtavakra's life too. We do not have any story about it, no one has written it, but certainly it must have happened because whatever Ashtavakra says is just this: 'You have done a lot of running—now stop. The divine is not attained by running, it is attained by stopping. You have sought enough, now drop the search. You cannot find truth by seeking because truth is hidden in the one who is seeking. Why are you running here and there?'

As Kabir says, 'The musk of the musk deer is in the navel—that fragrance is your own.' But when fragrance emanates from the navel of a musk deer, he goes mad. He starts running here and there, searching. Where does this scent come from? Who has produced this perfume? Where does it come from?—because whatever fragrance the deer knows comes from the outside: sometimes from flowers, sometimes from something else, but always from the outside. Today the fragrance comes from within, but still he thinks it must come from outside. He starts running. And the musk is in his own navel, the fragrance is his own!

The divine resides within you. As long as you seek it outside—in yoga, in hedonism . . . your search is useless.

An ordinary yogi takes you out of indulgence, Ashtavakra takes you out of indulgence and yoga both—beyond yoga, beyond hedonism. You will find that the worldly man has an ego, but have you seen the ego of a yogi? A worldly man gets angry. Have you heard the curse of a saint? A worldly man walks vainly with his head high, waving his flag. Have you seen the flags, the elephants, the pomp of the yogis? An ordinary man proclaims his wealth, announces his achievements. Have you seen the yogis boast that they have such-and-such powers, such-and-such abilities? But these things are all one and the same, there is no difference in them.

Unless yoga is transcended, unless a person is completely free of the idea 'I am the doer', nothing has happened. You have only changed colour. You are a chameleon, you simply changed colour. But only the colour has changed, not you.

'It has always been the observation of seekers that the realization of God is a very arduous phenomenon.' In a sense this is true. If you insist on attaining realization by running hard, then what can anyone do? If you want to touch your nose by reaching around your head, go ahead and do it. Certainly, when you touch your nose from the far side you will feel that touching one's nose is a very arduous phenomenon. This is because of you, not because of your nose.

If you stand on your head and try to walk, it is difficult to walk even five or ten steps. Then if you say that walking is an arduous phenomenon you are not lying; what you say is right. But you are standing on your head. For those who stand on their feet, walking is not a difficult thing.

You fast, overheat yourself in front of a fire, unnecessarily trouble your body, torture it, do a thousand kinds of idiocies—and then you say that to realize the divine is a very arduous phenomenon. What you say is right. What you could have reached easily, naturally, you are reaching by becoming unnatural, so you find it difficult. Your way of reaching is wrong. But why does man choose the impossible? It has to be understood. What is the joy of walking on your head when you have feet? There is pleasure in walking on the head. It is the pleasure of the ego.

Mulla Nasruddin was fishing in a lake. I watched for a while. I went on watching but he was not even getting a bite. It seemed there were no fish in the lake. I asked him, 'Nasruddin, it seems there are no fish in this lake. How long are you going to sit here? That other lake is nearby— why don't you go over there and fish? Here there is not a fisherman to be seen; all the fishermen are over there.'

Nasruddin said, 'What is the point in catching fish there? There are so many fish in that lake that there is no place for them to swim. If you catch fish there, so what? If you catch fish here, it is something!'

The impossible is attractive. The more impossible it is, the more the ego is strengthened by doing it. It is something if you catch fish here. What is the point if you do what everyone else is doing? Everyone walks on their feet. If you do the same, what fun is it? Walk on your head.

As I see it, there is no connection between arduousness and the divine. Arduousness is connected to the ego. The ego enjoys doing arduous things. Everyone does things the easy way. What's the point? If you tell someone that you walk on your feet, people will say, 'Have you gone mad? Everyone does.' But if you walk on your head, your name will be printed in the newspapers. People will start coming to you, they will bow their heads at your feet. You have achieved something: you are walking on your head!

Ego is worshipped when you do something impossible— like when Edmund Hillary climbed Mount Everest, the whole world came to know about it. If you climb a small hill near Pune and plant your flag on it and say, 'No reporter is coming, no photographer is coming. What is the matter? Why this discrimination? They made so much noise over Hillary, his name is set down now in history, but nothing is happening with me. He planted a flag—I am doing the same thing!' But to climb Everest is difficult—for fifty to sixty years people tried to climb it. Then one man finally succeeded—that's why there is this discrimination.

Eventually a road will be made. Sooner or later buses will start going there. Everest cannot keep itself safe from man for long now—when one man has reached its summit, a whole chain begins. Recently a woman reached there too. When even women reach, what is left in reaching it? Eventually everyone will be going. Within a short time, there will be hotels and buses and everything else. If you go when buses have started running and plant a flag, saying, 'This is where Hillary placed his flag. But I am being discriminated against, favouritism is being shown against me . . .'

Ego enjoys difficulties. Man makes many things harder so his ego can be fulfilled. We make many things difficult: the more difficult we make it the more juicy it becomes. Arduousness is not in realizing the divine; arduousness is juice for the ego.

What you say is right: 'It has always been the observation of seekers that the realization of God is a very arduous phenomenon.' These seekers are all egoistic. And when have seekers realized the divine? It has happened when seeking dropped away. You realize the divine only when seeking drops away, when you are not going anywhere—just sitting, at rest, in ultimate rest. It happens when the pilgrimage disappears into the void.

People usually think that if they realize the divine the pilgrimage will end. But it is exactly the opposite. If you drop the journey, the divine will be realized immediately. People think, 'When we reach the destination we will relax.' The situation is otherwise: if you relax, you reach the destination.

Relaxation is the key to meditation and samadhi. Effort is the key to the ego.

That's why you will find that the more effort-oriented a religion is, the more egoistic the monks of that religion are. A Jaina monk is more egoistic than a Hindu monk. A Jaina monk says, 'A Hindu monk? So what? Anybody can become one. A Jaina monk? It's a difficult thing—only one meal a day, many, many fasts, all kinds of arduous practices . . .'

Again, among the Jainas there are Digambara monks and Svetambara monks. The Digambara monks say, 'What is there to Svetambara monks? They wear clothes. The real monks are Digambaras.' Nowhere will you ever find the ego shining more than in a Digambara monk. His body will be dried out, just a skeleton—because of fasting, naked living, suffering in sun and fire—but his ego will be aflame. His conceit will be that of a Hillary.

There are at the most twenty Digambara monks in India, five or six thousand Svetambara monks, and five million Hindu monks. And if it is in my power I will make the whole world sannyasin. So there can be no ego in becoming my sannyasin . . . because I don't say to do this and do that. It is a very simple matter: put on orange clothes and you are a sannyasin!

If sannyas becomes easy then where is the juice for the ego?

People come to me. They say I should make a special ceremony for giving sannyas. Special ceremonies for sannyas! They are right in the sense that this is what happens when a Jaina initiation takes place. Loud music is played, a horse is brought in, there is a lot of festivity. It seems as if something great is happening, somebody is being enthroned. Sannyas has become like a royal throne. People start praising, applauding this great happening. And I give sannyas so silently that no one knows—I give it even by mail. I do not know who the fellow is, nor does he know who has given it. It is good.

As I see it, sannyas should be simple.

As I see it, the divine is realized in relaxation, not by ego. It is not a doing, not a seeking.

The divine is already attained.

Be a little lighter, be a little more peaceful, just stop. Suddenly you will find it was always here.

The last question:

> Osho,
>
> In our body there are some fifty trillion cells, and chemical reactions go on continuously. When you or Ashtavakra say, 'Be a witness,' whom are you addressing? If you are addressing the brain cells, it is meaningless, because mind is transient. If you are trying to wake up the soul then it is meaningless, as the soul is already awake. It is foolish to awaken it and say 'Know thyself.'
>
> Aren't you throwing people into illusion? And if people cease responding to pleasure and pain, won't they become like plants and animals?

Who is it that is saying there are fifty trillion cells in the body? Certainly it is not the cells. One cell cannot keep track of all the other cells—there are billions of cells in the body.

Who is saying this? Who asks this? Who discovered this? There is definitely someone inside you quite separate from the cells who counts and says there are twenty billion cells.

'In our body there are some fifty trillion cells, and chemical reactions go on continuously. When you or Ashtavakra say, "Be a witness," whom are you addressing?' That one, who says there are twenty billion cells.

'If you are addressing the brain cells, it is meaningless, because mind is transient.' No, we are not addressing the brain cells, we are talking to you. Ashtavakra is addressing you. He is not such an idiot as to address your brain cells, he is talking to you. Your being is beyond your cells. The fact is, you use the cells. It is like a driver sitting at the wheel of a car. The car is running, moving fast, moving at one hundred miles per hour. Still the driver inside is not the car. If a policeman pulls him over and he asks the policeman, 'Whom are you addressing? The motor?—the motor is propelling the car. Whom are you addressing? The petrol?—the petrol makes it run. The wheels?—they spin fast.'

What would the policeman say? The same as I say to you: 'I want to talk to you. It's you I pulled over.'

'If you are trying to wake up the soul then it is meaningless, as the soul is already awake. It is foolish to awaken it and say "Know thyself."'

You are absolutely right: the soul is already awake. There is no way to wake it up, nor are we trying to do that.

The situation is something like this. You lie down and knowingly fake sleep; you are lying awake with your eyes closed. It is very easy to rouse someone who is sleeping: shake him a little or throw water in his face and he will wake up. But the man who is lying awake with eyes closed pretending to sleep, how will you rouse him? Throw water; it won't do any good. Shake him, move him; he will roll over and keep on sleeping. Call his name; he hears but does not respond. This is your condition.

It is meaningless to rouse the awakened, but this awakened one is pretending to sleep; hence the need to awaken.

We are not waking up any sleeper, because the soul cannot sleep. It is the body that sleeps, and the body can be awakened. There is no meaning in awakening a soul that is already awake. You are absolutely right, you are speaking with great wisdom—but it must be borrowed. If it came from your own understanding you would never have asked.

Ashtavakra or I, we are awakening the one who is already awake but has forgotten that he is awake; who is awake but goes on pretending to sleep; who is playing at being asleep. And this is why there are difficulties in awakening anyone, great difficulties.

'Are you not throwing people into illusion?' Do you think people are not already in illusion? If they are not, then definitely I am throwing them into illusion. But if they are not in illusion, how can they be thrown into it? Can all these buddhas be thrown into illusion? And if people are in illusion, what I am doing is an effort to bring them out. However you are, I reverse it.

If you think you are in illusion, this is an attempt to awaken you. And if you think that you are already awakened, this is an attempt to throw you into illusion.

But who can throw you into illusion if you are already awakened? Remember, no one but you can throw you into illusion, and no one but you can awaken you. Someone can attempt to wake you up, but unless you cooperate, you will not wake up—because this is not a sleep which can be broken. You are faking it. Your cooperation is necessary. Cooperation means discipleship. Cooperation means that you go to someone who can awaken you. You tell him, 'It has become an old habit to deceive myself—please help me to come out of this habit.'

A young woman came to me and told me she was in the habit of taking an addictive drug. She wanted to stop it. She wanted badly to get off the drug, she was so desperate to be finished with it some way. But the drug addiction had gone deep into the cells of her body. When she did not take the drug, there was such severe pain and discomfort throughout the body that she couldn't sleep, couldn't get up, couldn't sit down, so she had to take it. And if she took it, she became depressed by the mess she was in. She had come to me to get off the drug, asking for my hand in support. This is the situation, this is your condition.

Your practice of remaining asleep life after life has deeply affected you. You are an awakened one under the illusion that he is asleep, a king considering himself a beggar. He has believed it for so many lives that now his habit . . .

Nothing will happen by only listening. You can listen to me, but nothing will happen through it—until you make it your own, until you accept it. No one but you can awaken you; otherwise one enlightened one would have been enough. He could have shouted loudly and awakened everyone. He could have beaten his drums and awakened everyone.

If a hundred people are sleeping here, one person is enough to awaken them. Actually, no one is needed; an alarm clock can awaken them. One man can come and beat a drum and all will get up, or strike a bell and all will get up. But why couldn't this happen when Buddha was here, when Mahavira was, Ashtavakra was, Krishna was, Christ was, Zarathustra was, when Lao Tzu was here? Why couldn't they have rung a bell loudly and awakened the entire earth? They rang the bell loud and long. If anyone was really sleeping they would have awakened—but here people are faking sleep. They lie with their eyes closed. They hear the bell and they think, 'Go on ringing it. We'll see who's going to wake us up!'

When you want to wake up you will.

I cannot throw you into illusion. You are already in illusion: what more illusion can you be thrown into? Do you think you can be led further astray? Do you think there is still somewhere you can be misled? Can you fall down further than this? Is there any place left to fall? Can the greed in you be increased an inch? Can the anger in you be increased even one gram? Can desires which overwhelm you be stronger still? You are standing at the end of the line. He who should be first stands last. He who should be a king stands like a beggar. You cannot go lower—there is no way to fall further.

There is no possibility for you to be more deluded. Even if someone wants to, he cannot do it to you. Yes, the most anyone can do is switch your illusion. If you are bored with one illusion, he'll give you another. And that is what the sadhus go on doing.

You start feeling fed up with worldly illusions, you feel bored, you have lived in them too much. Now nothing is real—you have seen it all. Now they create a spiritual illusion. They say, 'Come enjoy heaven. Do good deeds, renounce, do austerities, enjoy heavenly maidens. You have enjoyed and suffered much, but for nothing. Here you drink wine in small measure, mere handfuls; there, in the walled heavenly garden, springs of wine are flowing. You can drown in wine. What is here? In heaven there are golden palaces, trees of diamonds and jewels. Sit under the wish-fulfilling tree and ask for anything you want. You have suffered too much here.' But this is a new illusion.

I am not giving you any new illusion. I simply suggest you have seen enough illusion, now wake up a little.

How can witnessing be illusion? Think about it.

I simply ask you to be a witness. Whatever is, I ask you to watch it. If I asked you to do something, illusion would arise. If I asked you to give up this and do that, illusion would arise. I simply suggest that whatever you are doing; whoever you are, a yogi or a Zorba; whatever you are, Hindu or Mohammedan; wherever you are, in a temple or mosque—wake up, watch with alertness. How can there be illusion in being aware? For an awakened person there is no possibility of being in illusion. Dreams come in sleep; how can they come when one is wide awake?

'And if people cease responding to pleasure and pain will they not become like plants and animals?'

First, who told you that plants and animals are worse off than you? You just take it for granted. You should ask the trees and plants. Ask animals as well . . . look into the eyes of animals. This also is man's ego—he thinks he is above animals. And the strange thing is, animals have never been asked to offer testimony. You have made a one-sided decision, you have decided by yourself. If animals were writing books like your scriptures it would be written in them that man is the animal beyond cure.

I have heard that among monkeys it is said that man is a fallen monkey. Darwin says man has evolved from monkeys, but who is Darwin to decide? You should listen to the monkeys too. Both parties need to be heard. Monkeys say man is fallen. And what they say is understandable. Monkeys are above, up in the trees, and you are on the ground below—you are fallen. Monkeys are up above, you are below. Challenge any monkey to a fight, and see: has strength increased or decreased? Just see if you can leap from one tree to another—your bones will break. Is competence evolving or disappearing? Who told you that you are superior? Did you just take it for granted?

It is just ridiculous. One disease among the many diseases man has is to believe he is superior. If you ask men, they think they are superior to women—without even asking women. Women's testimony has never been taken. There was never any vote on it. Men wrote the scriptures, expressing what was in their minds, and women were prohibited from reading them, so they couldn't object. If she had known how to read, the pundit's wife would have harassed him for what he wrote. So women were prevented from reading: women should not read the Vedas, should not do this, should not do that. These male chauvinists went right to the limit: they said women cannot even be liberated. First they will have to be born as men, to come into life in a male body; then they can get enlightened.

Then ask among men. The white man considers himself superior to the black man. But ask the black man . . .

I have heard that an Englishman went to an African jungle to hunt, taking a black guide with him. They got lost in the jungle and then they saw a tribe of about a hundred savages with spears coming at them. The Englishman freaked out! He told his black guide, 'Our lives are in danger!'

The black said, 'Our lives? Leave me out of this! Just take care of yourself. Why should my life be in danger?'

The white man thinks he is superior, the black thinks he is superior. Ask the Chinese. It is written in Chinese books that the English are monkeys. They do not even count them as human.

This disease exists throughout the whole world. It has gone very deep in man. He goes on deciding things without consulting the other party. This is all the play of the ego. If you just look, leaving aside your ego, you will find that all are manifestations of the divine—animals, birds, plants, man, everything.

Sometimes the divine wants to be green, so it is green. Sometimes it wants to manifest in the song of birds, and it does. Sometimes it wants to become man, so then it becomes man. There is no stratification here, no hierarchy, no one above or below. All are simultaneously the infinite waves of the divine. In a small wave, it is the divine, in a big wave too, in a white wave it is the divine, in a black wave too, in grass it is the divine, in trees touching the sky too.

The religious vision says the divine is whatever exists at this very moment. In the divine how can anything be further ahead or behind? This would be very difficult. In making something higher and something lower, you are creating difficulties. In fact, there is only one. If you look as a witness, you will see all is one.

So the first thing is, don't ask, 'If people cease responding to pleasure and pain will they not become like plants and animals?' If they do, it is not a loss. Would there be some loss if Hitler became an animal or a plant? Yes, millions of people would be saved from death; no other harm would be done. What danger if Nadirshah became a tiger? He would have been satisfied with killing five or ten people, killing only for food. As a man, he covered the earth with corpses for no reason at all.

This much is certain—animals have not yet invented anything like the atom bomb. Animals use their claws to kill, a very ancient way. And they kill only for food. Man is the only animal who kills with no intention of eating. Man goes to the jungle to hunt birds and animals, and says it is his recreation, his sport. But if a lion attacks him, it is not recreation. He does not say, 'The lion is just playing—let him do it. It is his recreation.' You kill for sport? No animal kills for sport.

Another significant point is that no other animal kills its own kind. No lion kills other lions. No monkey murders the same species. Man is the only animal who kills his own kind. Ants don't kill ants. Elephants don't kill elephants. Dogs don't kill dogs. They quarrel and fight but they don't kill, they don't murder. Men are the only animals who murder one another.

What is it in man that you are so worried about losing? What would be lost? Trees and plants are beautiful, animals are very innocent. But I am not asking you to be like trees or plants or animals; I am only saying, 'Drop the ego.'

And the second thing is, I have never said to cease responding to pleasure and pain. Ashtavakra has not said that either. To maintain an equanimity in happiness and pain does not mean ceasing to respond to pleasure and pain. To maintain an equanimity in pleasure and pain means only this: 'I will remain a witness. If pain comes I will observe it; if happiness comes, I will observe it.'

This does not mean if you prick Buddha with a thorn he will not feel pain. If you prick Buddha with a thorn, he will feel more pain than you do, because he is more sensitive than you are. You have become stone-like, while Buddha is like a delicate lotus. When you prick Buddha with a thorn, he feels more pain than you do. But the pain is in his body. Knowing this, Buddha remains standing apart. He watches—pain is happening. He knows pain is happening, still he does not identify himself with pain. He knows, 'I am the knower; by inner nature, the knower.'

Ashtavakra does not ask you to cease responding. He doesn't say that if your house catches fire, don't run out, remain seated and you will become a buddha. He says that while running away, know that the house is burning, but you are not burning. And even if your body is burning, know that the body is burning, not you. He does not mean you should allow your body to be burnt—take your body away from the fire. He does not say to cause any hardship to your body.

To be unresponsive means to become stone-like, lifeless. The Buddha is not a stone. Have you ever met anyone more compassionate than Buddha? Ashtavakra could not have been a stone—a river of love flowed through him. The sensitivity of those whom springs of love flow through has increased, not decreased. A great compassion descended through him. But you can misinterpret it.

And whoever has asked the question seems to have some kind of scriptural intellect, a bit too much garbage in the intellect. He has read a little, heard a little, gathered a little information—now it churns around in him, not allowing him to listen, not allowing him to see. It goes on distorting things.

A poet says:

The travellers all stopped.
Water within half-jelled,
outside frozen ice.
On one side uncrossable marsh to the neck,
on the other an oceanic flood.
Wild winds blowing,
the jungle in disarray,
the travellers all stopped.
Doors closed, windows half open,
eyes peeping out.
Countless black rods of dusk
like arrows piercing the face of the sun.
Silent, hidden behind their masks,
frightened, hesitant,
the travellers all stopped.

All these masks and facades of intellect and scriptural knowledge and being pundits—how long will you go on hiding behind them? All these layers of thoughts—how long will you go on hiding behind them? Get rid of them. Awaken the pure consciousness within you. Look at things as a watcher, not a thinker, because a thinker means that the processes of the mind have begun.

So if you want to understand Ashtavakra, you will be able to understand him only as a pure consciousness. If you fall into thinking and deliberations, you will not be able to understand him, you will miss him.

Ashtavakra is not a philosopher, Ashtavakra is not a thinker.

Ashtavakra is a messenger, a messenger of consciousness, of witnessing. Pure witnessing, just watching. If there is unhappiness, observe it. If there is happiness, observe it. In unhappiness don't become identified with unhappiness. In happiness don't become identified with happiness. Let both come, let both go. Night has come, observe it. Day has come, observe it. At night, don't think you have become night. In the day, don't think you have become the day.

Remain detached, beyond, transcendent, above, far away.

Be identified with only one thing: you are the observer, you are the witness.

Hari-om-tat-sat!

3

The Lifting of the Veil

Ashtavakra said: You are the one observer of all, and in reality always free. Your bondage is this: you see the other—not yourself—as the observer.

'I am the doer', thus has the black serpent of ego bitten you. 'I am not the doer', drink this divine nectar of trust and be happy.

'I am the one pure awareness', thus having burned the forest of your ignorance with this fire of certainty and being beyond sorrow, be happy.

You are that bliss, that ultimate bliss, within which this imaginary world is projected like a snake on a rope. Knowing this, thus wander happily. He who considers himself free is free, and he who considers himself bound is bound; because in this world the proverb is true: 'As you think so you are.'

The soul is the witness, all-pervading, perfect, one, free, conscious, free from doing, absolutely alone, non-attached, desireless, peaceful. Because of illusion, it looks like the world.

'I am an individually projected life', drop this illusion and also the feeling of inner and outer, and awaken in the thought that you are the unchanging, conscious, non-dual soul.

THE FIRST SUTRA:

> Ashtavakra said: You are the one observer of all, and
> in reality always free. Your bondage is this: you see the
> other—not yourself—as the observer.

This sutra is extremely important. Understand each and
every word correctly. *You are the one observer of all, and in
reality always free.* Ordinarily we perceive our lives through
the eyes of others. We use the eyes of others like a mirror.
We forget the observer and become the observed.

And it is natural. A child is born: he does not know
anything of himself. Only by looking into the eyes of others
will he know who he is. You cannot see your own face, you
will have to look in a mirror. When you look at yourself in
the mirror you become the observed, you are no longer the
observer. How much do you know of yourself? As much as
the mirror reveals.

The mother says, 'My child is beautiful,' so the child
thinks he is beautiful. The teacher in school says, 'You are
intelligent,' and you begin to believe yourself intelligent.
If someone insults you, if someone condemns you, the
condemnation penetrates you deeply. That is why our
knowledge of ourselves seems to be so confused—because
it is made of many voices, of many conflicting voices.
Someone says, 'You are beautiful,' and someone else says,
'You? Beautiful? Look at your face in a mirror!' Both voices
are taken in—a duality is created. Someone says, 'You are
very intelligent,' and someone else says, 'I have never seen
such an idiot!' Both voices are taken in, both are collected.
A great uneasiness arises, a deep split is created.

This is why you are not certain about who you are. You
have collected such a crowd of opinions. You have looked
in so many mirrors, and each one has given you a different

message. Mirrors have no message about you, their message is about themselves.

You must have seen mirrors in which you become tall, mirrors in which you become fat, mirrors in which you become extremely beautiful, mirrors in which you become extremely ugly—you become an Ashtavakra. The reflection in the mirror is not of you. The reflection is the mirror's nature.

Conflicting opinions go on accumulating. You begin to believe that you are this accumulation of conflicting opinions. That is why you are always shaking, always afraid. How deep, this fear of public opinion! 'What if people think badly of me? What if they should think me a fool? What if they think I am immoral?' We become worried because we have shaped our being according to others.

Gurdjieff used to tell his disciples, 'If you want to know your soul, you will have to leave other people behind.' He was right. For centuries masters have been saying this. If you want to know yourself you will have to stop looking for your image in the eyes of others.

As I see it, many seekers, explorers of truth, left society not because it is impossible to know truth while remaining in society, but because it is very difficult to know one's own face correctly while living in society. Here people go on giving feedback as to who you are. Whether you ask or not, images of who you are go on pouring in from all sides. And by and by we begin to live by these images.

I have heard:

A politician died, and no sooner had he died than his wife—who had died two years earlier—welcomed him at the gate of the other world. But the politician said, 'I won't enter yet. Let me go to the national burning ground along with my bier.'

The wife said, 'What is the use now? The body is lying there—it is clay.'

He replied, 'It is not clay. Let me see how many people have come to bid me goodbye.'

The politician and his wife began to walk with the procession. No one could see them, but they could see. There was a huge crowd. There were news reporters and photographers. Flags had been lowered. Flowers were heaped on the bier, which came on a military truck. Great respect was being demonstrated. There were guns in front of and behind the bier, and soldiers accompanied the procession. The politician was deeply moved.

The wife asked, 'Why are you so happy?'

He said, 'If I had known that so many people would come when I died, I would have died earlier. I should have died much earlier; why did I wait so many years? But I lived so that a large crowd like this would come when I died.'

People live for the crowd, people die for the crowd.

What others say has become so important that you do not even ask who you are. You collect cuttings of what others say and make your self-image. This image is bound to be very unsteady, because people's minds go on changing. Not only do people's minds go on changing, their reasons also go on changing.

Somebody comes to you and says, 'You are a very virtuous person.' This is nothing but flattery. Does anyone consider you a virtuous person? No one here considers anyone else other than himself as being virtuous. Think about yourself—do you consider anyone else virtuous? Sometimes you have to say it, that is another matter. There are needs, life problems, and you have to assert a lie as the truth, call an evil man good, praise an ugly person as beautiful. You have to resort to flattery. This is exactly why flattery is so valued.

Why do people fall into the snare of flattery? Even if you tell the most idiotic person that he is a genius he does not deny it, because he has no idea about himself. He listens to whatever you say, he becomes whatever you say.

So reasons go on changing. One says beautiful, one says ugly. One says good, another says bad—this goes on accumulating. And on the basis of these opposing opinions you fashion your being. You are riding on a bullock cart that has bullocks pulling it in all directions, and the cart tries to move in every direction at once. Your very bones get tired. You are only dragged. You reach nowhere, you cannot move.

Today's first sutra says:

You are the one observer of all, and in reality always free. The individual is the observer, not the observed.

There are three types of people. Those who have become objects to be seen, performers—they are in the deepest darkness. Second are those who have become spectators. They are a little better than the first, but there is not much difference. Third are those who have become the observer. It is good to understand these three clearly.

When you become the observed, you become a thing; you have lost your soul. It is difficult to find a soul in a political leader. It is difficult to find a soul in an actor. He has become an object to be seen, he lives to be an object to be seen. His whole effort is to impress people: how to look good, how to look beautiful, how to look the best. It is not an effort to be the best, but an effort just to appear the best. One who becomes the observed becomes a hypocrite. He covers his face with a mask. He presents a good outward show but is rotting inside.

Second are those who have become spectators. They are the vast crowd. Naturally, the first type of people needs the second type; otherwise, how can people become performers? Someone becomes a politician, he gets a crowd to clap for him. There is great harmony between them. A leader needs followers. If someone is dancing, spectators are needed. If someone sings, listeners are needed; hence some busy themselves as performers and some remain spectators. Spectators are the vast crowd.

Western psychologists are very worried because people are becoming mere spectators. They go to the movies, switch on the radio, or sit in front of the television for hours. In America, the average person spends about six hours a day watching television. If there is a football game, they watch it; a wrestling match, they watch it; a baseball game or the Olympics, they watch that. Now they have become mere spectators, spectators standing at the side of the road—the procession of life passes and you go on watching.

There are some who have joined the procession. That is harder. There is much competition. To join the procession is not so easy. A lot of fighting and aggression are required. But spectators are also needed to watch the procession. They stand on the sides and watch. If they are not there, the procession too will disappear.

Imagine, if followers did not come, what would happen to the leaders? Alone shouting, 'Let our flag fly high!' they would look like great idiots, they would look insane. So spectators are needed, a crowd is needed; then even madness looks right. Imagine a cricket match is going on and no one comes to watch it. The match will be dead. The juice in the match is not in the match itself; it is in the thousands of people who gather to watch it.

Man is strange! He even goes to see horse races. The whole of this area of Koregaon Park is full of horse race enthusiasts. It is very strange—no horse would go to watch men run. Horses run and men come to see it. Man has fallen even below horses.

Life is spent watching, just watching. Spectators . . . You do not love, you watch lovemaking in films. You do not dance, you watch someone else dance. You do not sing, you listen to someone else sing. Is it surprising if your life becomes impotent, if all life energy is lost? There is no movement, no flow of energy in your life. You sit like a corpse. Your sole function is to go on watching. Someone goes on showing, you go on watching. These two types are abundant in the world, one bound to the other.

Psychologists say there are two poles to each illness. There are people that psychologists call masochists; they torture themselves. And there is another type which psychologists call sadists; they take delight in torturing others. Both are needed. So, when these two get together, it becomes a scene of great drama. Psychologists say you can't find a better couple than where the husband is a sadist and the wife a masochist. The woman enjoys torturing herself, the husband enjoys torturing others—a wedding made in heaven! One is blind, the other a leper—well suited, a perfect fit. Every illness has two polarities. The performer and the spectator are two poles of the same disease. Usually women like to be watched and men like to be spectators. In the language of psychology women are exhibitionists. Their whole interest is in ostentatious display.

Once, Mulla Nasruddin was swatting flies. There were too many around and his wife had asked him to get rid of them. He was standing near the mirror swatting them. He said, 'Look at these two she-flies sitting here.'

The wife remarked, 'This is too much! How do you know whether they are male or female?'

He replied, 'They have been on the mirror for the last hour—they must be female. What would a male do on the mirror?'

Women cannot live without a mirror. When they see a mirror, it pulls them like a magnet. Their whole life is spent in front of it: trying on clothes and dresses, trying on jewellery and adorning themselves. And the surprising thing is that, when the woman goes out, totally dressed up, if someone pinches her she becomes angry, but if no one pays any attention to her, then too she is unhappy—because so much preparation was made to be noticed, to attract attention. Otherwise, what was the need? Women do not bother to dress up in front of their husbands. Then the woman is indifferent to her appearance because she has already won her husband. But if she has to go out, she will take a lot of time to get ready. She will have spectators, she will be on stage.

Psychologists say man is a voyeur. His whole focus is in viewing, his whole interest is to see. Woman is not interested in seeing, she is interested in exhibiting herself. That is why a man–woman pair fit each other. Both sides of the illness are there simultaneously. And both states are unhealthy.

Ashtavakra says man's nature is to be a seer, an observer; it is neither to be a performer nor a spectator.

Never confuse these two again. Many times I have seen people make this mistake—they think they have become the observer when they have become a spectator. There is a very fundamental distinction between these two words. The dictionary may not show the difference. There, spectator and observer may have the same meaning. But in the dictionary of life there is a great difference.

A spectator is one whose eyes are on others.

And the observer is one whose eyes are on himself.

When the eyes are on the object you are a spectator, when the eyes are on the seer you are an observer. It is a revolutionary distinction, very fundamental. When your eyes stop on the object and you forget yourself, then you are just a spectator. When all objects of vision have departed, when you, and only you, are there—only awakening remains, only alertness remains—then you are an observer.

When you are a spectator, you become completely oblivious. You forget yourself completely, your attention gets stuck there. You go to the movies and for three hours you forget yourself, you don't even remember who you are. You forget all worries and anxieties. This is why crowds rush there. There is so much worry, anxiety, trouble in living—a method of forgetting is needed. People become completely one-pointed. Only at the movies is their total attention focused. They see . . . actually there is nothing on the screen, just shadows go on flickering, but people are all attention. They forget their illness, their anxieties, their old age, and even if death comes they will forget that.

But remember, you have not become an observer in the theatre; you have become a spectator. You have forgotten yourself, you have no memory of who you are. You have lost all memory of the energy of seeing which is within you. You have stopped at the object in front of you, you are totally drowned in it.

To be a spectator is a kind of self-forgetting. And to be an observer means now all objects of observation have disappeared. The screen is empty, now no film moves on it. No thoughts remain, no words remain; the screen becomes absolutely empty, blank and shining, white. Nothing left to see, only the seer remains. And now you take a plunge into the seer. You become the observer.

Performers and spectators—humanity is divided between these two. Very rarely an observer is born—an

Ashtavakra, a Krishna, a Mahavira, a Buddha. Very rarely someone is awakened and becomes the observer.

You are the one observer of all. And the beauty of this sutra is that no sooner do you become an observer than you know that the observer is only one, not many. Objects are many, spectators are many. It is the nature of objects and spectators to be many: it is a web of lies. The observer is only one. For instance, the moon is out, a full moon. In rivers and puddles, in pools and ponds, in the ocean, in streams—everywhere it is reflected. If you wander the earth counting all the reflections there will be trillions. The moon is one, reflections innumerable. The observer is one, the performers are many, the spectators are many. They are only reflections, they are shadows.

When a person becomes free from being a performer or a spectator, has no desire to exhibit and be seen, and has no desire to see, when he knows that the trap of seeing and showing is false—no longer interested, he attains non-attachment, freedom from desire. Now there is no desire for anyone to say you are beautiful, you are good, you are virtuous. Even if you inwardly wish people to think you virtuous, then know that you are still caught in the same old web. If you wish in your heart that people know you are religious, then you are still caught in the same web. The world is still with you. It has assumed another shape, taken a new mode, but the same old trap continues. The same old pattern continues.

What will you get by seeing? You have seen so much. What did you get? What will you get by exhibiting? Who can give you something real for your display?

Putting aside these two, putting aside this duality and plunging into the observer, one finds that there is only one; this full moon is only one. In these pools, puddles, ponds, lakes it looked numerous. They were separate mirrors, so there seemed to be many moons . . .

I have heard that a king built a whole palace with mirrors. He put mirror after mirror inside and it became a looking-glass palace. Once, a dog—the king's own dog—was shut in at night. He was left inside by mistake. You can understand that dog's condition—it is the same as man's condition. He looked all around and saw nothing but dogs. A dog in every mirror. He barked—he freaked out!

When a man is afraid he wants to make others afraid. He thinks perhaps his fear will be less if others are also frightened.

The dog barked, but naturally, as there were only mirrors there, in mirror after mirror dogs barked back. The sound returned to him—it was his own echo. He barked all night, ran, charged the mirrors, and became covered in his own blood. No one else was there, he was alone. He was found dead in the morning. There were bloodstains all over the place. His story is the story of man.

There is no other here. The other does not exist. Only love is. Here only one is. But this will not be understood until you have caught hold of that one within you.

You are the one observer of all, and in reality you are always free. Ashtavakra says: *In reality . . . free.* Do not think this just a fantasy. Man is very strange: he thinks the world is real and these statements of truth, just fantasies. He considers unhappiness to be real, and if a ray of happiness descends, he considers it a dream, a deception.

People come to me and they say, 'We feel great joy, but the doubt arises that perhaps it is an illusion.' They have lived in misery for so many lives that they have lost the confidence that there can also be joy. Joy begins to seem impossible. They are so used to weeping, so used to unhappiness, so familiar with the thorns of life that they do not trust their eyes when they see flowers. They think,

'This must be a dream—an unreal sky flower; it cannot be, it should not exist.'

That is why Ashtavakra says: *And in reality . . . free.* One is not bound. Bondage is impossible, because only the divine is, only one is. There is nothing that binds, nor anything to be bound. . . . *in reality . . . always free.* This is why a man like Ashtavakra says, 'If you wish you can be free this very moment—because you are already free. There is nothing preventing freedom, there was never any bondage—you only believed you were bound.'

Your bondage is this: you see the other—not yourself—as the observer. There is only one bondage: you consider the other, not yourself, as the observer. And there is only one liberation: to know yourself as the observer.

Begin trying this experiment: You are sitting near a tree, you are looking at it. Then gradually, continuing to look at the tree, begin to see that one who is looking at the tree—just a little adjustment. Ordinarily the arrow of consciousness moves towards the tree. Let this arrow move in both directions. Let it bear fruit in both directions—it should see the tree and at the same time try to see the one who is seeing. Do not forget the seer.

Catch the seer more and more. You will miss again and again—it is an old habit of many lives. You will miss, but try to catch the one who sees again and again. And as the seer comes into your grasp, sometimes only for a moment—in that moment you will feel an emergence of unknown peace. A blessing has showered. A ray of benediction has descended. If it happens like that for a moment, in that moment you will enjoy the ecstasy of liberation. And this ecstasy will transform the flavour of your life, change the flow of your life. Words are not able to change your life stream, scriptures do not transform.

Experience transforms, the taste transforms.

You are listening to me here . . . One can listen in two ways. While listening, if your attention is fixed only on what I am saying, and you forget yourself, then you are not an observer, not a listener, not witnessing what you hear. Your attention gets stuck on me and you become a spectator. You can become a spectator not only with the eyes, but with the ears also. Whenever your attention gets stuck on the object you become a spectator.

While listening, listen to me and at the same time keep looking at that one too, catch hold of him, keep touching him—that one who is listening.

Certainly you are listening, I am speaking. But don't notice only the speaker, keep track of the listener too. Remember him again and again continuously. Gradually you will find that the moments you were in touch with the listener are the only moments you heard me; the rest is useless. When you listen in touch with the one who is listening then you will hear exactly what I am saying. And when you listen out of touch with the one who is listening, then who knows what you will hear? Something neither Ashtavakra nor I have said. Then your mind will weave all sorts of webs. You are unconscious: in unconsciousness how can you understand the words of consciousness?

These are statements of consciousness. These are words of another world. When you listen in sleep, you will weave dreams around these words. You will spoil the colour of these statements. You will paint over them. You will stretch their meanings in your own way. You will comment on them, and in your very commentary these very unique words will become corpses. Your hands will touch only Ashtavakra's corpse—you will miss the living Ashtavakra, because to touch the living Ashtavakra you will have to touch your observer. There, is the living Ashtavakra.

Think about it. You are listening to me. As you go on listening, listen also to the one who is listening. Let the arrow be double-ended—towards me and towards you also. There is no harm if you forget me, but you should not be forgotten. And a moment comes when neither you remain nor I remain . . . a moment of such deep peace, when two do not remain, only one remains. You are the one speaking, you are the one listening. You are the one seeing, you are the one being seen. This is the moment that Ashtavakra is indicating:

The one observer of all, and in reality always free. Bondage is dreamlike. Tonight you will sleep in Pune, but during your sleep you may be in Calcutta, you may be in Delhi, in Kathmandu—you may be anywhere. When you wake up in the morning you will find yourself again in Pune. If you went to Kathmandu in your dreams, to return you won't need to travel by air, nor catch a train, nor come back by foot. You won't need to travel at all. In the morning your eyes will open, and you will find yourself in Pune. In the morning you will find that you never went anywhere. You went somewhere in your dreams, but is going somewhere in dreams really going?

Your bondage is this: you see the other—not yourself— as the observer. There is only one bondage: we are not conscious of ourselves, we are not conscious of our observer.

This is one meaning of the sutra. There is another meaning that is also worth considering. Whosoever has written on Ashtavakra has usually given it this meaning, so it is necessary to understand the other meaning too. The second meaning is also right. Both together are right.

Your bondage is this: you see the other—not yourself— as the observer. You are listening to me; you think the ears are listening. You are looking at me; you think the eyes are looking. How will the eyes see? If you think the eyes are the observer you are mistaken. The one who sees is behind the eyes. The one who hears is behind the ears. If you touch my hand, you will think your hand is touching my hand. It is wrong. The one who touches is hidden within the hand; how will the hand touch?

If you die tomorrow the corpse will be lying there. People will sit holding the hand but there will be nobody inside the body to be touched. The corpse will be lying there, the eyes will still be open; it will look like everything is being seen but nothing will be seen. The corpse will be lying there . . . there may be music, a band playing, sound waves strike the ears, vibrations will reach you, but nothing will be heard. He who heard, he who saw, he who touched, he who tasted—that one has gone.

The experiencer is not the sense organs, but rather someone hidden behind the sense organs.

The other meaning of the sutra is to know yourself as the observer and not as the body, not as the eyes, the ears, the sense organs. Know only the inner consciousness as the observer.

> 'I am the doer', thus has the black serpent of ego bitten
> you. 'I am not the doer', drink this divine nectar of trust
> and be happy.

'I am the doer', thus has the black serpent of ego bitten you. Our belief is everything. We have fallen into dreams of belief. We become whatever we believe about ourselves. This idea is very thought-provoking. This is the very essence of the Eastern experience: whatever we have believed about ourselves, we become.

If you ever see a hypnotist giving a demonstration, you will be amazed. If he hypnotizes a man, then under hypnosis tells him, 'You are a woman—stand up and walk,' the man starts walking like a woman. It is very difficult for a man to walk like a woman. For that, a certain body structure is needed. To walk like a woman, a belly with an empty space for the womb is needed; otherwise one cannot walk like a woman. Or one can do it only after long practice. But when a hypnotist puts a man to sleep and tells him under hypnosis, 'Stand up! You are a woman, not a man—walk!', he walks like a woman.

Or he may hand him an onion and say, 'Here's an apple—go ahead and eat it.' He eats the onion. And if you ask him how it tastes he says it is very good! He doesn't even suspect that it is an onion—he can't smell it.

Hypnotists have experienced this, and by now it is scientific fact. There has been much experimentation on it. Lift the hand of an unconscious, hypnotized person and put an ordinary rock in it. Tell him it is a hot coal, and he will throw it away with a jerk, shouting, 'I am burned!' It would be okay if it only went this far, but a blister forms on his hand!

You must have heard of people who walk on fire. This too is a deep state of hypnosis. If you believe you won't be burned, the fire doesn't burn you. It is a matter of belief. If there is the slightest doubt, there will be trouble—you will be burned. There have been many incidents where people have felt courageous and simply walked on fire: 'When so many people are walking, then we can too.' But if the worm of doubt is inside anyone, he is burned.

An experiment was done on this at Oxford University. Some Buddhist monks from Sri Lanka were invited to fire walk. Every year on the Buddha Full Moon they walk on fire in remembrance of the Buddha. This is absolutely right. To walk on fire in remembrance of the Buddha is right because Buddha's whole teaching is that you are not the body.

If we are not the body, then how can fire burn us? In the Gita, Krishna has said, 'Neither fire can burn you nor weapons pierce you.' So, many monks walk on fire on the Buddha Full Moon in Sri Lanka.

Some of them were invited to Oxford and they walked on fire there too. While they were fire walking at Oxford one monk was burned. About twenty monks walked—and only one was burned. It was looked into, to find out how it happened. The monk had come only to see England, he had no trust that he could walk on fire. His intention was something else, he had come only as a tourist; he only wanted to see England. And he thought, 'These nineteen people are not getting burned—why should I burn?' But inside there was a worm of doubt and he was burned.

There was another incident that same night. A professor, an Oxford University professor, was sitting watching. He had never seen, had never heard about fire walking. He watched and felt so much trust that he got up and started walking on fire. He was not a Buddhist, not religious—he didn't know anything. He just watched so many people walking and he felt—the feeling came from such depths, the trust became so strong that he got up in deep ecstasy and began dancing on the coals.

The monks were shocked because they had the idea that Buddha was protecting them. This man was no Buddhist. He was English, and wasn't even religious. He didn't go to church, so Jesus wouldn't bother about him. He had nothing to do with Buddha, he had no master at all . . . just trust.

In deep trust, trust fulfils itself.

'*I am the doer*', *thus has the black serpent of ego bitten you. 'I am not the doer*', *drink this divine nectar of trust and be happy.* Listen to this statement: Ashtavakra says again and again: 'Be happy.' He is saying it can happen this very moment!

I am the doer . . . This is our projection and we create our ego in accordance with this projection. The doer means the ego. *I am the doer* . . . we create the ego out of this, so the bigger the doer, the bigger the ego. If you have never done anything special, how can you have a big ego? You have built a big house—your ego becomes as big as the house. You have created a great empire, so the limits of your ego extend to its limits. Because of this, some mad people have set out to conquer the world. Try to conquer the world? Who has ever conquered it? People come and go—who has been able to conquer the world?

But people try to conquer it, making claims that their ego is so vast, it is bigger than the whole world: 'I will surround it. I will make the borders, I will define the whole universe.' Alexander and Napoleon, Tamerlane and Nadir Shah—all mad people—attempted to conquer the world. This desire to conquer the whole world is the desire of the ego.

You may have seen someone . . . when he became a minister or chief minister, did you see his stride? Then when he is out of office look at him: out of office he gets into such a bad state. The man is the same, but his strength is lost. The poison of the ego which gave him that quickness, which gave him that high, which brought a lightness to his step, which kept his head high and his back straight—this is all lost. What happened? A moment before he looked so powerful, the next moment he has become so feeble. Once they are out of office politicians do not live long. They remain strong as long as they are winning elections, but as soon as they are defeated they lose strength.

Psychologists say that people die earlier if they retire than if they don't. There is a difference of ten years, more or less. A man who would have lived to be eighty, if he is retired at sixty he dies at seventy. The single cause of early death is that he is no longer in power; no longer a collector, a commissioner, a police inspector or even a constable or schoolteacher. A schoolteacher too has his arrogance. He has a realm of his own: he holds sway over thirty or forty boys. He keeps them in submission—he is emperor of the classroom.

It is reported that when Aurangzeb put his father in prison, his father told him, 'I don't feel at home here. Can you do something for me? Send me thirty or forty young boys so I can open a school.'

It is said that Aurangzeb remarked, 'My father may be in jail but the old pride of being an emperor remains. Now he will have dominion over just thirty or forty boys.'

Even the most insignificant schoolteacher is king in the world of thirty or forty children. The mightiest kings never have so much power over their subjects. When the teacher says, 'Stand up!' they stand up, and when he says, 'Sit down!' they sit down. All are in his hands.

Just a schoolteacher, a collector, a deputy collector, a cabinet minister, anyone whatsoever—as soon as he retires he becomes weak. No one greets him on the streets anymore. He doesn't seem to have any purpose anywhere. He seems to be superfluous, as if thrown on to the rubbish heap, or put in the junkyard. Now he is not needed anywhere. Wherever he goes people endure his presence, but from their expressions he understands them to be saying, 'Just move on. Why have you come here anyway? Excuse us—now let us do our work.'

The same people who used to flatter him avoid him. Those people who used to massage his feet have disappeared. Suddenly the balloon of his ego is shrinking, as if the balloon has burst; air has escaped, it is punctured. He begins to shrink. There doesn't seem to be any reason in living. The wish to die starts coming to him. He begins to think of dying because now life has no meaning.

People die sooner after retirement because the whole strength and juice of their lives was in the area of their work. Somebody was a head clerk, so he had five or ten clerks he used to torture. It doesn't matter who you are—even if you were just a peon, you have your pride. When you enter an office, look at the peon sitting there. He sits in the hall on his stool, but look at his arrogance when he says, 'Stop! Wait!'

Mulla Nasruddin was working as a policeman and he stopped a woman for speeding. He quickly pulled out his papers and started writing. The woman said, 'Listen, don't waste your time writing—the mayor knows me.' But he went on writing. The woman said, 'Did you hear or not? The chief minister knows me too.' But he just went on writing. Finally the woman placed her last stake. She said, 'Can you hear or not? Indira Gandhi knows me too.'

Mulla said, 'Stop talking all this nonsense. Do you know Mulla Nasruddin?'

The woman replied, 'Which Mulla Nasruddin is that? What do you mean?'

He said, 'My name is Mulla Nasruddin, and if I know you then something is possible. Whosoever else knows you . . . even if God himself knows you, this report is going to be written and you are going to be prosecuted.'

Everyone has his pride. The policeman too has his arrogance; he has his own world, his own realm. If you are caught inside it he will harass you.

The ego lives within the boundaries of what you can do. You can see that an egotistical person feels very helpless in saying yes.

Examine yourself carefully. I am not giving you a yardstick with which to check others. Use it for self-analysis.

To say no gives pleasure because one feels powerful in saying no.

When a child asks if he can go and play outside, his mother says, 'No!' There is no harm in playing outside. If the child cannot play outside where can he play? And the mother also knows he is going to—he will raise an uproar, he too will show his strength. There will be a clash of wills and politics will be used. He will scream and shout; he will throw things. Then she will say, 'Go and play outside!' But when she is the one saying, 'Go and play outside,' it is okay. Then he goes, obeying her orders.

Mulla Nasruddin's son was creating an uproar and Mulla told him again and again, 'Sit down and be quiet! Do as I say. Sit down and shut up.'

But the boy was not listening. What son listens? Finally, becoming angry, Mulla said, 'Make as much mischief as you like. Now let's see if you disobey my orders. Now it is my order: Make trouble! Now let's see if you disobey my orders.'

'No' comes easily. You keep it ready on your tongue. Look carefully: ninety times out of a hundred there is no need to say no, but you don't miss any opportunity to say it. When you get a chance to say no you seize it immediately. You feel helpless when you have to say yes. You feel insignificant when you have to say yes. To say yes means you have no power.

Therefore, the very egotistical become atheists. To be an atheist means they have said the final no. They have said that even God is not, forget about anyone else. An atheist has made the final, the ultimate denial. The theist has accepted the ultimate, he has said yes, God is. To say God is means, 'I am not.' And to say no to God means, 'Only I am. No one is above me, no one is beyond me. No one can set limits on me.'

Our doing gives strength to our ego. Keep this sutra of Ashtavakra in mind: 'I am the doer,' thus has the black serpent of ego bitten you. You are uselessly disturbed and miserable. This misery is not coming from somewhere outside—we ourselves have created the unhappiness we suffer. The bigger the ego, the greater the misery. Ego is a wound, and the slightest puff of air gives pain.

It is impossible to make an egoless person miserable. And it is impossible to make an egotist happy. The egotist has made a decision not to be happy—because happiness comes from a mood of yes, from a mood of acceptance. Happiness comes from realizing, 'I am nothing—I am a drop in the ocean. A drop of the ocean—and only the ocean is. What is my being?'

To the same extent that one's experience of non-being deepens, showers of happiness begin to flood over you. He who becomes void is filled, he who stands proudly is made void. 'I am not the doer,' drink this divine nectar of trust and be happy.

'I am not the doer . . .' Ashtavakra calls this feeling divine nectar. 'I am not the doer . . .' This is ambrosia.

You should understand another meaning also. Only ego dies, you never die; hence ego is death, poison. The day you know there is no such thing as ego, then there is only the divine inside of you—you are one with it, one ray of it, one drop of it—then there is no death for you, then you are immortal.

With the divine you are deathless. With yourself you are going to die. With yourself you are alone—against the world, against existence. You are engaged in an impossible battle in which defeat is certain. With the divine everything is with you. In it defeat is impossible, victory is assured.

Take all with you when you start the journey. When it can happen by cooperation, why struggle? When it can be attained by bowing down, why try to take it by fighting? When it can be attained by simplicity, by innocence, why uselessly cause trouble?

'I am not the doer,' drink this divine nectar of trust and be happy. Janak has asked, 'How can I be happy? How can happiness happen? How can liberation be attained?' Ashtavakra is not giving any methods. He does not say do this or that. He says look in this way, let your looking be like this. It is all a matter of looking. If you are unhappy it is rooted in wrong looking. If you want to be happy, then right looking . . .

Drink this divine nectar of trust and be happy. This definition of trust needs to be understood. Distrust means you do not accept that you are one with the whole. From this, doubt arises. How can there be distrust if you accept you are one with the whole? Wherever existence takes you, it is good. We didn't come here through our own wish, we don't go through our own wish. We don't know why we are born nor do we know why we die. Before birth no one asked us whether we wanted to be born. Before death no one will ask us whether we want to die.

Everything is happening here by itself. Who asks us? Why should we uselessly bring ourselves into it? We shall disappear again into that one from whom life has emerged. And the divine has given life, how can we distrust it? How can we distrust the source from which this beautiful life has emerged? That in which these flowers bloom, these lotuses bloom; that which is behind this moon and stars, this man, these animals and birds. Here there is so much song, so much music, so much love—why should we distrust it?

Trust means we do not consider ourselves separate, we are not foreigners. We know that we are one with this existence. With the very declaration of this oneness life is showered with happiness.

Drink this divine nectar of trust and be happy. Be happy right now: *drink this divine nectar of trust and be happy*. Be happy this very moment.

> 'I am the one pure awareness,' thus having burned the forest of your ignorance with this fire of certainty and being beyond sorrow, be happy.

Go beyond misery right now. All unhappiness disappears when you realize this, that 'I am pure awareness, I am only the witness, I am only the observer.'

The disease of ego is the only disease.

I have heard:

Once, Mulla Nasruddin participated in a poetry festival in Delhi. When the festival was over the master of ceremonies distributed the prizes to the poets. Mulla was not pleased—he expected a bigger prize than he got. He was very angry and he said, 'Do you know who I am? I am the Kalidas of Pune!'

The master of ceremonies must have been clever. He said, 'That's great. But tell us which neighbourhood in Pune you are the Kalidas of?' Each neighbourhood has its Kalidas, each street its Tagore. Each person thinks he is unique, that he is incomparably brilliant.

In Arabia there is a saying that when God makes a man, he whispers in his ear, 'Never has a better man than you existed.' And he says it to everybody. This joke is very deep. And every person lives with this idea in his head, 'No man greater than me has ever existed, I am the highest being ever created. Who cares whether anyone believes me or not? That is their problem. But I am the highest in creation.'

A man who lives with this conceit makes himself miserable. Expectations that can never be fulfilled arise from this false idea. His expectations are infinite—but life is very small. One who lives in expectations is bound to be unhappy.

There is an art to live this life in quite a different way—void of expectations, without demanding anything, filled with gratitude for whatever one has, in thankfulness. This is the technique of one who trusts.

What you have is so much . . . but only when you see it.

I have heard:

A man went to the river to end his life. A Sufi fakir was sitting on the riverbank and he asked, 'What are you doing?'

The man was just about to jump in. He said, 'Don't stop me. It's too much! This life is nothing, everything is meaningless. I never got anything I wanted, I always got what I wanted to avoid. God is against me, so why should I continue this life?'

The fakir said, 'Wait, stay one more day—then you can die. What's the rush? You say you don't have anything?'

The man replied, 'Nothing at all. If I had anything, why would I come to take my life?'

The fakir said, 'Come with me. The king of this place is my friend.'

The fakir took him to the king and he whispered something in the king's ear. The king said, 'I can offer you a million rupees.' The man heard only this, he couldn't hear what the fakir had whispered. The king said, 'I can give you a million rupees.'

The fakir went to the man and whispered in his ear, 'The king is ready to buy both your eyes for a million rupees: will you sell them?'

Ego is a contagious disease. When a child is born, he has no ego. He is absolutely egoless, innocent. He is an open book in which nothing is written—a blank book. Then letters are gradually inscribed, then the ego is gradually created. Parents, family, society, school, university: all go on strengthening the ego. All our methods of education, our culture, our society and civilization give birth to this one disease, give birth to the ego. Then this ego pursues us like a ghost our whole life.

If you want to know the meaning of real religion, it is this: real religion is nothing but the medicine for the disease given to you by society, culture and civilization.

This religion is anti-society, anti-culture, anti-civilization. This religion is rebellion. This religion is revolution.

The whole meaning of the religious revolution is to drop what has been given to you by others, what has been taught by others. Do not cling to it: it is your misery, it is your hell. Besides ego there are no burdens in your life. Besides ego there are no fetters, no chains.

I am the one pure awareness, thus having burned the forest of your ignorance with this fire of certainty and being beyond sorrow, be happy. Ego means mixing one's consciousness with something else. A man says, 'I am intelligent'; now he has added ego to his intelligence. His consciousness becomes contaminated.

Have you noticed: when someone adds water to milk, we say the milk has become contaminated. If he then says no, it is not contaminated, he has added only the purest water, still you would say it is contaminated. Whether the water was pure or impure is not the question—water was added. It does not make any difference that you added pure water; the milk has still become contaminated. If you look a little closer, you will see that not only has the milk become impure, but the water has also become impure. Separately, water and milk were pure; mixed, both are contaminated. Confusion arises from the mixing of opposites, from the mixing of different types.

No sooner is consciousness added to something different that the trouble begins. You say you are intelligent. Intellect is a mechanism—use it. Do not become an intellectual. This is real intelligence—not becoming an intellectual. When you say you are intelligent, then the difficulty has started— water in the milk. Then it doesn't make any difference how pure your intelligence is. When you say you are a person of character, water is added to milk. It doesn't make any difference how pure your character is—bad character or good character, both have egos.

I have heard an old story:

In Russia, during the time of the czars, three criminals were imprisoned in Siberia. The three always argued among themselves who was the greatest criminal and they also argued who would be jailed the longest. This usually happens in jail—people inflate their crimes when they talk. It is not only you that talks of a greater bank balance than you have. When a guest comes you borrow furniture from your neighbours and carpets to spread on your floor. It is not only you who deceives others. You are not the only one who, seeing others, begins reciting 'Hari Ram, Hari Ram.' Or when someone comes you spend a longer time praying and ring the worship bells louder, but when no one comes you finish everything quickly. It is not that you are the only one doing this. If a guest is in the house, you go to the temple to give an impression that you are religious. In jail, prisoners do the same thing.

Those three prisoners used to argue among themselves. One day the first prisoner said, 'When I was sent to prison in Siberia, when I reached this jail, there were no motor cars.'

The second one said, 'So what's so great about that? When I was jailed, there weren't even bullock carts.'

The third said, 'Bullock cart? What's a bullock cart?'

They were trying to prove who had been jailed the longest. Ego exists there too.

I have heard . . .

A new criminal arrived at a jail. There was an old gangster already in the cell he was sent to. The gangster asked him, 'How long are you going to stay?'

He replied: 'I was sentenced for twenty years.'

He said, 'Then stay near the door. You will be leaving soon. Set up your bed just by the door.'

Criminals have egos too. In doing wrong one inflates one's ego; in doing good one also inflates it. But in both conditions consciousness is contaminated.

Ashtavakra says: 'I am the one pure awareness . . . I am neither intelligent nor of great character, nor characterless; I am neither beautiful nor ugly; I am neither old nor young; neither white nor black; neither Hindu nor Mohammedan; neither Brahmin nor Sudra. I have no identification—I am the one who sees all of these.'

When you light a lamp in your house its light falls on the table, on the chair, on the wall, on the wall clock, on the furniture, on the cabinet, on the carpet, on the floor, on the ceiling—it falls on all. If you are there, it falls on you too. But the flame is neither the wall, nor the roof, nor the floor, nor the table or chair. Everything is illumined by its light, but the light is separate.

Pure consciousness is your light, is your awareness. The light of that awareness falls on your intellect, on your body, on your actions—but you are not any of these. As long as you identify yourself with anything, ego will arise. Ego is the identification of consciousness with some other thing. As soon as you drop all identification—you say I am only pure knowing, I am pure awareness, I am purely a buddha—then you begin to return to your home. The moment of liberation is coming closer.

Ashtavakra says: *'I am the one pure awareness,'* thus *having burned . . . with this fire of certainty . . .* What is this certainty, this trust?

This trust will not happen through listening.

This certainty will not happen through intellectual understanding—you have understood it many times, and still you forget it again and again.

This certainty comes from experience.

If you experiment a little, trust will come. When experience comes, trust comes. And when trust comes, the revolution happens.

> . . . having burned the forest of your ignorance with this
> fire of certainty and being beyond sorrow, be happy.
> You are that bliss, that ultimate bliss, within which
> this imaginary world is projected like a snake on a rope.
> Knowing this, thus wander happily.

There is no reason for unhappiness here. You uselessly live in a bad dream and go on getting disturbed. In nightmares, have you noticed . . . someone sleeps with his hand on his chest, but in his sleep he thinks a ghost is sitting on him. He put his own hand on his chest, it is his own weight, but in sleep that weight creates an illusion. Or in putting his own pillow over his chest, it seems that a mountain has fallen on him. He tries to scream and shout—the scream won't even come out. He wants to move his hands and feet—his hands and feet won't move. He falls into such a panic. And when his sleep is broken, he finds that he is drenched in sweat. When sleep is broken, when he wakes up, he understands there was no enemy, no mountain has fallen on him. He had put his own pillow on his chest, he had put his own hand on his chest. His heart is still pumping wildly, as if he has run for miles. The dream is broken, but its effects still continue. The sufferings we call worldly sufferings are only misunderstandings of our awareness.

This imaginary world is projected like a snake on a rope. Sometime you must have seen a piece of rope lying on the road in the dark, and immediately the idea of a snake comes. When the idea comes, a snake is projected on to the rope. You run, you scream and shout. You might even fall over while running and break a limb. Later on you will find out that it was only a rope. But what use is that now? The limb is broken. But if you have even a small lamp of awareness, a little light, then even in the darkest night you can see that a rope is a rope, not a snake.

In this very awareness, bliss and ultimate bliss are born, *thus wander happily.* You have the key—you have the light. You have kept the light covered wastefully. Take the cover off!

Kabir has said, 'Open the curtain of the veil.' Push aside the curtains of thought, of passion, of expectation, of fantasies, of dreams. These are the veils. Push them aside. Look with unveiled eyes. People sit veiled head to foot, and because of those veils they cannot see anything. They are pushed here and there, and they fall into ditches.

This imaginary world is projected like a snake on a rope. Knowing this, thus wander happily. Understand this knowing; grasp it, be acquainted with it. Then move happily. This existence is ultimate bliss. This existence doesn't know unhappiness. Unhappiness is your creation.

It is difficult to understand this. We live in such misery, how can we believe that misery does not exist? The one who ran when he saw a piece of rope won't believe there is no snake. The one who was sleeping with a pillow on his chest and thinks that a mountain has fallen on him cannot believe in that moment that in fact a mountain has not fallen on him. This is our situation. What can we do?

Move a little from the observed towards the observer.

See everything, but do not forget the one who sees.

Hear everything, but do not forget the one who hears.

Do everything, but remember you are not the doer.

Buddha used to say, 'Move on the path and remember that within no one is moving. Within, all is unmoving.' And this is how it is. Have you seen the wheels of a moving vehicle? The axle remains still, while the wheels move. In the same way the wheel of life moves, but the axle remains still. You are the axle.

> He who considers himself free is free, and he who considers himself bound is bound; because in this world the proverb is true: 'As you think so you are.'

This is a significant sutra: *He who considers himself free is free.* He who knows that he is free is free. For freedom nothing else has to be done. Just to know that you are free is enough. Freedom will not come from your doing, freedom comes from your knowing. Freedom is not the result of action, it is the fruit of knowing. *He who considers himself free is free, and he who considers himself bound is bound.* He who thinks, 'I am in chains,' is in chains. He who thinks, 'I am liberated,' is liberated.

Try it and see. For one day decide that during these twenty-four hours it is true—that you are free. Try remaining free for twenty-four hours. You will be surprised, you won't believe it yourself. If you think you are free, there is no one to enslave you, and you are free. If you think you are enslaved, then everything binds you.

I had a friend, he was a professor with me. During the Holi festival he drank bhang—a hemp drink—and created a disturbance in the street, he made a scene. He was a very gentle and simple man. There is danger in a gentle person; such a person has much repressed within. He was not a troublemaker. Even his name was Bholeram, 'simple-hearted'. He was honest and simple. There is a danger in such a nice man—he should avoid things like bhang. The bhang washed off his superficial, sweet temperament and all the repressions lying beneath, which had been unexpressed his whole life, came out. He went out in the street and raised an uproar and created trouble. He harassed some woman, was arrested and locked up at the police station. And he was an English professor!

At around two in the morning someone came and informed me that my friend had been arrested, and he wanted me to get him out before morning, otherwise it would be a big mess. With difficulty we got him released just before dawn. We got him out, but he was so upset—such a nice man—he was so disturbed that everything became impossible. For three months he suffered. Whenever a policeman appeared on the road he would hide, thinking, 'He is coming to arrest me.' We lived together in one room. If he heard a police whistle at night, he would dive under the bed. I would ask what he was doing: he would say they were after him.

Eventually his condition deteriorated so much that he could not sleep, nor would he allow me to sleep. He would say, 'Wake up! Did you hear? Those people . . . There are voices in the air. They are sending out messages on the radio, inquiring where Bholeram is!'

I would say, 'Bholeram, go to sleep.'

He would reply, 'How can I go to sleep? My life is in danger! They will arrest me. They are keeping a file against me.'

Finally, I was so harassed, and not seeing any way out, he stopped going to the college—he took leave and stayed at home. Around the clock he had this one obsession, becoming what psychologists call paranoid. He created everything out of his fear, his paranoia.

He was a good man, and I had never thought that this could happen. But now I experienced what imagination man is capable of. 'The walls,' he would say, 'have ears. People are listening everywhere!' If he saw anyone walking near the house then he thought he must be looking for him. If anyone was standing around laughing, he must be laughing at Bholeram. If people were talking among themselves they were conspiring against him. The whole world was against him.

I could see no other way, there was only one possibility: I had a friend who was a police inspector. I explained everything to him and asked him to come one day with Bholeram's file.

He said, 'If there were a file on him I would bring it, but there is no file, not even a record. This man has never done anything, he took bhang once and created some sort of scene. The matter is finished—there should not be any fuss about it now.'

I told him, 'Bring any file, even fill it with blank papers, but it should be thick because he says it is a big thick file. And remember, it should have Bholeram's name printed on it. Don't worry about it, just give him two or three slaps, and put him in handcuffs too. Refuse to let him go until I give you a ten-thousand-rupee bribe. Then too, only "perhaps" he should be released.'

The police came, bringing everything with them. They slapped him two or three times and Bholeram was very happy to get slapped. He said to me, 'Look! Isn't it happening like I told you it would? Here is the file: "Bholeram" is written in big letters on it. Tell me, where have all your wise explanations gone now? Now this is happening: I am in handcuffs! Bholeram is finished!'

But in a way he was happy, and at the same time miserable. He was crying, but he was happy to see that his projection had proved right. Man is so insane! If your projection of suffering proves right, your ego is satisfied, you are proved right. He felt that everyone else was proved wrong, that all those who were trying to advise him were not right; finally, he alone proved right.

With great difficulty, I pleaded and persuaded the inspector. I had already told him not to agree with what I would say too soon; otherwise Bholeram would suspect that we were in conspiracy.

The inspector said, 'It cannot be done. He should be sentenced for life.' He continued talking like this and looked at me to see how he was doing. With great difficulty I finally persuaded him, and with folded hands I requested him to accept the bundles of bills as a bribe. Then he burned the file in front of us. From that day Bholeram was free of fear—he was okay now. The whole episode ended there.

This is your situation, more or less. He who considers himself free is free, and he who considers himself bound is bound; because in this world the proverb is true: 'As you think so you are.'

What happens to you is what you have thought. Your thinking has created your world. Change your thoughts.

Wake up! See in a new way. Everything will remain as it is, only your way of seeing, of thinking, of knowing will change—then everything will change.

He who considers himself free is free, and he who considers himself bound is bound; because in this world the proverb is true: 'As you think so you are.'

As you think so you are.

The soul is the witness, all-pervading, perfect, one, free, conscious, free from doing, absolutely alone, non-attached, desireless, peaceful. Because of illusion, it looks like the world.

The witness, all-pervading, perfect . . . Listen to these words. Ashtavakra says you are perfect, you don't need to become perfect. Nothing can be added to you. However you are, you are complete. You don't need any improvement. You don't have to climb any ladder—there is nothing above you. You are perfect, you are the divine, all-pervading; the witness, one, free; you are consciousness, free from all doing, non-attached. No one binds you. You have no companion, you are alone; you are in supreme aloneness. You are desireless.

You don't have to become all these. This is the difference in Ashtavakra's message. If you listen to Mahavira, he says you have to become these things. Ashtavakra says you already are. This is a great difference, no small difference. Mahavira says you have to be non-attached, you have to become desireless, you have to become perfect, you have to become all-pervading, you have to become the witness. Ashtavakra says you are all these, you just have to wake up. You have to open your eyes and see.

Ashtavakra's yoga is a very natural yoga. As Kabir says, 'Oh sadhu, the natural samadhi is best.'

'I am an individually projected life', drop this illusion and also the feeling of inner and outer, and awaken in the thought that you are the unchanging, conscious, non-dual soul.

What you have believed in up to now is nothing but reflected projections. It is only your belief, your opinion. Moreover, people around you share the same beliefs. In this way your opinions are strengthened. Ultimately, man borrows his opinions. You learn from others. Man imitates. All are unhappy here, so you also become unhappy.

There was a rare buddha in Japan: Hotei. As soon as he was enlightened, as soon as he woke up, he began laughing. And he continued laughing his whole life, traveling from village to village. In Japan they call him 'The Laughing Buddha'. He would stand in the middle of the marketplace and laugh. And his name spread far and wide. People used to wait for Hotei's arrival. He had no other message than standing in the middle of the marketplace and laughing. A crowd would collect and they too would begin laughing.

People used to ask him, 'Please tell us something more.'

He would reply, 'What more is there to say? You are unnecessarily crying. You need a fool to make you laugh. This is my only message: Laugh! There is nothing missing, just have a good belly laugh. The whole existence is laughing: you are unnecessarily crying. Your crying is absolutely private. The whole of existence is laughing: the moon and stars, flowers and birds are all laughing, and you go on crying. Open your eyes and laugh! I have no other message.'

He laughed, and went on wandering from village to village. It is said he made all of Japan laugh. And people gradually began to get glimpses from laughing and laughing with him. It was his meditation, his very samadhi. People began to experience that they could laugh, they could be happy—without any cause.

The very search for causes is wrong. As long as you look for a reason before you laugh, you will never laugh. If you think you will be happy when there is a reason for it, then you will never be happy. Looking for reasons one becomes more and more unhappy. Cause belongs to suffering, happiness is your nature. Cause has to be created, suffering has to be created. Happiness is. Happiness is already present. Just let happiness manifest. This is what Ashtavakra says again and again: *thus wander happily* . . . being beyond sorrow, be happy . . . *drink this divine nectar of trust and be happy*.

Man is perfect, he is one, he is free. His projections are the only barrier.

'I am an individually projected life', drop this illusion and also the feeling of inner and outer, and awaken in the thought that you are the unchanging, conscious, non-dual soul. Becoming free of the feeling of outer and inner . . . Your being is neither outside nor inside. Outside and inside are only mind distinctions. Being is outside, being is inside— all outside and inside are in being. Only being is.

Drop . . . the feeling of inner and outer, and awaken in the thought that you are the unchanging, conscious, non-dual soul.

This translation is not right. The original sutra is: 'drop . . . the feeling of inner and outer, and awaken in the feeling that you are the unchanging, conscious, non-dual atma.' Thought is not a correct translation here. 'Awaken in the feeling that you are the unchanging . . . soul.'

Know that you are, feel that you are. Awaken to such a feeling. Thought is again becoming intellectual. Thought makes it only superficial. It cannot come from the head, it can only come from the heart. This experience is like love, not like mathematics. It is not like logic, it is like a song, whose singing goes on sinking deeper and deeper and, touching the innermost life energy, makes it vibrate.

Awaken in the feeling that you are the unchanging . . . soul. You are not this revolving wheel of life, you are the axle in the middle. The axle is unmoving.

As long as you think you are on the earth, you are on the earth. But the moment you are ready, the moment you dare to fly into the sky, that is the very moment you can start flying.

Wake up! You have seen plenty of dreams—now wake up.

Awakening is the key.

Nothing else is to be done—not any sadhana, not any yoga, not any yoga postures. Just wake up.

Hari-om-tat-sat!

4

Meditation: The Only Medicine

Osho,
     What is the relationship between meditation and
witnessing? In what way are mind and ego dissolved by
them? Is surrender possible without attaining complete
egolessness? To what extent are orange clothes and the
mala helpful for meditation and witnessing? Also, please
explain the difference between witnessing, wakefulness
and right remembering.

Human life can be divided into four circles.

The first circle is of action, the world of doing. It is the
outermost. Moving within a little we come to the world of
thought. Moving a little further in we come to the world of
feeling, devotion, love. Moving still further within we reach
the centre—the world of the witness.

The witness is our nature, because there is no way
to go beyond it. No one ever has, and no one ever can.
To become the witness of the witness is impossible. The
witness is simply the witness. You cannot go deeper
than it. It is our foundation. Our house is built on the

foundation of witnessing—built of feeling, of thought, of action.

This is why there are three yogas: karma yoga, gyan yoga, bhakti yoga—the yogas of action, knowledge and devotion. These are the three methods of meditation. Through these three disciplines one can make efforts to reach the witness.

The yoga of action means action plus meditation. Karma yoga is the effort to go directly from doing to witnessing. Meditation is the process and witnessing is the goal.

You have asked, 'What is the relationship between meditation and witnessing?' Meditation is the path, witnessing is the destination.

Witnessing is the culmination of meditation.

And meditation is the beginning of witnessing.

A karma yogi is one who adds meditation to doing, who links meditation to the world of action—action plus meditation.

Then a gyan yogi is one who adds meditation to thought. He links meditation to the world of thought. He begins to think meditatively. A new practice is added: whatever one does is done with awareness. When the state of thought plus meditation is established, the journey towards witnessing begins.

Meditation is a change of direction.

Whatever meditation is joined to becomes a vehicle for moving towards witnessing.

And the third path is bhakti yoga—adding meditation to feeling, a deep joining of meditation and feeling, the wedding of meditation and feeling. So, while feeling, become meditative.

Through these three paths one can approach the witness. But the method that brings you is meditation, the fundamental thing is meditation. It is just like a doctor giving you medicine, saying to take it with honey, and you say you don't eat honey, you are a Jaina. Then he says to take it with milk, and you say you cannot drink milk because milk is a form of blood, you are a strict Quaker—you don't drink milk, it is like eating meat. So the doctor says take it with water. But the medicine is the same—honey, milk or water, it doesn't make any difference. They are only to help swallow the medicine, to get it down the throat. Medicine won't go down by itself.

Meditation is medicine.

There are three types of people in the world. Some people cannot live without action. Their whole life flow is in working. If they try to sit quietly they cannot; they have to do something or other. There is energy, flowing energy. There is no harm in this, but the masters say, swallow the medicine of meditation with the action. You can't stop doing, but you can add meditation to doing. You say, 'I can't sit a single moment without doing something. I just can't. Sitting is not within my power, it's not my nature.'

Psychologists call them extroverts: they are always occupied, they need to do something or other. Until they fall down exhausted and sleep it is not natural for them to stop working. Activity is their nature.

The master says, 'Good. Do it riding on action. Make this your horse. Mix your medicine with this and swallow it. The real question is the medicine. Start working meditatively. Whatever you do, don't do it unconsciously, do it with awareness. Stay awake while doing.'

Then there are some who say doing has no attraction for them, but thoughts come rushing in waves. They are thinkers—they have no juice for doing. They have no interest in the outer, but great waves arise within, a great tempest. And they cannot be inside for a single moment without thoughts. They say, 'If we sit silently more thoughts come. When we sit silently more thoughts than usual come. Just mention worship, prayer, meditation, and a great deluge of thoughts—armies—come in wave after wave and drown us. What should we do?'

The master says, 'Drink meditation mixed in with your thoughts. Don't stop your thoughts, but when thoughts come observe them. Don't get lost in them, stand a little apart, at a distance. Calmly watching your thoughts, you will gradually attain witnessing. Add meditation to your thoughts.'

Then there are some who say, 'We have no trouble with thoughts, no trouble with doing. We have an excess of feeling. Tears flow, the heart is overwhelmed, drowning—in love, in affection, in trust, in devotion.'

The master says, 'Make this your medicine. Add meditation to this. Let tears flow—flow filled with meditation. Let the thrill be there, but filled with meditation. The essence is meditation.'

These differences between bhakti, karma and gyan are not differences in medicine. The medicine is one. You can see this in Ashtavakra. Ashtavakra says take a direct leap. Swallow the medicine straight. He says, what use are these practices?

That is why Ashtavakra is not a gyan yogi or a bhakti yogi or a karma yogi. He says to drop straight into witnessing. These crutches are no use—this medicine can be swallowed directly. Drop these crutches, drop these vehicles—you can run directly. You can be the witness directly.

As far as Ashtavakra is concerned, the witness and meditation are not different. But as far as other methods are concerned, the witness and meditation are different. For these other paths, meditation is the process and witnessing is the destination.

For Ashtavakra the path and destination are one. So he can say to be blissful right now. One whose path and goal are different cannot say, 'Right now.' He will say, 'Move! The journey is long; climb, then you will reach the mountain.' Ashtavakra says, 'Open your eyes: you are sitting on the mountain! Where are you going? How to go anywhere?'

Ashtavakra's sutra is extremely revolutionary.

Neither gyan, nor bhakti, nor karma yoga—none of these have reached his height. It is pure witnessing. Look at it like this: the medicine doesn't even need to be swallowed, just understanding is enough, awareness is enough. There is no need for help—you are already there. But people are incapable of understanding it.

A Sufi story:

A man went in search of truth. The first religious man he met was sitting under a tree, just outside his own village. He asked, 'I am searching for a true master. Please tell me the characteristics of a true master.'

The fakir told him the characteristics. His description was very simple. He said, 'You'll find him sitting under such-and-such a tree, sitting in such-and-such posture, his hands making such-and-such gestures—that is enough to know he is the true master.'

The seeker started searching. It is said that thirty years passed while he wandered the whole earth. He visited many places, but never met the master. He met many masters, but none were true masters. He returned to his own village completely exhausted. As he was returning he was surprised, he couldn't believe it: that old man was seated under the same tree, and now he could see that this was the very tree that the old man had spoken of—'he will be sitting under such-and-such a tree.' And his posture was exactly as he had described. 'It was the same posture he was sitting in thirty years ago—was I blind? The exact expression on his face, the exact gestures . . . !'

He fell at his feet saying, 'Why didn't you tell me in the first place? Why did you misdirect me for these thirty years? Why didn't you tell me that you are the true master?'

The old man said, 'I told you, but you were not ready to listen. You were not able to come home without wandering away. You had to knock on the doors of a thousand houses to come to your own home, only then could you return. I said it, I said everything—'beneath such-and-such a tree'. I was describing this very tree, the posture I was sitting in, but you were too fast, you couldn't hear correctly, you were in a hurry. You were going somewhere to search. Searching was very important for you, the truth was not so important.

'But you have come! I was feeling tired, sitting continuously in this posture for you. You were wandering for thirty years, but think of me sitting under this tree! I knew some day you would come, but what if I had already passed away? I waited for you—you have come! You had to wander for thirty years, but that's your own fault. The master was always here.'

It happens many times in our life that we cannot see what is near, and what is far attracts us. The distant drum sounds sweeter, we are pulled by distant dreams.

Ashtavakra says that you are what you are seeking.

And you are it right here, right now.

What Krishnamurti has been telling people is exactly Ashtavakra's message. No one understood Ashtavakra, nor has anyone understood Krishnamurti. And your so-called saints and sannyasins are very angry because Krishnamurti says there is no need for meditation. He is absolutely right—no need for devotion, no need for action, no need for knowledge. Ordinary sadhus and saints become very nervous: 'No need whatsoever? He is misleading people!' It is these sadhus who mislead.

Krishnamurti is straightforwardly giving Ashtavakra's message. He is saying there is no need because there is only a need if you have lost something. Just get up and shake off the dust! Splash a little cold water on your eyes; what more is needed?

In Ashtavakra's vision witnessing and meditation are one, because the goal and the path are one. But for all other paths and religious schools meditation is a method; witnessing, its final fruit.

'In what way are mind and ego dissolved by them?' Mind and ego are not dissolved by witnessing: in witnessing, you find out that they never existed. They can be dissolved only if they exist.

It is like this: you are sitting in a dark room and think there is a ghost. It is only your shirt hanging there, but you are scared, and in fright, your imagination adds hands and feet to it. He is standing there frightening you! Someone says to light a lamp, and you ask how will lighting a lamp make ghosts go away. But lighting a lamp does drive away the ghost because there isn't one there. If there were, lighting a lamp wouldn't drive it away. What has a lamp got to do with scaring away ghosts? If there were a ghost, a lamp would not drive him away. But he doesn't exist, he is illusory—that's why he goes away.

You suffer from thousands of diseases which are not there. This is why the ash from some sadhu will cure you; not because ash has driven out your illness. Are you mad? Has ash ever cured a disease? If so, the whole science of medicine would be useless. Ash cannot cure illness, it only gets rid of the idea that you were ill.

I have heard a story about a doctor—he himself told it to me. He was living near the Bastar tribal area and a tribal man came to him from deep within Bastar. The doctor was visiting a village, a tribal village. This man was sick, but the doctor had nothing to write with; there was no pen or paper in the village. He found a cloth and wrote the name of the medicine on it with a piece of rock, and told him, 'Take it with milk for a whole month, and you will be fine.' The man came back after a month. He was completely okay—healthy, robust. The doctor asked, 'Did the medicine work?'

He said, 'It worked great. Now write on one more cloth for me.'

The doctor asked, 'What do you mean?'

He said, 'That piece of cloth is finished. I drank it all up! It was great medicine.'

He had come to him completely cured! Now it wouldn't be right for the doctor to explain anything; that would be inappropriate. He told me, 'Since he was cured I didn't say anything: medicine is what makes you well. Why should I confuse him by telling him, "You idiot, I just wrote out the name of the medicine, but you never bought it!" He drank the prescription, but it worked.' The disease must have been false, imaginary.

Psychologists say that ninety out of a hundred illnesses are imaginary. And as understanding increases it is possible that 99 per cent are imaginary. One day perhaps 100 per cent of diseases will be found to be imaginary.

This is why the world has so many medical systems that work. Use allopathic medicine and the patient gets well. Use Ayurvedic or homeopathic or the Greek-Islamic systems, or naturopathy, and the patient is cured. Even a charm or a talisman will cure him.

It is surprising. If he were really sick then only one particular method would work to cure the disease, every method could not work. There is no disease. It is only what you believe in: someone believes in allopathy so it works—and the doctor's name is more important than the medicine.

Have you ever noticed that when you return from seeing a great doctor, your pockets empty from paying such huge fees, you are already half cured? If this same doctor wrote you free prescriptions it wouldn't have any effect on you. The fees you have paid out do more than his medicine. Once you have the idea that he is a great doctor—the greatest—it is enough.

You ask, 'In what way are mind and ego dissolved by them?' They are not dissolved. If they existed, they would be dissolved. In witnessing, you find out, 'Idiot, you are needlessly lost! Your own imagination has projected mirages—it was all imagination.' They don't dissolve. In witnessing, you become alert and find out that they never existed.

'Is surrender possible without attaining complete egolessness?' This is a significant question. The questioner asks, 'Is surrender possible without attaining to complete egolessness?' But the questioner's mind is being tricky— perhaps unconsciously. He has added 'complete' to 'egolessness', but not to 'surrender'. Without complete egolessness, complete surrender is not possible. As much ego as you drop, that much surrender is possible. If you drop 50 per cent of your ego, then 50 per cent surrender is possible. Are dropping the ego and surrender two different things? They are two ways of saying the same thing.

You say that without completely dropping the ego then surrender is not possible, that complete surrender is not possible. Don't deceive yourself by thinking, 'What is the need of surrender because unless the ego is completely dropped . . . ?' And who knows when it will drop and how it will drop.

Surrender is possible to the extent that the ego drops. Don't wait for completeness: do as much as you can. Do that much and the next step becomes available.

It is like a man travelling on a dark night. He has a small candle in his hand that shines light only four paces ahead. If the man says, 'How can one travel ten miles with this? Four paces of light and ten miles of darkness—I will get lost.' Then we tell him, 'Don't worry, take four paces, and when you have taken four paces the light goes ahead four more paces. You don't need ten miles of light to start walking. Four paces is enough.'

How much ego . . . Let go of one drop, then let go of another. In letting go of one drop the opportunity to let go of the next drop comes. Walk four paces, and the light goes four paces ahead. Don't make the excuse that you will surrender only when the ego is completely dropped. Then you will never do it. You have made your protection very carefully. You surrender as much as your ego drops—it is true. Then drop as much as you can—gather as much surrender as you can. Perhaps the taste of it will make you more ready; its bliss, its ecstasy will give you more courage. Courage comes from tasting.

A man can say, 'Until I have completely learned swimming I will not go in the water.' He is right; his calculation is right, his logic is correct. 'What if I go in the water without learning, and drown? Why get into so much trouble? First I will learn to swim perfectly.' But where will you learn it perfectly? On your bed? Where will you completely learn swimming? You have to go in the water.

But no one is telling you to plunge into the ocean—go in at the edge, go in up to your neck, go in only as far as your courage tells you. Learn to swim there and gradually your courage will increase. You can go a foot deeper each time, until you are able to swim in the full depth of the ocean. Once you know swimming . . . and to know it you will have to go in. Stay near the shore. I am not saying to jump straight off a mountain into a deep river. Stay near the shore, make friends with the water. Become acquainted with the water, move your arms and legs.

What is swimming? The skilful thrashing about of your arms and legs. Everyone knows how to thrash around. Even if you throw someone into the water who has never swum before, he will start thrashing around. The difference between this and a swimmer is only of a little skill; there is no difference in what they are doing. The person who has never swum before is also throwing his hands and feet about but he has no trust in the water, no trust in himself. He is afraid he is going to drown. That fear will drown him— water has never drowned anyone.

You may have seen that a dead body floats to the surface, a corpse will float on water. Ask the corpse, 'What trick did you learn? When you were alive you drowned; dead, you are afloat!' The corpse is not afraid: how can the river drown it? It is not the nature of water to drown anything, water lifts things up. This is why weight appears to decrease in water. In water you can lift up and carry a man who is heavier than you. In water you can lift a huge rock. The weight of things is less in water. Just as the earth has gravitation, the earth pulls down, water raises upward. Water has the nature of raising things. If you are drowning you are causing it, water has never drowned anyone. Don't unknowingly blame the water. Water has never drowned anyone.

Ask a scientist: he will also say that it is a miracle that a man can drown, because water uplifts. You drown in your freak-out. You scream and shout, you open your mouth, you drink in water and take on more weight—and you drown. You cause your own death. A swimmer learns only this: water lifts you up! His trust in water becomes stronger. He understands that weight decreases in water. Our weight in water is much less than on land.

You must have seen when you throw a bucket into a well that while the bucket is filling and is in the water it is weightless. Start pulling it up and it becomes heavy. The water supports you; how can it drown you? A learner slowly, slowly becomes acquainted with this fact. Trust arises. Trust comes that water is not an enemy but a friend. It won't drown you.

A skilled swimmer doesn't thrash his arms, doesn't move them, but can remain on the surface—like a lotus flower. He is a man just like you; there is no difference except that trust has arisen in him. He trusts himself, he trusts the water—a friendship has arisen between them.

It happens the same way in surrender. In surrender, the fear is that you may drown, so you want to climb out on to the bank. I am not telling you to surrender one hundred degrees—one degree will do. Doing it gradually you will come to know, the taste will grow, juice will arise, the energy will flower.

You will be surprised how much has been wasted due to the ego, how much comes from a tiny bit of surrender. New doors open—doors of light. New breezes flow in your being . . . a new thrill, a new spirit. All is fresh. You will see life for the first time. For the first time you are removing the smokescreen from your eyes. The presence of the divine will begin manifesting itself. Surrender, and the divine comes near. Because you begin to be erased, the divine begins to manifest.

Is existence far away? You don't see it because of your heavy ego. You don't see it because your eyes are filled with ego. Become capable of seeing it with your naked eye. Gradually courage will increase—trust, self-confidence. You will surrender more and more. One day you will take the total jump. One day you will say 'Enough!' Up until now you have wasted yourself in trying to save yourself.

One day you will understand and let go, then you will let yourself drown and be saved.

Blessed are those who are ready to be drowned, because no one can drown them. Unfortunate are they who are saved because they are already drowned—if not today, tomorrow their boat will crash and be broken up.

And there is one more thing to consider about ego and surrender. The mind is very clever—it finds excuses. Mind says, 'So who is first? Is dropping the ego first or is surrender first? Should I surrender so the ego drops, or should I drop the ego so surrender happens?'

When you go to the market to buy eggs you don't ask, 'Which is first, the chicken or the egg?' If you ask this you will never return home with your eggs. You just buy your eggs and go without first making sure which is first—the chicken or the egg.

Many people have debated it. The question of the chicken or the egg is very ancient. Which comes first? It is very difficult to find an answer. As soon as you say the egg comes first difficulties begin, because the egg must have come from a chicken—so the chicken comes first. As soon as you say the chicken came first, again the problem arises, because how will the chicken come without an egg? It is a circle. The question is misleading. The question is misleading because the chicken and the egg are not two. The chicken and the egg are two stages of the same thing. You raise a question by putting one ahead of the other, making them two. The chicken is a form of the egg—the completely manifested form. The egg is a form of the chicken—the unmanifested form—like a seed and a tree.

Egolessness and surrender are just like this.

Which comes first? Don't waste time arguing. If you bring up the chicken you have brought up the egg. If you bring up the egg you have brought up the chicken. If one comes, the other comes along with it wherever you begin from. If you can drop the ego, start by dropping the ego. If you can't drop the ego, then start by surrendering. If you surrender, the ego drops. I am not saying it will completely drop; it will drop as much as you surrender. If surrendering appears difficult, then drop the ego. Surrender will come as much as you drop the ego.

There are two kinds of religion. One is the religion of egolessness, the other is the religion of surrender. One type of religion gives emphasis to the chicken, the other to the egg. Both are correct, because when there is one, the other comes by itself.

For instance, both Mahavira's religion and Buddha's religion have no place for surrender; they say just drop the ego. Where will you surrender? There is no divinity in front of whom you can surrender. Mahavira says, 'No shelter, no divine feet: there is no place you can go to surrender. Whose feet can you go to? Go without surrender, just drop the ego.'

Hindus, Mohammedans, Christians—these are religions of surrender. They don't say much about dropping the ego, they say, 'Surrender to the divine. Find shelter somewhere, some feet where you can bow your head—the ego will go by itself.'

Both are right because they are two sides of the same coin. If you take the 'heads' side of the coin home or the 'tails' side home, what difference does it make? The coin will come home. They are two sides of one coin. But you have to start somewhere. Don't just sit around figuring it out.

'To what extent are orange clothes and the mala helpful for meditation and witnessing?' If you are ready, everything can be helpful. If you are ready, a path can be made from very small things.

It is said that when Rama was building his bridge across the ocean to Sri Lanka the squirrels brought tiny stones and grains of sand. They too had a hand in it, they too helped build the bridge. There were others who brought huge rocks. The small squirrels did what they could.

Don't expect much from changing the colour of your clothes, because if everything were changed just by changing one's clothes, it would be very easy. Don't expect that just by putting a mala around your neck much will happen, transformation will happen. Transformation is not so cheap. But also don't think it is only a squirrel's job; what can it do? Rama thanked the squirrels too.

These small devices are helpful too. Helpful like this: you suddenly return to your village in orange clothes. The whole village will look at you in amazement. You will not be able to live in that village the way you used to. You will not be able to remain hidden in that village the way you used to. You will bring an individuality with you to the village. Everyone will ask what happened. Everyone will remind you that something has happened. Each one will question you. Each one will awaken your remembering. Each one will give you an opportunity, reminding you again and again to become the witness.

One friend took sannyas and then he began weeping—a simple person. And he said, 'There is just one problem: I am a wine drinker, and certainly you will ask me to drop it.'

I said, 'I never ask anyone to drop anything. Drink, but drink meditatively.'

He said, 'What do you mean? Can I drink wine even as a sannyasin?'

I said, 'It's up to you. I have given you sannyas; now you explore it.'

He came back a month later, saying, 'You tricked me! I was standing in the pub when a man came and touched my feet, saying, "What are you doing here, Swamiji?" I ran away from there, saying to myself, "A swamiji in the pub?"'

He told me, 'You tricked me. Now I am afraid to even go towards the pub. What if someone does something like touch my feet or bow down to me? Now it's fifteen days since I've been there.' A remembering happened. Mindfulness was awakened! Using these orange clothes you won't be able to get angry the same way you did up until yesterday. Something will tug on you. Something will tell you to just forget it. It feels very awkward in these orange clothes.

I give you orange clothes just to create a little difficulty, nothing else. If you are a thief, you won't be able to remain a thief so easily. If you are mad for money, greedy, then your greed will not have the same strength. If you are in politics, running after the prestige of political office, you will suddenly find it is meaningless. This small thing, these clothes, will become very symbolic. They have no significance of their own, but when you dress yourself in them, you gradually find that what was a very small thing—the seed was very small—has gradually become big, has gradually changed everything. It will change your activity, it will change your habits, it will change your style of behaviour and movement. There will be a new grace in your life. People's expectation of you will change. People's eyes will look at you differently.

Changing your name, you will become disconnected from your old name. Changing your clothes, you will become free of your old pattern. This mala around your neck will go on reminding you of me. It will become a bridge between you and me—you will not be able to forget me so easily. And people will start setting you apart. And their separating of you will be a great help in your being a witness.

But I am not saying that just by doing this everything will happen—just change the clothes, put on the mala and know it is over, the journey is complete. It all depends on you. They are like signposts, like milestones on the side of the road on which is written 'Twelve miles', 'Fifty miles', 'One hundred miles to Delhi'. The stone does not have much significance. Milestone or not, if it is one hundred miles to Delhi, it is one hundred miles. But these lines written on stone are encouraging, these arrow signs make the traveller feel lighter. He says, 'Okay, only one hundred miles to go, fifty miles to go, twenty-five miles to go.'

In Switzerland, in place of milestones they have put 'minute-stones'. If you stop your car at some mountainous place you will be surprised looking at the signpost how far the last one was—thirty minutes away. The next station—fifteen minutes away. It is a meaningful indication—Swiss people are skilful at making watches so it is no great surprise. Their awareness of time is very deep. They don't write miles, they write time: 'Fifteen minutes' distance'! It conveys how deep the awareness of time is in these people.

If you wear orange clothes it conveys something about you. Everything conveys a message. How you sit, how you move, how you look—everything conveys something about you.

We never dress soldiers in loose clothes, no one in the world does. If they were dressed in loose clothes they would be defeated. Dressing soldiers like that could prove dangerous. We dress soldiers in tight clothes, so tight that they always feel uncomfortable and they want to just jump out of them. Tight clothes arouse fighting instincts.

Sitting in tight clothes one is always ready to fight. Wearing loose clothes one is a little relaxed. Only an emperor wears loose clothes, or a sannyasin, a fakir. Have you ever noticed that when you climb stairs wearing loose clothes, you go one step at a time; wearing tight clothes you take them two at a time. Wearing tight clothes you are filled with anger. If anyone says some small thing you are upset. In loose clothes you remain relaxed.

Small things make a difference. Life is made of small things. The bridge of life is constructed with tiny little stones brought by the squirrels. What you eat, what you wear, how you rise and sit—ultimately all these have their effect. You are the combination of all these. Here a man is walking along wearing flashy, gaudy, colourful clothes— it conveys a message. A woman is walking along wearing vulgar, obscene clothes that show off her curves—it conveys a message. A man is wearing plain and simple clothes, loose, comfortable—a message is conveyed about him.

Psychologists says that if you quietly observe someone for half an hour—how he wears his clothes, how he gets up, how he sits, how he looks—you will learn so many things about the man you won't be able to believe it. Our every way of moving, every gesture, is ours. We are changed by a change in gesture; our gestures change because of a change in us.

So these are just signs. These will be with you. These will go on directing you. These will give you a little help in keeping alert.

'And please explain the difference between witnessing, wakefulness and right remembering.' There is no difference; these are all synonyms, used by different traditions. Krishnamurti uses 'wakefulness'; Buddha has used 'right remembering', 'mindfulness'; Ashtavakra, the Upanishads, the Gita, all use 'witnessing'. The difference is only of tradition, but they all indicate the same direction.

The second question:

> Osho,
> During your first discourse on Ashtavakra many people were weeping profoundly. What does this mean? Are those who were crying weak-hearted, or is it the power of your voice? Please throw some light on this.

One thing is certain: the questioner is a hard-hearted man. He sees only weakness in tears. It is clear that tears have dried up in the questioner's eyes, the eyes have become barren like a desert. Flowers don't bloom in them—tears are flowers of the eyes.

The questioner's feelings have died. The questioner's heart has become blocked. The questioner lives only through intellect. He has given the final rites for his dead feelings. He must be living in thoughts. Love and compassion, the regard for life, romance, bliss—he must have rejected the possibility of these. No current seems to flow. His heart must be dried up like a desert. So the first thing that came to him is that people crying here are weak-hearted.

Who told you that crying is a sign of weakness? Meera wept unrestrainedly; cascades of tears flowed from Chaitanya's eyes. No, they are not a sign of weakness, they are an indication of feeling, an indication of the strength of feeling. And remember feeling is deeper than thinking. As I said earlier, first is the level of activity, then the level of thought, then feeling, then the witnessing centre.

Feeling is the closest to the witness.

Devotion is the closest to the divine. Action is very far away; the journey is very long from there. Thought too is far away; it too is a long journey. Devotion is very near.

Remember, tears are not necessarily caused by unhappiness, although people are acquainted with only one kind of tears—those of unhappiness. Tears also flow in compassion, tears also flow in joy; tears flow in giving thanks, in gratitude. Tears are only a sign that something is happening inside that is difficult to contain—unhappiness or joy. Something is happening inside that is so abundant that it starts to overflow. And if it is sadness—sadness so deep that it is difficult to contain inside—it will flow in tears. Tears are a discharge. Or, if joy becomes too full, tears of joy will flow. Tears are an outlet.

Tears are not necessarily connected with sadness or joy—they are connected with over-abundance. Whatever becomes excessive, tears will absorb and wash away. So an over-abundance must have happened inside those who were crying, some sweet pain must have penetrated their heart. They must have heard the murmuring of the unknown. A ray of the far unknown must have touched the heart. Something must have descended into their darkness. Some arrow must have filled their heart with pain and ecstasy—they could not stop their tears.

There is no relationship between this and the power of my words, because you were also listening. If it were only the power of my speaking then even you would have cried, everyone would have cried. No, it is related more to the heartfulness of the listeners than to my speaking. Those who could cry, cried. And crying is a great power.

Humanity has lost a very unique capacity—men especially have lost it. Women have saved it a little, women are fortunate. The tear glands in human eyes are the same in man and woman; nature has made the tear glands identically. The intention of nature is clear: the eyes of both are made for crying. But the male ego has slowly, slowly controlled everything. Gradually men have begun to think that crying is feminine; only women cry. Men have lost much from this—they lost devotion, they lost feeling, they lost joy, they lost gratefulness. From this they lost the greatness of suffering, because suffering also purifies, cleanses.

This is why a great calamity has entered men's lives. You will be surprised that worldwide the number of men that go mad is twice that of women. And this number would greatly increase if wars were stopped, because men release their madness in war, release it in great quantity! If wars were completely stopped for one hundred years, it is feared that 90 per cent of all men would go mad.

Men commit suicide more than women—double the number. The common belief is otherwise, you think that more women commit suicide. They talk about it, but they don't do it. They take pills or something and sleep, but they take the pills in a calculated way.

So women make more suicide attempts, but unsuccessfully. They are calculating in their attempts. Actually, women don't want to commit suicide—suicide is only a way to express their complaint. They are saying that this life is not worth living, a better style of living is needed. A woman who commits suicide is telling you that you have become so stony-hearted that you won't pay any attention to her unless she is ready to kill herself. She is only attracting your attention.

This is very unseemly—that she has to use dying as the means to attract your attention. Man has certainly become exceptionally hard, has become stone-like.

Women don't want to die, they want to live. When too much trouble comes on the path of life—there is no one who listens, no one who pays attention—they use suicide as a method to make you pay attention. But when men commit suicide they succeed. Men commit suicide in insanity.

More men are mentally ill. Why? There are many reasons, one among them is tears. Psychologists say men must learn how to cry again. To not cry is not a strength. What you call strength is callousness. Strength is not so hard, strength is gentle. You have seen streams falling down the mountains, cascading, falling—gentle water. Rock is very hard. Rock certainly thinks it is strong, and that flowing water is weak. But finally the flowing water is victorious, the rock is reduced to sand and carried away.

The divine is with the gentle.

'The divine is the power of the powerless.'

A flower has bloomed and near it is a rock. Of course, the rock appears strong, the flower weak. But have you ever seen the flower's power—the power of life? Who bows down to a rock? You don't take a stone to offer to the divine's feet. Do you think the stone is very strong so you give it to your beloved? No, you won't do this. You pick flowers, and give them to someone. A flower has strength. A flower has majesty. Tenderness is its strength. Its blossoming is its strength; music, fragrance is its strength. Its weakness is also its strength. It opens in the morning, and it wilts by the evening—this is its strength. But it blossoms. A rock never blossoms, it just is. A rock is dead. The flower is alive—and it will die because it has lived. A rock will never die, because it is already dead.

Become tender. Call tears back again. Let them fill your eyes with song and poetry; otherwise you will remain deprived of many things. Your god will remain rational, not the heart's experience; only a theory, not a taste and an experience of truth.

Those who let tears flow are fortunate—they are strong. They don't care what you say, they don't bother what other people say. When someone is crying totally he is not concerned with criticism. Strength is needed to cry without your being concerned and saying, 'What will people say?' Let them talk! A bad reputation? Let it be. 'Leave me to cry my heart out.'

When a man cries, wails like a baby, then think of his strength. He is not bothering about all of you. He is not worried, like others, about what people say: 'Me, a university professor and crying? If a student should see!' Or, 'Such a big businessman and crying? If a customer should see!' Or, 'Such a strong husband and crying?

My wife is nearby, and she will be after me when we go home.' Or, 'I am a father and crying, and if my son sees, if the babies see . . . Control yourself!' Your ego holds back, controls. Egoless, you would cry. Ego always keeps itself under control. Egoless you flow, there is a flow in you. A poet says:

> Whatever burns up goes out,
> once out it can't be rekindled.
> Those burned up in love, O Rahim,
> are rekindled again and again.

Coals burn—'They burn themselves and go out'—but a moment comes when they finally go out, then you will not be able to burn them again. Has anyone ever succeeded in making ash into burning coals again? 'Whatever burns up goes out, once out it can't be rekindled.' Once they are out they will never burn.

'Those burned up in love, O Rahim . . .' But of those whose hearts have been wounded by love's arrow, what does Rahim say? 'Those burned up in love, O Rahim, go out but are again rekindled.' They burn up again and again, they go out again and again and are re-lit again and again. The fire of love is eternal, immortal.

Those who listen to me with love will be able to cry. Those who listen to me only with the intellect will take from me a few conclusions, some knowledge. They will take ashes—not live coals of love. They will take ashes that can never be re-lit. Remember, the fire has gone out. As soon as I have said the words to you they go out. When you receive intellectually it is ash, when you receive through the heart it is a burning coal.

In those in whom the coal of love is born, the fire will burn, then go out, then burn again. It will cause you much anguish. It will cleanse you. It will bring a total transformation of your life.

If you can open your heart and cry, it means the burning coals of love have reached you. If you cannot cry, it has reached only the intellect. A little ash will be collected. You will become somewhat knowledgeable, you will become quite skilful at explaining to others, you will become accomplished in debate, in arguing. But the main point will have been missed. Where you could have taken live coals you returned only with ashes. Even if you call it holy ash it won't make any difference—ash is ash.

> The fire is lit, melodies of pain arise from my heart;
> in the sorrows of your love I have become a fiery tongue.
> Because of intellect wandering the path;
> I've become the dust of a passing caravan.

'The fire is lit, melodies of pain arise from my heart.' Those tears were tears of the heart catching fire.

When you see someone crying go and sit near him. That is a moment of divine satsang—it is not to be missed. If you cannot cry, at least you can go and sit next to someone who is crying. You can take his hand in yours, and perhaps you too can catch the infection.

'The fire is lit, melodies of pain arise from my heart.' Let the fire be lit! These orange clothes are a symbol of fire. They are a symbol of the fire of love.

'In the sorrows of your love I have become a fiery tongue.' And when anguish arises within your heart, the feeling of *virah*—divine longing—arises when there is fire in every breath, a tongue of fire—'in the sorrows of your love I have become a fiery tongue.'

'Because of intellect wandering the path.' Because of intellect I have gone astray.

'Because of intellect wandering the path; I've become the dust of a passing caravan.' And because of intellect my situation has become like the dust left behind when the caravan has passed. I have become dust. Nothing besides dust ever sticks to the hands of intellect.

> Because of intellect wandering the path;
> I've become the dust of a passing caravan.
> When the heart became lighted, O Krishnamohan,
> boundaries have disappeared, and I have become limitless.
> When the heart became lighted, O Krishnamohan . . .

If love has struck, if the arrow of love has struck the heart, if the embers of fire are aglow . . .

'When the heart became lighted, O Krishnamohan, boundaries have disappeared, and I have become limitless.' In that moment boundaries are broken—you become boundless. Tears are your first step towards the infinite. Tears indicate that you are melting, your fixed boundaries have melted a little; you have become soft, you have become warm, you have dropped your cold intellect a little. A fire is lit, heat is arising. These tears are not cold, these tears are very hot. And these tears bring news of your melting. Just as when snow melts, when your ego begins melting inside, tears flow.

> When filled with desire each breath was speaking fire;
> now love has descended: I am speechless.

When you were full of intellect, full of desires, full of thoughts of a million and one things, the tongue was sharp and fast.

'When filled with desire each breath was speaking fire; now love has descended: I am speechless.' Those tears are indications of a state beyond language. When something happens and there is no way to express it, if you don't cry what will you do?

When you become incapable of speaking, the eyes say it with tears. When the intellect becomes incapable of speech, one says it by dancing.

Meera danced. Something happened that she couldn't find words to express.

Tying the ankle bells, Meera enters the dance . . .

She wept, wept continuously. Something happened that was impossible to express in words, words seemed very confined. Only tears could say it—she said it with tears.

No, don't keep this idea that these people are weak. These people are strong. Their strength is of tenderness. Their strength is not of fighting and violence, their strength is of the heart. If you consider these people weak you will never cry. I emphasize again and again—don't think these people are weak. Be envious of them. Look within again and ask: 'What happened that I am unable to cry?'

A person filled with feeling is the closest to his own centre. And the closer someone comes to himself, the more he experiences anguish. The further you are from home the easier it is to forget it. As soon as the home is near, memories of it come stronger.

You sit, completely forgetting God. The word 'god' falls on your ears, but it creates no stir. You hear it, but it is just a word. God is not just a word. The question is not merely of hearing. 'God' will give a jolt to those who have a little fire of life within—the very word will give a shock.

If you love me from the heart,
then why do you make me cry?

The bhakta, the devotee, is always complaining to God:

> If you love me from the heart,
> then why do you make me cry?
> In this deep darkness of your light,
> why do you hide your glance from mine?
> Even coming close, you never came close;
> you never call me close.
> For what do you live around me?
> For what do you come around me?

If you have heard me rightly, then many times you will feel the divine is very near.

'For what do you live around me? For what do you come around me? . . . Even coming close, you never came close; you never call me close . . . If you love me from the heart, then why do you make me cry? In this deep darkness of your light, why do you hide your glance from mine?'

One who goes deep into feelings comes so near to the divine that he begins to experience the heat of the divine's flame. Eyes begin to meet eyes. Boundaries begin to cross over each other. They begin to transcend each other's borders.

What is being said here is not mere talk, it is to transform you. It is not talking just for talking's sake, it is to change you completely—from the very roots.

The third question:

Osho,
　　　Culture is a product of dharma plus *dharana*, religion plus concepts—or concepts plus religion. And society and its traditions are created from this culture. You have said that religion is against everything. If religion remains

opposed to everything, then is it not possible that it will create anarchy, chaos? Please explain.

The meaning that you are taking of dharana being derived from dharma is not right. Dharana is not religion. The word dharma comes from a root meaning 'that which gives support to everything, which maintains everything'. It is not a concept, but that which sustains everything. That which supports this vastness, this moon, these stars, this sun, these trees and birds, man and the endless expanse of existence—what supports all this is dharma.

Religion is not related to concepts. Your concept may be Hindu, someone's may be Mohammedan, someone's Christian—but it is not related to dharma. These are concepts, these are intellectual ideas. Religion is the name for that essential truth which sustains everything, without which everything would be dispersed. That which joins all, which is the totality of all, which bridges all.

It is like making a garland of flowers. Here is a heap of flowers and there a garland. What is the difference? The pile is chaotic. No flower is connected with any other flower, all the flowers are disconnected. The garland is strung on a thread. The thread is not visible, it is hidden in the flowers, but it joins one flower to another.

This whole existence is strung on a thread called dharma. This, which joins us to trees, the moon and stars, which joins stones and pebbles to the sun, which joins everything, which is the connection of all—this is dharma.

Culture is not created from dharma. Culture is made from cultural conditioning. Dharma is known when all conditionings have been renounced. Sannyas means renouncing conditioning.

Hindu culture is different; Mohammedan culture, Buddhist culture, Jaina culture—all are different, separate.

There are thousands of cultures in the world because there are thousands of conditionings. Someone faces east when he prays, someone turns to the west to pray—this is conditioning. Someone wears these clothes, someone those; someone eats this kind of food, someone eats that kind of food—this is all conditioning.

Cultures will remain on earth, and they should remain because the greater the diversity, the more beautiful is the earth. I don't want the world to have only one culture—that would be idiotic, very dull and boring. Hindu culture is needed on the earth; Mohammedan, Christian, Buddhist, Jaina, Chinese, Russian—thousands of cultures are needed because variety makes life beautiful. Many types of flowers are needed in a garden. Just one type of flower will make the garden monotonous.

Cultures must be numerous—they are numerous and they should remain so. But religion should be one, because dharma is one. There is no other possibility.

That is why I call Hinduism a culture, I call Islam a culture—not religion. It is good, cultures are beautiful. Make mosques in their unique style, temples in a different architecture. Temples are beautiful, mosques too are beautiful. I would not want only temples on the earth and that mosques should disappear—beauty would be greatly diminished. I would not want only Sanskrit to remain with us and Arabic to disappear—beauty would be much diminished. I would not want only the Koran to remain with us, and the Vedas, the Gita and the Upanishads to disappear—the earth would become very poor.

The Koran is beautiful. It is a rare literary masterpiece, it is poetry of great height—but it has nothing to do with the religion I am talking about. The Vedas are lovely, a rare proclamation of the earth's aspirations to touch the sky. The Upanishads are very sweet. A sweeter expression has never been given. They should not be lost. All these should remain—but as culture.

Dharma is one. It is that which connects us all—Hindus, Mohammedans and Christians too. It is that which connects animals, men, plants—everything. That which flows as green in plants, as the bloodstream in man; that which moves inside you as breath, which is present inside you as the witness. Dharma, religion, connects everything.

Don't think of religion as a synonym for culture. Religion has nothing to do with culture. There can be culture in Russia, where there is no religion. There is culture in China, where now there is no religion. There can be an atheistic culture, as well as a theistic one. Religion has nothing to do with culture. Religion is not concerned with your day-to-day lifestyle. Religion is concerned with your being. Religion is your pure existence, your nature. Culture is your outer shell, your etiquette, your behaviour in everything concerned with these—how to stand, how to speak, what to say, what not to say.

Tradition never becomes religion. Religion is not tradition. Religion is the timeless, eternal truth. Man makes traditions—religion already is. Traditions are man's creation, they have been invented by man. Religion precedes man, man has been made by religion. Understand this difference.

Never mistakenly assume that tradition can be religion. And a religious person can never become traditional. Jesus had to be crucified, Mansoor had to be murdered, Socrates had to be poisoned—because a religious person can never be orthodox. A religious person is a great revolution. He is a continual declaration of the eternal, of the timeless. Whenever anyone proclaims the eternal and the timeless, the orthodox, the straight conformists, freak out. They become very nervous. They say he will bring chaos, anarchy.

There is chaos now. What you call order, governance—what nonsensical order is this? This whole life is full of strife, full of so many crimes. This whole life is filled with suffering—and still you are afraid of chaos! What is in your life except hell? What fragrance of happiness is there? Which flower of bliss blooms? What flute is playing in your life? It is just a heap of ashes. Still you say chaos will come.

So a religious person can be rebellious, but not an anarchist. Understand this.

A religious person is the truly orderly person because he has made a connection with the infinite. He is joined to the deepest root of life. How can he be chaotic? Yes, he can lose his connection with you, be a little outside of your established patterns, your order. He is related to the ultimate. He has become disconnected with the false—he is connected to the raw truth. He has broken off from the rotten and become connected with the brand new, the ever new.

Your culture and society are like plastic flowers. The life of a religious person is like a living flower. Plastic flowers look like flowers, but in reality they are not. They seem to be, they look like them at a distance, but they are false.

If you tell the truth just because the conditioning to tell the truth has been forced on you, then your truth isn't worth a penny. If you don't eat meat because you were born in a Jaina family and the conditioning that eating meat is a sin has been forced on you—you are so deeply conditioned that just seeing meat you become nauseated—then don't think you are religious. It is just conditioning.

A person born in a Jaina household is frightened by meat, becomes nauseated when he sees it—not just seeing it, he is afraid of the very word 'meat'. Anything that can be associated with meat will nauseate him, even a blood-red tomato will frighten him—this is only conditioning. If this person were born in a meat-eating household he would enjoy eating meat, because there the conditioning would be to eat meat; here, eating meat is not the conditioning.

Conditioning is your bondage. I am not telling you to start eating meat. I am saying to allow that manifestation of consciousness to come inside you as it came inside Mahavira. It was not conditioning. It was his own experience that to trouble anyone else is ultimately to trouble oneself, because we are all one, joined together. It is like someone slapping his own cheek. Sooner or later, what we do to someone else is going to return to us. This experience became so deep for Mahavira, this awareness became so manifest to him, that he stopped causing suffering to others. He stopped eating meat not because he was taught that eating meat is a sin, he stopped eating meat through witnessing. This is religiousness.

If you were born in a Jaina household and don't eat meat, it is only conditioning. This is a plastic flower, not a real flower. Send this Jaina to America, and in two to four years he will start eating meat. Seeing meat eaten everywhere, at first he will be disturbed, at first he will turn up his nose, but gradually he will get used to it. Then seeing others eating meat at the same table, gradually, his nose, his nostrils will accept the smell of meat.

Then the influence of another conditioning begins. There everyone says, 'If you don't eat meat you will become weak. Listen! How will you perform in the Olympics without eating meat? You won't be able to win a single gold medal. Gold medal? You won't even win a bronze one. Look at your condition. You have remained enslaved for a thousand years, what strength do you have? What is your life expectancy? How many thousands of diseases do you suffer from?'

Certainly the life expectancy in the meat-eating countries has now reached to more than eighty years; the average is eighty to eighty-five. Soon it will be one hundred. Here we are stuck at around thirty or thirty-five.

'How many Nobel Prizes have you won? If vegetarianism purifies the intelligence then you should be winning all the Nobel Prizes. Intelligence doesn't appear to have become highly developed. And remember, Rabindranath Tagore who won the Nobel Prize was not a vegetarian. Has a single Jaina won a Nobel Prize? What's the matter? They have been vegetarian for two thousand years, and in two thousand years your intelligence still hasn't become pure?'

So meat-eaters have arguments. They say, 'Your intelligence becomes weak because you don't get the right proteins, the right vitamins, enough energy. Your body is weakening—you will not live long. Your strength is decreasing.'

In America one hears every day, sees in the papers, that some ninety-year-old man has married. You are shocked. You say, 'What kind of insanity is this?' But a ninety-year-old man gets married because he is still capable of sex. It is proof of strength. A ninety-year-old man fathers a child too. It is proof of strength.

As soon as someone goes and lives in the West, he hears these arguments and sees these proofs and sees the vast prosperity of its culture. Gradually he forgets.

If Mahavira had to go to the West he would not eat meat. He is a natural flowering. He would say, 'Okay, I will live two or four years less—what's the harm? What is the use of living longer? What will you do living longer? You will eat up a few more animals—what else?' If anyone had asked Mahavira, he would have said, 'Look behind you a little; if you live one hundred years, then look back at the long line of birds and animals you have eaten. You have eaten a whole cremation ground! You have eaten a whole population. Heaps of bones are lying all around you. One man eats so many animals in his life—thousands of birds and animals will pile up. Just think of how many lives you have destroyed. For what? Just to live? Why live more? To destroy more animals?'

If someone were to tell Mahavira that he would become weak, then he would say, 'What will I do with strength? Am I to hurt someone? Am I to kill someone? Am I going to war?'

If someone were to point out to Mahavira, 'Look, you have been enslaved for one thousand years,' he would say, 'There are two positions: either become a master of someone or a slave.' Mahavira would say, 'It is better to become a slave than a master—at least you won't torture anyone, you will be tortured. It is better to be deceived than to be a deceiver—at least you didn't deceive anyone. It is better to be a victim of theft than to be a thief.'

If someone were to tell Mahavira, 'Look, you didn't win any Nobel Prizes,' he would say, 'What will I do with a Nobel Prize? It is a toy . . . good for children to jump around and play with. What can I do with it? I have come to earn some other prize. That prize is given only by the divine, no one else can give it. That prize is of the ecstasy of witnessing. It is of sat-chit-anand, truth-consciousness-bliss. You keep your Nobel Prize. Give it to children to play with. It is a toy.'

There is no prize in this world comparable to the prize of inner bliss. If the body is gone, youth disappears, money is spent, all is gone but the inner nectar is saved, then all is saved. He who loses the inner loses all. He who saves the inner, saves all.

But usually when a Jaina goes to the West he returns corrupted. Why? He was already corrupted—a paper flower, it was false, made through conditioning.

Understand the difference between culture and religion. Religion is your inner nature and culture is what you have been taught by others. No matter how carefully someone teaches, anything learned from others will not liberate you, it will enslave you. So when I say religion is rebellion, revolt, I mean rebellion against tradition, rebellion against conditioning, rebellion against spiritual slavery.

But a religious person cannot be an anarchist. If a religious person is anarchistic, who here will be disciplined? A religious person will become highly disciplined. But his discipline will have a different flavour. It flows outward from the inside. It is not imposed by anyone else. It is spontaneous. It is like a spring of inner energy bursting open. It is like a river flowing with the energy of the water, no one is pushing it.

But you are as if someone has tied a cord around your neck and you are being dragged along, and someone is whipping you from behind to keep you moving.

The man who lives in culture is forcefully dragged along, dragged against his will. A religious person is dancing. Even when he approaches death he goes dancing. You are dragged even in life. You always experience that you are under compulsion. You always experience that you are missing something that others enjoy, others have all the fun.

People come to me saying, 'We are simple and virtuous straightforward people. There is such injustice in the world. The cheats enjoy everything, thieves and criminals have everything.'

I tell them, 'The very idea arising in you that they are enjoying indicates you are not simple, not virtuous, not straightforward. You are just like them, only you are less courageous. You also want to have fun like them, but you must pay the price for that and you are afraid to pay. You too are a thief, but one needs courage to steal and your courage is gone. You too want to cheat and make a pile of money, but one could be caught cheating, arrested, so you stop. If you are assured that no one will catch you, that there is no one to catch you, there is no fear of being arrested—you will immediately become a thief.'

A religious person feels compassion for those who cheat because he feels, 'These poor people are missing ultimate bliss. They are missing my experience.' A religious person does not envy the irreligious, he feels compassion. He cries inwardly that these poor people will lose everything in collecting a few scraps of gold and silver. They will be finished while making their mud houses, their sandcastles. They wander in trivia, when an experience of the eternal is possible. He is compassionate. There is no question of jealousy, because he has something more vast. And because of this vastness there is a discipline in his life. There is no higher discipline than this discipline.

A religious person is rebellious, but not undisciplined. His discipline is his own, it is inner. His discipline is self-discipline.

And what you call organized, what you call order—what has that order given? War, violence, vice, hatred, hostility. What has it given?

A poet says:

An earth burns for clouds;
love is born so as to writhe in pain.
If a friend asks for my life, no problem;
I have even given life for the enemies.
Sinners have always saved me;
it is for the good people that I have sinned.
Whenever questions came, all masks were on;
I have been given life as a puzzle.
I always germinate a crowd of dreams,
for the barren city, for the desolate places.
What world of robbers have I come into?

Here hands are chopped off for bracelets.
Life has squeezed me so much:
I have sold my eyes so I can see.

What is here? Even eyes are sold—in the hope that someday one will be able to behold the beloved. The soul is sold—in the hope that someday one will meet the divine. What have you attained here? Where is order here? What could be more anarchic than this? Hate in every direction, hostility, strangling competition, envy, jealousy. No one is anyone's friend, all are enemies of one another. Here nothing is attained—what is it you are calling order?

Order is possible only when there is joy in life. Joy brings an order. Order comes as a shadow of joy.

Remember, an unhappy man can be an anarchist. A happy man cannot be disorderly—an unhappy man will be an anarchist. What has he got? He becomes eager to break and destroy. He who has gained nothing from life will begin breaking and destroying in frustration. He who has received from life, who is fortunate—how will he destroy it?

This order—this facade of order—don't take it as order. It is the conspiracy of the politicians. And those that you understand to be your leaders, those that you understand to be your guides, are brigands. These are the very ones stealing from you.

Now walk on with some other support.
Too self-serving had become the banks.

Now even to take the support of the riverbank doesn't feel right.

Now walk on with some other support.
Too self-serving had become the banks.

The walls you are standing under thinking them to be shelters
will collapse any moment.
Surely some miracle has happened today,
musical resonances are coming from the ruins.
It is no wonder if the limits of hope have shattered;
the swords are out of their sheaths.
What will happen to the boat, nobody knows;
the sails are conspiring with the thunderstorm.

'What will happen to the boat, nobody knows; the sails are
conspiring with the thunderstorm.'

Thousands of helpless sighs are buried here;
these graves are not merely a heap of stones.

Here, sails are conspiring with the thunderstorm. Here,
the ones you understand to be helpers are exploiting you.
And those you think are your leaders are sitting on your
chest. Have you noticed: when someone gets into office he
starts talking law and order. And out of power a politician
begins talking revolution; just with his being out of power
the question of revolt arises. Then everything is wrong,
everything should be changed. And just coming into power
the question of law and order arises. Everything is good,
change is dangerous. Now it is necessary to be disciplined.

Everywhere in the world it has always been like this.
Politicians only have lust for power, they are not concerned
with order or revolt. Yes, when they are not keeping
order, when the power is not in their hands, then they say
everything is wrong—then a revolution is needed. And as
soon as they come to power, revolution isn't needed any
more because the work of the revolution is complete. Its
work was this—to bring him to power. The job is done.
Then whoever mentions revolution is an enemy.

And those that speak of revolution also have nothing to do with it. It is an amazing thing to watch—it is happening every day, and still man does not become alert. All revolutionaries become counterrevolutionary when they come to power. And all ousted politicians become revolutionaries as soon as they step down from office. Political office has great magic! Sitting in office—order, because now order is in your favour. Stepping down— revolution; now revolution is in your favour.

A religious person has nothing to do with order, nothing to do with revolution. A religious person is concerned with self-discipline. A religious person wants to wake up. With the help of outer things you have been seeking for a long time; but no order, no harmony could be created. Now wake up! Seek on your own. Be a light unto yourself. You have travelled far with the help of outer lamps and gone astray—and only astray, falling into ditches and ruins, being injured.

Light your own lamp, and move on your own.

No one outside can give you order. Create your own order. Let your life be filled with discipline from within.

Hari-om-tat-sat!

5

The Inner Sky

Ashtavakra said: O son, long have you been caught in the bondage of perceiving yourself as the body. Cut this bondage with the sword of knowing 'I am awareness' and be happy.

You are alone, void of action, self-illuminated and innocent. Your bondage is this: that you practise samadhi.

You are permeating this universe, you are the thread within it. You are pure consciousness by nature, do not become small-minded. You are without expectations, unchanging, self-sufficient, the abode of serenity, of boundless intelligence, and unperturbed. Hence have faith only in consciousness.

Know that which has form is false, and know the formless as unchangeable and everlasting. From this true understanding one is not born in the world again. Just as a mirror exists in the image reflected in it, and also exists apart from the reflection, God is within and outside this body. Just as the one all-pervading sky is the same within and outside a pot, the eternal everlasting Brahman is the same in all.

THE FIRST SUTRA:

> Ashtavakra said: O son, long have you been caught in
> the bondage of perceiving yourself as the body. Cut this
> bondage with the sword of knowing 'I am awareness' and
> be happy.

In Ashtavakra's vision—and this is the purest vision, the
ultimate vision—bondage is only a belief, bondage is not real.

There is an episode in Ramakrishna's life . . .

For his whole life he had been worshipping Mother
Kali, but at the very end he began to feel, 'It is duality; the
experience of oneness has still not happened. It is lovely,
delightful, but the two still remains two.' Someone loves a
woman, someone loves money, someone politics; he loved
Kali—but love still was divided in two. Still the ultimate
non-duality hadn't happened and he was in anguish. He
began looking out for a non-dualist, a Vedantist—for some
person to come who could show him the path.

A paramahansa named Totapuri was passing by.
Ramakrishna invited him to stop with him and asked, 'Help
me to attain oneness with the divine.'

Totapuri said, 'What's difficult in that? You believe
there are two, so there are two. Drop the belief!'

Ramakrishna replied, 'But dropping this belief is very
difficult—I have lived with it my whole life. When I close
my eyes the image of Kali is standing there. I drown in that
nectar. I forget that I am to become one; as soon as I close
my eyes there are two. When I try to meditate, it becomes
dual. Help me out of this!'

So Totapuri said, 'Try this: when the image of Kali is
before you, pick up a sword and cut her in two.'

Ramakrishna said, 'Where will I find a sword?'

What Totapuri said is the same as what is said in Ashtavakra's sutra. Totapuri said, 'From where did you bring this image of Kali? Bring a sword from the same place! She too is imaginary. She too is an embellishment of your imagination. Through nurturing it your whole life, through continuously projecting it your whole life, it has become crystallized. It is just imagination.' Not everyone sees Kali when they close their eyes.

After years of effort a Christian closes his eyes and Christ comes to him. A devotee of Krishna closes his eyes and Krishna comes to him. A lover of Buddha closes his eyes and Buddha comes to him. A lover of Mahavira closes his eyes and Mahavira comes to him. Christ doesn't come to a Jaina, Mahavira doesn't come to a Christian—only the image you project will come. Ramakrishna's effort was with Kali, and the image became almost solid. It became so real from constant repetition, from continuous remembering, that it seemed Kali was standing in front of him. No one was standing there.

Consciousness is alone. There is no second there, no other.

'Just close your eyes,' Totapuri said, 'raise the sword and strike.'

Ramakrishna closed his eyes, but as soon as he closed them his courage vanished. Raising his sword to strike Kali? The devotee has to raise his sword and strike God!—it was too hard.

To renounce the world is very easy. What is worth holding on to in the world? But when you have established an image deep in the mind, when you have created poetry in the mind, when the mind's dream has become manifest, then it is very difficult to renounce it. The world is like a nightmare. But a dream of devotion, a dream of feeling is not a nightmare; it is a very sweet dream. How does one drop it? How does one break it?

Tears would start flowing from his eyes and he would become ecstatic . . . his body would begin shaking. But he didn't raise his sword—he would completely forget about it.

Finally Totapuri said, 'I've wasted many days here. It's no good. Either you do it or I'm going to leave. Don't waste my time. Enough of this nonsense now!' That day Totapuri brought a piece of glass with him, and he said, 'When you begin to be absorbed in delight, I will cut your forehead with this piece of glass. When I cut your forehead, gather courage inside, raise your sword and cut Kali in two. This is the last chance—I am not staying any longer.'

Totapuri's threat of leaving . . . It is difficult to find such a master. Totapuri must have been a man like Ashtavakra. Ramakrishna closed his eyes and Kali's image appeared to him. He was about to bliss out—tears were ready to flow from his eyes, overwhelmed, joy was consuming him— he was about to become ecstatic, when Totapuri held his forehead and, where the third-eye chakra is, made a cut from top to bottom with the piece of glass. Blood began to stream from the cut, and this time Ramakrishna found courage. He raised the sword and cut Kali in two pieces. When Kali fell apart he became non-dual: the wave dissolved in the ocean, the river fell into the ocean.

It is said that he stayed immersed for six days in this ultimate silence. He was neither hungry nor thirsty—there was no consciousness of the outside, no awareness. All was forgotten. And when he opened his eyes six days later, the first thing he said was, 'The last barrier has fallen!'

This first sutra says:

> O son, long have you been caught in the bondage of perceiving yourself as the body.

You have started believing this bondage is your being. 'I am the body, I am the body, I am the body!'—you have repeated this, life after life. From this repetition we have become the body. But we are not the body. This is our misperception, this is our habit. This is our self-hypnosis, and we have believed it so deeply we have become it.

There is another episode in Ramakrishna's life . . . He did the sadhanas, the spiritual practices, of all religions. He is the only person in the history of mankind who tried to attain the truth through the paths of all the religions. Ordinarily a person reaches by one path. When you have reached the summit of the mountain, who bothers about other paths? Do you then walk up the other trails? Who cares? You have attained. The trail you came on, you came on; what's the use of walking on all the others? But Ramakrishna reached the summit of the mountain again and again, then descended. He climbed by a second path, then by a third path. He is the first person who practised the sadhanas of all the religions and attained to the same peak through all of them.

Many have talked about synthesis—Ramakrishna is the first to create a science of synthesis. Many people have said that all religions are true, but it has just been talk. Ramakrishna made it a reality. He gave it the strength of experience, he proved it with his life. When he was doing Islamic sadhana he became a real Mohammedan fakir. He forgot Rama and began chanting, 'Allahoo . . . Allahoo.' He began listening to the verses of the Koran and lived right on the steps of the mosque. If he came near a temple he didn't even lift his eyes, let alone bow in greeting. He had forgotten about Kali.

In Bengal there is a sect, the Sakhis. When Ramakrishna practised the sadhana of the Sakhi sect . . . The Sakhis believe that God alone is male, everyone else is female—Krishna is God, everyone else is his *sakhi*, his girlfriend—so in the Sakhi tradition, men also consider themselves women. But what happened in Ramakrishna's life had never happened in the life of any follower of the Sakhi tradition. A man can believe on the surface he is a woman, but he remains a man, inside he knows that he is a man. Members of the Sakhi sect take an idol of Krishna to bed with them—this is their husband. But what difference does it make? But when Ramakrishna did this sadhana something unprecedented happened—scientists too will be surprised that such a thing happened. He did the sadhana of the Sakhis for six months and after three months his breasts started to swell, his voice changed, he began walking like a woman, and his voice became sweet like a woman's. His breasts were growing, becoming the breasts of a woman's; the male structure of his body began to change.

This much is possible, because man too has breasts, though undeveloped—women's are developed. So it is possible that undeveloped breasts become developed; the seed does exist. Up to this point nothing great has happened. Many men's breasts become enlarged—this is not such a great surprise. But when six months were nearly over he started menstruating. This was a miracle! To menstruate is completely against the science of the body. This had never happened to any man.

What happened during these six months? The belief, 'I am a woman'—this idea became so strong, this feeling echoed so deep in his being, in every pore . . . In every cell of the body it echoed: 'I am a woman.' No opposing feeling remained, he completely forgot about being a man; then it happened.

Ashtavakra is saying we are not bodies; it is just that we believed we were and we became bodies. Whatever we believed, we became. The world is our belief. And the moment we drop our beliefs we can immediately be transformed. And to drop it nothing real has to be changed, only an idea must be dropped.

If we were really the body, transformation would be very difficult. We are not really the body. In reality we are hidden inside the body as consciousness—the witness, the observer.

O son, long have you been caught in the bondage of perceiving yourself as the body. Cut this bondage with the sword of knowing 'I am awareness' and be happy. Raise the sword of awareness. 'I am awareness'—raise this sword of understanding, chop away the idea that 'I am the body,' and you are happy.

All suffering is of the body. Birth, illness, old age, death—all are of the body, and when there is identification with the body there is identification with all the pains of the body. When the body is worn out then we think, 'I have become worn out.' When the body becomes ill we think, 'I have become ill.' When the body approaches death we are frightened that we are dying. Beliefs . . . only beliefs.

I have heard that one night Mulla Nasruddin and his wife were lying in bed . . . They had no children, and his wife was very eager to have a child. As they were about to fall asleep the wife said, 'Listen, if we have a child where will we put him to sleep?—because there is only one bed.'

So Mulla slid a little towards the side, saying, 'We will put him right here between us.'

And the wife said, 'And then if we have a second?'

Mulla slid over a little more saying, 'We can put him here too.' Miserly fellow!

The wife said, 'And if a third comes?'

Mulla slid over further and was just going to say, 'Put him right here,' when he fell off the bed with a crash. His leg was broken. The neighbours gathered, hearing all the noise—he was crying loudly—and they asked, 'What happened?'

He said, 'This child—the one who does not yet exist— broke my leg. And when a non-existent child can cause so much trouble, what to say of a real one! Excuse me, but I don't want any children. This experience is enough!'

Sometimes . . . no, not sometimes, usually we live like this— believing. We follow our belief, and when we follow our belief real consequences come, even if the belief is false. There was no child, but a real leg was broken. The effect of the false can be real. If the false is believed deeply enough, its consequences will actually happen.

Psychologists say many of the various experiences of our world are more belief than reality.

A psychologist was doing experiments at Harvard University. In one, he sealed up a big bottle, carefully packed it, and brought it to his classroom. Fifty students were there. He put the bottle on the table and told the students, 'There is ammonia gas in this bottle. I want to do an experiment to find out how much time it takes for the smell of this gas to spread when I take the lid off. So when the smell reaches you raise your hand. As soon as you detect it raise your hand. I want to find out how many seconds it takes to reach the last row.'

The students sat attentively. He opened the bottle. As soon as he opened it he quickly covered his nose with a handkerchief—ammonia gas! He stood aside. Before two seconds had passed someone in the first row raised his hand, then a second, then a third. Then a hand came up in the second row, then the third row. In fifteen seconds the ammonia gas had reached the whole of the class—but there wasn't any ammonia in the bottle! The bottle was empty.

An idea—so consequences happened. They believed it, so it happened. When he said there wasn't any ammonia gas, the students said, 'Whether there was or not we smelt it.' The smell was projected. It was as if the smell came from within—there was nothing outside. They thought, so it came.

I have heard . . .

A man was sick in the hospital and a nurse brought juice for him, orange juice. Just before she brought the juice another nurse had given him a bottle to put his urine sample in—for testing. He enjoyed practical jokes, so he poured the orange juice into the bottle and put it aside.

When the nurse came to take the bottle she was startled that it had such a strange colour. The man said, 'You are surprised too—its colour is rather strange. Okay, let me recycle it through the body one more time, that will fix the colour,' and he lifted the bottle to his mouth and drank the contents.

They say the nurse passed out: she thought the man was drinking urine. And he had said, 'I will pass it through my body one more time and the colour will be corrected, it will be put right.' What kind of man is this? But it was only orange juice. If she had known it was orange juice she would not have passed out. Her becoming unconscious was real, though it came from belief.

In life you can find thousands of such incidents around you where belief has done something, where belief becomes actualized.

'I am the body'—we have believed this for many lives, and believing it we have become the body. Believing it we have become small. Believing it we have become limited. Ashtavakra's fundamental premise is that this is self-hypnosis, autohypnosis. You have not become the body, you cannot become the body. There is no way to do it—how can you become what you are not? What you are, you are right now; you only have to cut away false beliefs.

Cut this bondage with the sword of knowing 'I am awareness' and be happy. Right now awaken in joy . . . because all our miseries are parasites of the belief that we are the body. Buddha also dies, but does not suffer at death. Ramakrishna dies, but does not suffer at death. Ramana Maharshi dies, but does not suffer at death.

When Ramana died he had cancer. The doctors were very surprised: it was a very difficult illness and it caused much suffering, but Ramana remained the same as ever, as if the illness made no difference. It made no change at all. The doctors were disturbed. It was not possible; how could it happen? Death was at the door and the man was relaxed, unwavering. We can understand the discomfort of the doctors: so much suffering but the man was calm, unwavering. We can understand their discomfort, their reasoning, because the body appears to be all to us. One who knows that, 'I am not the body . . . death is coming, but it is the death of the body. And pain is coming, but that too comes to the body.' A new consciousness has manifested that stands back and watches. And this distance between the body and consciousness is as the distance between the earth and the sky. There is no greater distance than this. In your inner world the most distant things in existence are meeting. You are the horizon where the earth and the sky meet.

That which is born, remains, grows, changes, deteriorates and perishes: you are not that.

That which observes all of this . . . You have seen your childhood, and you have also seen childhood depart: if you were your childhood-self then who could remember now that there was a childhood? You would have disappeared with the childhood. You have seen your youth: you saw it come, you saw it go. If you were your youth then who is it who remembers now? You would have gone with your youth. You watched your youth come, you watched it go—obviously you are other than this youth. It is such a simple thing, such a clear thing. You have seen suffering, seen pain arise, seen the clouds of pain gathering around you—and you have seen suffering depart. You have seen unhappiness, you have seen happiness. A thorn has pierced your skin, you observed pain. The thorn is removed, and now there is no pain. You see it—you are the seer. You stand beyond. You cannot be touched, no event can touch you. You are a lotus floating on water.

> You are alone, void of action, self-illuminated and innocent. Your bondage is this: that you practise samadhi.

This is an amazing, revolutionary statement. It is impossible to find such a revolutionary statement in any scripture of the world. When you understand it completely, a deep gratitude arises.

Patanjali has said, 'Yoga is the cessation of *chitta-vritti*—projections of the mind.' In yoga it is an accepted idea that until the mind stops projecting a person cannot know himself. When all mental projections become quiet, a person can know himself.

Ashtavakra is speaking against Patanjali's sutra. Ashtavakra is saying, 'You are alone, void of action, self-illuminated and innocent. Your bondage is this: that you practise samadhi.' Samadhi cannot be practised, samadhi cannot be prepared for, because samadhi is your nature. Mental projections are lower states. Trying to stop them is like entering a dark house and trying to fight with darkness.

Understand this. Bring your swords, spears, staffs and fight with darkness; call soldiers, strong men and start pushing darkness out. Will you ever be victorious? As a definition it is accurate—the absence of darkness is light. But understand this definition. It is true that the absence of darkness is light. It is true that the quieting of mental projections is yoga, but don't take it the other way.

The absence of darkness is light, but don't start trying to get rid of darkness. The actual situation is just the reverse: the presence of light is the absence of darkness. Light a lamp and darkness disappears by itself. Darkness does not exist—darkness is only an absence.

Patanjali says that you will know your being once you calm the projections of the mind. Ashtavakra says that when you know your being, the projections of the mind will become quiet. Without knowing your being, projections cannot be stilled. Mental projections arise because the being is not known. If you think you are the body, desires of the body arise. If you think you are the mind, desires of the mind arise. The desires of whatever you identify with will shadow you, will reflect in you. Whatever is near you, it affects you.

It is like placing a coloured stone next to a crystal: the colours of the stone will shine on the crystal. Put it with a red stone and the crystal appears red. Put it with a blue stone and the crystal appears blue. This is from the proximity of the stone and the crystal. The crystal doesn't become blue, it only seems to.

Darkness only seems to be, it is not. The non-existence of light is called darkness. Darkness has no reality of its own, no existence of its own. Don't start fighting with darkness.

Yoga and Ashtavakra's vision are opposites. Hence I say, if you want to understand Ashtavakra, you should try to understand Krishnamurti—Krishnamurti is a modern version of Ashtavakra. What Krishnamurti says in a modern idiom, in today's language, is the essence of Ashtavakra's message. The followers of Krishnamurti think he is saying something new. There is nothing new to be said, whatever can be said has already been said. Whatever facets life can have, have all been explored somewhere. Man has been seeking from time immemorial. There is nothing new to be said under the sun; only the language changes, the packaging changes, the clothes change. New ideas change according to the times, but what Krishnamurti is saying is exactly this.

Ashtavakra's language is very ancient, Krishnamurti's language is very modern. But those who can understand a little will see that they say the same thing.

Krishnamurti says that yoga is not needed, meditation is not needed, mantras and asceticism are not needed. All of these are practices. Practice has to be done for what is not our nature. What practice can be done to find our inner nature? Drop all practices, look into yourself, and your nature will become manifest.

You are alone, void of action, self-illuminated and innocent. Look at this declaration. Ashtavakra says you are innocent. Don't even think yourself a sinner. Let the sadhus and priests say thousands of times that you are a sinner, to cleanse yourself of sins, to repent, that you have done bad karma—become released from it. Remember Ashtavakra's sutra: You are free of action, how can you do anything?

Ashtavakra says there are six life waves. These six waves are hunger and thirst, sadness and happiness, birth and death. Hunger and thirst are waves of the body. If there is no body there is neither hunger nor thirst. These are needs of the body. When the body is healthy, hunger increases. When the body is ill, hunger decreases. If the body is out in the sun, thirst increases because sweat will evaporate. There is more thirst in hot weather, less thirst in cold. These are needs of the body, these are waves of the body.

Hunger and thirst are of the body; sadness and happiness are of the mind. When someone leaves you there is unhappiness because the mind grabs hold, makes attachments. When you meet someone, a beloved, there is happiness. When a beloved leaves, unhappiness. When you meet a disagreeable person, unhappiness; when the disagreeable person leaves, happiness. This is the play of the mind, the play of affection and disgust, the play of attraction and repulsion.

Inside one in whom mind has ceased to exist there is no sadness, no happiness. These are waves of the mind.

And birth–death: birth and death are waves of life energy. At birth breathing starts; at death breathing stops. As soon as a baby is born the doctor is concerned that he should start breathing, start crying—crying, because to cry he will need to breathe. In the spasms of crying the breathing passages will open. In the spasms of crying the closed lungs will start functioning. If the child doesn't start crying within a few seconds the doctor will hang him upside down and spank him, forcing the breathing to start.

Breathing is birth. Breathing means the process of life. When a man dies, breathing is finished, the process of life stops. This goes on moment to moment. As the breath comes in, life comes in. As the breath goes out, life goes out.

Birth and death are happening every second. Every incoming breath is life. Every outgoing breath is death. So life and death are happening every moment. These are waves of life energy.

Ashtavakra says, these are the six waves and you are beyond these six waves, you are the observer of these.

Buddha based his whole system of meditation on the breath. Buddha said one technique is enough: go on watching the incoming and outgoing breaths. What will happen from watching the breath come and go? Slowly, as you see that the outgoing breath has gone out and that the incoming breath has not yet come in, you will find a short gap in between where the breath stops, where it is neither going out nor coming in. Between each half breath there is a momentary gap—where breath does not flow, does not move, does not stir. It goes out, stops for a moment, then comes in. It comes in, stops for a moment, then goes out. You will begin to see a gap. In this very gap you will find that you are: this coming and going of the breath is the play of life force. And if you become capable of watching the coming and going of the breath, then the seer is separate from the breath, is other than the breath.

Our body is the outermost circumference, mind is a circle within, and life, a circle deeper within. It is possible for the body to be crippled, broken, destroyed, and still man goes on living. The mind can be split, insane, non-functional, and still man goes on living. But without breath man will not live. Injure a man's entire brain, still he will go on living—lying in a coma, but still alive. Limbs can be cut off so only breathing remains; man goes on living. If the breath stops, even if everything else is okay, the man will die. These are the six waves, and the observer is beyond these six.

You are alone . . . No one is your companion. The body is not your companion, the breath is not your companion, thoughts are not your companions. *You are alone* . . . There is no companion within—what to say of the outside! Husband, wife, family, friends, beloveds—none are companions. There is none who is near, none who is related. To be near is only an outer phenomenon. From within, no union can be made with anyone.

You are alone, void of action . . . Don't even raise the question of your karmas, your acts. If you should ask Ashtavakra, 'You say one can be liberated right now, so what happens to the fruits of our past actions? What happens to the sins of lifetimes? How do we get released from them?' Ashtavakra will say, 'You have never done them. Out of hunger, the body may have done something. Out of vital energy, life may have done something. Out of its own needs, the mind may have done something. You have never done anything. You are ever separate in non-doing. Doing has never happened through you; you are the observer of all actions. Liberation is possible right now.'

Consider it: if we have to destroy the whole web of past actions, we can never become liberated. It is impossible. We have done so many acts over infinite time—just estimate how many. If we have to be released from all these actions then the release will take an infinite time, and during this infinite time you won't be sitting idle, you will still be doing something, so karmas will again accumulate. This chain will be endless. This chain will never finish, it will never come to any conclusion.

Ashtavakra says that if to be free you have to become free of the impressions of past actions, then liberation can never happen. But liberation does happen. You cannot become free—you *are* free. The existence of liberation is the proof that the being has never done any act. You are not a sinner, you are not a saint; you are not virtuous, not unvirtuous. There is no hell anywhere, there is no heaven. You have never done anything; you have only seen dreams, you have only thought you were doing. You were sleeping within—the body was doing. Those bodies that did those things are long gone: how can the fruit of their actions be yours? You were sleeping inside—the mind acted. The mind that acted is disappearing every second.

I have heard that a former maharaja saw that his drawing room was dirty. He scolded his servant, Jhanku, saying, 'There are spiderwebs all over the drawing room. What have you been doing all day long?'

Jhanku said, 'Your Majesty, some spider must have made those webs—I have been dozing in my room.'

You were dozing inside, some spider must have made the webs! The body has spun webs, the mind has spun webs, the life energy has spun webs—you were sleeping. Wake up! Awakening, you find that you never did anything. Even if you wanted to do something you couldn't do it. Your nature is inaction. Non-doing is your natural state.

You are alone, void of action, self-illuminated and innocent. Did you hear this proclamation? You are innocent! Throw away what the pundits and priests have taught you! You are innocent. Their teaching has been very harmful; they have made you a sinner. They have taught you in a thousand ways that you are bad . . . they have filled you with humiliation and guilt. You are innocent, you have committed no wrong.

Your bondage is this: that you practise samadhi. Look at this revolutionary statement! *Your bondage is this: that you practise samadhi.* You are making efforts for samadhi to come to fruit, for meditation to flower, for liberation to happen—practices, rites, rituals. *Your bondage is this: that you practise samadhi.* This is your bondage. Raise the sword of awareness and sever it!

Now these two will become clear to you: the path of yoga and the path of awareness are completely different. The ancient name for the path of awareness is *sankhya.*

Sankhya means awareness, yoga means sadhana, techniques. Sankhya means simply wake up, nothing needs to be done. Yoga means there is much to be done before awakening happens. In yoga there are means; in sankhya there are only ends. There is no path, only the destination, because you have never left the destination to go anywhere else, you have just been sitting in your inner temple. You don't have to come back—just know that you have never gone anywhere.

You are alone, void of action, self-illuminated and innocent. Your bondage is this: that you practise samadhi. You are bound only by this, that you are seeking liberation. The search for liberation creates a new bondage.

A man is enslaved by the world, then he freaks out and begins to seek liberation. Here he renounces house and home, renounces his family, renounces business and money; then he is enslaved in a new bondage—he becomes a monk. New restrictions: how to move and sit, how to eat and drink—he creates a new slavery.

Have you observed that a monk's condition is like that of a prisoner? A monk is not free, because a monk thinks that first he has to accept restrictions to become free. This is a hilarious idea! For liberation, first one has to accept restrictions! To be free no restrictions are needed.

Krishnamurti has a book, *The First and Last Freedom.* It is the most up-to-date expression of Ashtavakra. If you are to be free then become free at the very first step. Don't think you will become free in the end. You can be free only on the first step, not on the second. If on the first step you make preparations for freedom, these very preparations will create bonds. Then to get rid of these new bonds you will have to make new preparations. These preparations will again make new bonds. You will get rid of one and be bound by the next. You will escape from the ditch and fall in the well.

Look how worldly people and sannyasins are both bound. Their slaveries are different, but the distinction is nothing. It seems that whatever you do will enslave you unless the basic stupidity is broken.

I have heard that someone's woman had run away, so he went to look for her. Searching everywhere he reached the jungle and there a sadhu was sitting under a tree. The man asked, 'Have you seen my woman going this way? She has run away from home. I am terribly upset.'

The sadhu asked, 'What is her name?'

He said, 'Her name is Trouble.'

The sadhu said, 'Trouble! You have given her a great name. All women are trouble, but only you have actually given the name. So what is your name?' The sadhu was eager to know—this man seemed to be very clever with names.

He said, 'My name is Foolish.'

The sadhu started laughing. He said, 'Drop this search. Wherever you sit "Trouble" will come. You don't need to go anywhere. You being "Foolish" is enough. Trouble will find you.'

When someone renounces the world and escapes, this renunciation does not destroy his weak-mindedness, his foolishness, his stupidity. He takes this stupidity and sits in the temple making new bondages. That stupidity weaves new webs. First enslaved by the world, now enslaved by sannyas, he cannot remain without bondage.

Freedom is on the first step. There is no planning it. Planning means to be bound in plans. Make preparations, and you are enslaved in preparations. Then this will have to be renounced. How long is it going to go on? It will be endless.

I have heard: a man was afraid to enter a graveyard. His house was on the other side of the graveyard, so he had to cross it every day. He was so afraid that he wouldn't come out of his house at night; by dusk he would return home, trembling.

Finally a sadhu took pity on him. He told him, 'Stop worrying about it and take this charm. Always keep this charm tied to your wrist; then no ghost or spirit can bother you.'

It worked. By tying the charm on his wrist his fear of ghosts disappeared. But now a new fear caught hold of him: What if the charm got lost? Naturally, that charm had protected him from ghosts . . . now he could cross the graveyard in the middle of the night with no fear. There had never been ghosts there—it was only his own fear. The charm released him from that fear, but he was caught in a new fear, of losing the charm. He took the charm with him when he went to bathe, checking again and again to see that he had it. He was terrified now that while he slept at night someone would open the charm, someone would steal it. The charm became his life.

The fear continued in the same way—if not of ghosts then of losing the charm. Now if someone substitutes something else for the charm, what difference will it make? This man is not going to change his fearfulness.

It is not a question of ghosts; it is a question of fear. So you can push fear around from one place to another. Lots of people go on playing this kind of volleyball. Throwing the ball from here to there, from there to here, they just go on throwing and playing. And meanwhile the whole of life passes you by.

Ashtavakra says, practising for samadhi is the cause of bondage. If you are to be free, then declare your freedom, don't go on getting ready. So I say, look at this revolutionary statement. This statement is rare, it is incomparable.

Ashtavakra says to declare your freedom here and now. Don't prepare for it. Don't say that first you must get ready, and then . . . because the preparations will enslave you. Then how to drop the preparations? One disease is dropped, another disease is taken up. This is just switching shoulders.

You have seen people carrying a body on a stretcher to the burning grounds: they go on switching shoulders. Tired of carrying the weight on one shoulder, they shift to the other shoulder. They get a few minutes' relief; then the other shoulder starts to hurt, and again they switch. You are doing this life after life. You only find a short relief from this, you never find the ultimate rest from it.

Stop carrying these dead bodies. Make your declaration! If you want freedom, then in a second, in a fraction of a second, it can be declared.

People ask me why I give sannyas to each and every one. I say that everyone is entitled to it—it is only a question of declaring it. There is nothing else needed, it only has to be declared. This declaration has to be enthroned in your heart, that 'I am a sannyasin,' and you have become a sannyasin, that 'I am enlightened,' and you are enlightened. Your declaration is your life.

Find the courage to declare. Why make small declarations? Proclaim 'Aham Brahmasmi—I am Brahman!' and you have become the ultimate.

In the next sutra Ashtavakra says:

> You are permeating this universe, you are the thread within it. You are pure consciousness by nature, do not become small-minded.

Why be involved with trivial things? Sometimes you are involved with, 'This house is mine, this body is mine, this money is mine, this business is mine . . .' What trivial things the mind gets involved in!

You are permeating this universe, you are the thread within it. This whole existence is infused by you. The whole expanse of Brahman is permeated by you. *You are pure consciousness by nature, do not become small-minded.*

Why make small claims? Make a great proclamation. Proclaim this: 'I am pure consciousness, I am pure intelligence!' *Do not become small-minded.*

We have made such trivial claims, and we become what we declare. In this, India's contribution to the world is unique because India has made the world's greatest proclamations. Mansoor proclaimed in the Mohammedan world, 'Ana'l haq!—I am the truth.' They murdered him. They said, 'This man is making too great a claim. 'I am the truth'—only God can say that. How can man say it?' But we didn't murder Ashtavakra, nor did we murder the seers of the Upanishads who said, 'Aham Brahmasmi—I am Brahman,' because we understood one thing: man becomes the proclamation he makes.

Why make a small claim? When the evolution of your life is dependent on your claim, then claim the most expansive, claim the infinite, the omnipresent. Make the divine proclamation. Why be satisfied with anything less? Why be miserly? You are miserly in your very declaration. Then make your miserly claim and you will become it.

Say yes to the small, you will become small. Say yes to the infinite and you will become infinite. Your belief is your life.

> You are without expectations, unchanging, self-sufficient,
> the abode of serenity, of boundless intelligence, and
> unperturbed. Hence have faith only in consciousness.

This one conviction is enough. Not practice—faith, conviction. Not practice—trust. This much faith is sufficient—that you are pure consciousness. This is the greatest magic in the world.

Psychologists say that when you tell someone again and again that he is unintelligent, he becomes unintelligent. People aren't as stupid as they look. They are the Supreme Being. They have been called stupid, told they are stupid. It has been repeated by so many people and they have listened to it so many times that they have become idiots. They could have become buddhas, but they have become *buddhus*, idiots.

Psychologists say that if you meet someone in good health on the street and say to him, 'Oh! What happened to you? Your face looks yellow. You seem to have a fever. Let me feel your pulse . . . you are sick! Your legs seem to be shivering,' at first he will deny it, because he hadn't thought until a moment before. He will say, 'No, no! I am completely fine. What are you talking about?'

You may say, 'Okay, suit yourself.' Then a little later another person comes to him saying, 'Wait! Your face has gone completely pale. What's the matter?' Now he won't be able to say so boldly that he is completely fine. He will say, 'Yes, I'm feeling a little out of sorts.' He will begin accepting it. His courage will start slipping.

Then a third man comes and starts saying the same thing. Now he will return home feeling, 'My condition is very bad. Now there is no sense in going to the market.'

You may have heard this story:
Once a Brahmin bought a goat and was taking it home. Three or four thieves thought the goat could be snatched away from him. But the Brahmin was strong and to steal from him would be no easy job, so they decided to try diplomacy, a little trickery.

One came up to him on the road saying, 'Well done! How much did you pay for the dog?'

That man, that Brahmin said, 'Dog! Are you blind? Or only mad? It is a goat! I am bringing her from the market. I paid fifty rupees for her.'

The thief said, 'It's up to you but, you know, seeing a Brahmin carrying a dog on his shoulders . . . Dear brother, to me it looks like a dog. Could there be some mistake?'

The Brahmin went on his way, wondering what kind of man that was! But he touched the feet of the goat just to check, saying to himself, 'It is a goat.' Another of the gang was waiting across the road. He called over to the Brahmin, 'What a fine dog you have bought!'

Now the Brahmin did not have the courage to insist it was not a dog: who knows, maybe it was a dog—two men could not be wrong. Still he said, 'No, no, it's not a dog.' But it was weaker now. He said it, but the foundation was shaken. He said, 'No, no, it's a goat.'

The man said, 'It's a goat? You call this a goat? Then, respected Brahmin, the definition of goat needs to be changed. If you call this a goat, then what will you call a dog? But it's up to you. You are a scholarly man; you can change it if you want. It's just a name. Perhaps you say dog, perhaps you say goat—a dog it remains. Nothing changes just by calling it a goat.'

The man went away. The Brahmin put the goat down and looked: it was definitely a goat . . . a goat like any other goat. He rubbed his eyes and splashed them with water from a roadside tap. He was nearing his own neighbourhood: if people saw a Brahmin carrying a dog on his shoulders it would be a blow against worship in the temple and against scholarship. People paid for his worship—they would stop paying, they would think him mad. Again he thoroughly inspected the animal, making sure it was a goat. But what was with those two guys?

Again he shouldered the goat and started off, but now he moved a little nervously. What if anyone else saw him? Then he came across the third fellow. He exclaimed, 'What a fine dog! Where did you get it? I too have wanted to have a dog for a long time.'

The Brahmin said, 'Friend, you just take it! If you want a dog, take it. It is really a dog. A friend gave it to me, you please relieve me of it.' And he ran home before anyone could find out that he had bought a dog.

This is how man lives. You have become what you believe. And there are cheats and scoundrels all around—you have been led to believe all kinds of things. They have their own motives. The priest wants to convince you that you are a sinner, because if you are not a sinner how will he continue to pray for you? It is in his interest that a goat be taken for a dog. A pundit—if you are not ignorant what will become of his scholarship? How will he run his business? A religious teacher—if he explains to you that you are inactive, free of doing, that you have never committed sin—then what need is there of him?

It is as if you go to a doctor and he explains that you are not sick, that you have never been sick, you cannot be sick, health is your nature—then the doctor is committing suicide. What will happen to his business? Go to a doctor in robust health, go when you are not at all sick; then too you will find that he discovers some problem. Go and try it. Go in absolutely top form, when you are not sick at all; just go and do it, tell the doctor that you just want him to do a check-up. It is not easy to find a doctor who will say you are not ill.

Mulla Nasruddin's son became a doctor. I asked Mulla, 'How is your son's practice going?'

He said, 'Things are going very well indeed.'

I asked how he figured that things were going well. He said, 'Things are going so well that many times he tells patients that they are not sick. Only a great doctor can say it, one whose practice is going well, going so good that now he doesn't want to be bothered, he doesn't have time.' Mulla said, 'This is how I figured it's going well. Many times he tells people there is nothing wrong with them!'

There are many businesses—they have their own interests. Thousands of businesses are riding on your back—pundits, priests, religious teachers. They need you to be a sinner, it is necessary that you have done evil. If not, what will happen to those who explain how to be released from bad karma? What will happen to those messiahs who come to save you? If Ashtavakra is right, then all messiahs are useless. Then there is no need for your release—you are saved, you are liberated.

Ashtavakra has no such profession. Ashtavakra doesn't want to do business with you. He speaks straightforwardly, he is giving crystal-clear truths: *You are without expectations, unchanging, self-sufficient, the abode of serenity, of boundless intelligence, and unperturbed. Hence have faith only in consciousness.*

Only one conviction is needed: 'I am the witness.' It is enough. Such a self-confident person is religious. There is no need for any other conviction. There is no need for faith in God, no need for faith in heaven and hell, no need for faith in the law of karma. One faith is enough, and that faith is that you are the witness, unchanging. And as soon as this conviction is strong within you, you will find yourself becoming unchanging, steady.

A psychologist did an experiment. He divided a class in two, half the children here, half there—in separate rooms. He told the first group, 'This problem is very difficult; none of you will be able to solve it.' He wrote an equation on the board and said, 'It is not within your capacity. It is so difficult that even the students of the next class couldn't do it. But I am doing an experiment—I want to know if anyone among you can come close to solving it; if anyone can find a method, or make two or three steps in the right direction. But it is impossible!' He repeated again and again, 'It is impossible. Still, you must try.'

He went into the other room with the rest of the students from the same class. He wrote the same equation on the board and said, 'This problem is so easy it is unlikely that any of you will be unable to solve it. Children in the lower class have solved it too. So I am not giving you this as any kind of examination, it is so easy you are bound to solve it. I only want to know if there is anyone in the class who will have any difficulty with it.'

The question was the same, the class was the same, but there was a great difference in the results. In the first group only three out of fifteen students could solve it. In the second group, twelve out of fifteen students solved it; only three could not. Such a big difference. The same question! The deciding factor was the attitude with which the problem was presented.

Ashtavakra does not say that religion is arduous, he says it is very easy. Those who say it is difficult, make it difficult. Those who say it is almost impossible, a razor's edge— they are frightening you. They say it is like climbing the Himalayas, only rare beings can climb—then you drop the idea, thinking, 'I am not such a rare being. It is beyond me. Let the rare ones climb, I am not going to get into this trouble. I applaud these rare beings—they can go ahead! But I am a simple person; just leave me in this ditch.'

Ashtavakra says it is very easy. It is so easy, you don't need to do anything, just observing with alertness is enough.

This is the highest declaration of man's genius. It is to make man aware of the highest possibility of human life. Religion is the ultimate miracle of man's genius. In contrast, politics is the most inferior expression of human intelligence; religion is the most superior.

Once a politician fell seriously ill. The doctor advised, 'Don't do any mental work for two or three months.'

The politician asked, 'Doctor, do you have any objection to my doing a bit of politics?'

The doctor replied, 'No, none at all. Do as much politics as you want, just don't do any mental work.'

The brain doesn't function at all in politics. In politics there is violence, not intelligence. There is grabbing, scrambling, struggling; not peace. There is no rest, only restlessness. There is ambition for greatness, jealousy, aggression—there is no soul.

Religion is non-aggression, non-violence, freedom from competition. It is not struggle; it is surrender. Nothing needs to be taken from anyone else; there only needs to be the declaration of what one already has. When we have so much, what need is there to steal from others? Only those who don't know themselves can steal. They are fighting over bits and pieces when God is enthroned inside, dying over bits and pieces while the ultimate expanse is present within. The ocean is present, and they crave droplets!

Only those who don't know themselves can be in politics.

And when I say politics, I don't mean only those who are in political parties. By politics, I mean all those people who are struggling in some way: struggling for money, money politics; struggling for power, power politics; struggling for renunciation, the politics of the renunciate.

Among the renunciate there is great rivalry that no other renunciate should get ahead. An Olympics goes on among the renunciate, that no mahatma becomes more important than you. One mahatma will go out to defeat another. If the Olympics is ever hosted by India, there should also be a competitive event for the mahatmas.

But wherever there is competition, there is politics. The basic sutra of politics is, 'What I don't have, someone else has; I can seize it and make it mine.' But what you take from others, how can it become yours? How will stolen goods become yours? What has been seized will be taken away. If not today, then tomorrow someone else will take it from you. And if no one succeeds in taking it from you, death will surely take it. Only that which you don't have to take from anyone else is yours. Then even death will not be able to take it.

Yours is what you had before you were born, what you will still have after death. Seek that one.

And to search for that one, Ashtavakra says you don't need to practise: only be alert, only witness.

Many times you feel you are running unnecessarily, but how do you stop? It is not that you haven't felt it is a meaningless rat race. You have, but how do you stop? And the training for the rat race goes very deep. You have forgotten how to stop—your legs are in the habit of running, the mind is in the habit of running. Your training is such that you can't sit still. Training for sitting has disappeared.

A poet says:

A complaint came to my lips
but who to tell it to, it will be meaningless.

> Swallowing the pain, I kept moving along,
> refusing to sit, refusing defeat.

And people still think it is defeat to just sit. If they sit, they think they are defeated. If they sit, they think it is escapism, running away! If they just sit, the passing thousands will look with condemnation . . . so people keep moving.

Complaints that all is useless come often to the mind . . . but who to tell? Who will understand? Here everyone is like you. No one tells anyone. People go on moving, each hiding his own wound.

'A complaint came to my lips but who to tell it to, it will be meaningless.' If you meet an Ashtavakra or a Buddha, it is meaningful to say it. Here, whom can you tell?

'Swallowing the pain, I kept moving along . . .' People swallow the pain and move on.

'Refusing to sit, refusing defeat.' And this becomes the idea of the ego: 'Sitting defeated' means finished, gone under, dead. Keep going, keep doing something or other. Keep trying to accomplish something or other. If not, you will be lost.'

And those who just sit, attain. Those who stop, attain. The divine is not attained by running, it is attained by stopping.

Ashtavakra says, attain in ultimate ease.

Just sit sometimes. Find some time to only sit, not doing anything. Zen monks have a meditation technique: Zazen. Zazen means just sitting, not doing a thing. It is a very deep method of meditation. To call it a method is not right because there is no method; just sitting, not doing anything. Zen says the same as Ashtavakra is saying: Sit down! Sit for a while and relax. Leave this turmoil for a while. Leave all ambition for a little while. Leave the mind's running around, leave its rat race. Simply sit a while, and sink into yourself.

A light will gradually begin spreading inside you. Perhaps you won't see it at first. It is like returning home in the bright afternoon sun. At first the house seems dark inside. The eyes are used to the sun. Sit a little while, and the eyes will adjust, and the room becomes lit. Slowly, slowly, light comes into the room. It is the same inside. You have been going out, going out for many lives, so it seems dark inside. The first time you go in nothing will be visible . . . nothing but darkness. Don't freak out. Sit . . . let the eyes get adjusted to the inside. The pupils have been used to bright sun.

Have you ever thought: in the sun the pupil becomes small? If you look in a mirror right after being in the sun, the pupil will appear very small because so much sunlight cannot be taken in—it is more than enough, so the pupil contracts. Contracting is automatic. Then when you go into the dark the pupil has to expand, the pupil has to enlarge. After sitting in darkness for a while, again look in the mirror and you will find the pupil enlarged.

For the third eye, it happens exactly the same as with the outer eyes. To look outside, the pupil should be small; to look within, the pupil should be large. It has been a long and ancient practice. But to destroy that practice, no new practice is needed—just go on sitting.

People ask, 'What will we do sitting? Just give us "Ram, Ram", some mantra to chant, we will repeat it—give us something to do.' People say, 'We want crutches, we want help.' As soon as you practise, bondage starts. Just sit!

By sitting I don't mean sitting down; you can remain standing, you can lie down too. Sitting means, don't do anything, in the twenty-four hours just spend some time in non-doing. Become free of action. Remain empty. Let what is happening, happen. The world is flowing by, let it flow.

It is moving, let it move. Sounds come, let them come. A train passes by, a plane flies over, there is some noise—let it be, you just go on sitting. Don't concentrate—you just sit. Samadhi will gradually start becoming strong inside of you. You will suddenly understand what Ashtavakra means— what it means to be free of practice and rituals.

> Know that which has form is false, and know the formless as unchangeable and everlasting. From this true understanding one is not born in the world again.

Then you are what the Buddha has called *anagamin*—a person who never returns after death. We come back because of our desires, we come back because of our politics; we come back because of desires and hopes. One who dies knowing, 'I am the knower' does not enter again. He is released from this useless wheel—from coming and going.

Know that which has form is false, and know the formless as unchangeable and everlasting. From this true understanding, one is not born in the world again. Know that which has form is false . . . Within us, what has form is illusory; what has no form is the truth. Look at a whirlpool sometime. What is a whirlpool but waves arising in water? When it becomes calm, where has it gone? There was no whirlpool, it was just a wave in the water, it was just a shape that arose in the water. Likewise, we are just waves of the divine. When the wave is gone, nothing is left behind. Not even ash is left, not a trace remains. It is like writing on water, it disappears as you write—in the same way all that happens in our life are only waves.

> Just as a mirror exists in the image reflected in it, and also exists apart from the reflection, God is within and outside this body.

You have seen that when you stand in front of a mirror there is a reflection. Does something happen to the mirror? A reflection happens, which means that nothing happens. Move aside and the reflection is gone—the mirror remains just as it was. Your reflection is made by your coming before it; step aside and it is gone. But in the mirror nothing is made and nothing moves aside. The mirror remains in its own nature.

This sutra of Ashtavakra says: Stand before a mirror, a reflection is made in the mirror, but is a reflection really made? It seems to be. But don't be fooled by the reflection. Many are fooled by reflections.

And this sutra says that reflective mirrors are surrounding you; outside, inside, mirrors are reflecting in mirrors, and there is nothing at all. In just the same way the divine exists inside and outside of this body. God is within, God is without, God is above, God is below, God is in the west, God is in the east, God is in the south, God is in the north—in every direction, the same one. We are small whirlpools, small waves rising in that vast ocean.

Don't get confused by thinking of yourself as a wave—think of yourself as the ocean. Just this much difference in belief: it is the difference between slavery and freedom. See yourself as a wave and you are bound, see yourself as the ocean and you are liberated.

> Just as the one all-pervading sky is the same within and outside a pot, the eternal everlasting Brahman is the same in all.

Just as the one all-pervading sky is the same within and outside a pot . . . Consider a pot: it is the same sky inside the pot, the same sky outside. You may smash the pot, but the sky is not smashed. You can make a pot, but it doesn't distort the sky. No matter how the pot is shaped—crooked or round—the sky takes no form. We are all vessels of clay, earthen pots. It is the same reality outside it, the same reality inside it—don't place too much value on the thin wall of clay. This wall of clay makes you into a vessel—don't be too tightly identified with it. If you believe you are this wall of clay, you will go on being made into pots of clay, your belief will pull you back here again and again.

No one else brings you into the world. Your fixation that you are a pot brings you back. Once you know that you are the emptiness inside the pot. Lao Tzu's statement is meaningful. Lao Tzu says, 'What is the meaning of the sides of the pot? The real meaning is in the emptiness inside the pot. If you fill it with water, the water fills the space, not the sides.'

When you make a house, do you call the walls the house? That is not right. The empty space left inside is the house. You live in this, you don't live in the walls; the walls are only a boundary. In reality, we live in the sky. We all exist as digambaras, sky-clad. What difference do the walls make? We remain in the sky, inner or outer. Today the wall exists, tomorrow it will fall—the sky always exists.

If you mistakenly take the house as the walls, take the pot as layers of clay and take yourself as a body, this will be your bondage. Just a small mistake in reading the sutra of life and everything goes wrong; a very small mistake . . .

Once Mulla Nasruddin boarded a bus. Absorbed in thought he took a seat and lit a cigarette. 'It is clearly written that smoking is forbidden on the bus,' the conductor angrily said. 'Didn't you read it? Don't you know how to read?'

'I read it, but there is so much written in the bus. Which of them should I do?' Nasruddin said. 'Look at this: it says here, "Always Wear Handloom Saris!"'

One need only be a little careful to avoid such mistakes. The body is very close—to read the language of the body is very easy. And the body is so close that its shadow falls on the inner mirror and is reflected. You are in the body, but you are not the body. The body is yours, you are not the body's. The body is your means, you are the end. Use the body, don't lose your mastership. Though living in the body, remain beyond the body—like a lotus in the water.

Hari-om-tat-sat!

6

The Touchstone of Truth

THE FIRST QUESTION:

Osho,
Through studying texts like Vedanta and the
Ashtavakra Gita, I have learned that whatever is worth
attaining has already been attained. Making efforts for
it is going astray. I have deepened this trust, so why has
self-realization not happened? Please show me the path.

Never think that what you understand from scriptures is
your own understanding. Never think what you understand
from words has become your own experience.

Hearing Ashtavakra, many people will feel, 'Far out!
Everything is already attained.' But it is not attained this way.
What connection is there between your listening to Ashtavakra
and attaining? 'It has already happened': but this must be your
own experience. This recognition, the realization, must be
yours, it cannot be an intellectual conclusion.

Intellect will quickly accept it. What could be easier
than, 'It has already happened. Good, our troubles are over.
Now there is no need to search, no need to meditate, no
need to worship or pray—it has already happened.'

Intellect is ready to accept—but not because it has grasped the truth. It accepts because then the difficulties of the path can be dropped, efforts of sadhana dropped, and the need to continue meditating dropped. Soon you look around and find that you have not attained. If it could happen merely by the intellect grasping it, there could be spiritual universities. There is no university of spiritual study. It is not attained from scriptures, it is attained by your own spontaneous, inspired wisdom.

Listen to Ashtavakra, but don't be in a hurry to believe. Your greed makes you hurry. Your greed will tell you, 'This is very handy. We already have the treasure, so the whole bother of attaining it is over. Now there is nowhere to go, now there is nothing to do.'

You always wanted to attain without effort. But remember, the desire to attain is still there behind all this: to attain without doing! Previously you thought of striving to attain; now you think of attaining without effort—but the desire to attain is still there. This is why the question arises, 'Why has self-realization not happened yet?'

The one who has understood it—he will say, 'To hell with self-realization! What would I do with it?' If you had understood Ashtavakra, no other question could arise. The statement, 'Self-realization has not happened,' indicates that while accepting what Ashtavakra says, you are watching from the corner of your eye: Is it attained yet or not? Your eye is still focused on attaining.

People come to me and I tell them, 'Meditation cannot go deep as long as you continue desiring. As long as you expect to attain something—bliss, God, soul—meditation will not go deep, because thinking of attaining is greed. It is ambition, it is politics. It is not yet religion.' They say, 'Okay, we'll meditate without expecting anything, but we will attain, won't we?'

There is no difference. They are ready to stop desiring because, 'You say this is the way to attain, so we won't think of it—but still, we will attain it, won't we?'

You are not able to rid yourself of greed. Hearing Ashtavakra many people will very quickly accept that it has happened. If it could happen so quickly . . . and it is not that there is much of a barrier to it happening. The only barrier is the foolishness of your desiring. The happening is so near!

Ashtavakra is right—it has already happened. But only when all desire for attaining disappears then this 'It has happened already' will be understood. Then you will know from your totality that it is attained. But at the moment it is just an intellectual game: 'If a great master like Ashtavakra said it, it must be right.' You are hurrying to believe. Your belief is impotent. Without doubting you have quickly accepted it. In this country the habit of doubting anything written in scriptures has disappeared. If it is in the scriptures, it must be right.

One day Mulla Nasruddin came carrying a very handsome umbrella. I asked him, 'Where did you get it? Such fine umbrellas are not made here.'

He said, 'My sister sent a gift.'

I said, 'Nasruddin! You have always said that you don't have any sisters.'

He replied, 'It is true.'

Then I said, 'Yet this gift is sent by your sister?'

He said, 'If you don't believe me: here, it is written on the handle, "A gift for my beloved brother, from your sister." I was coming out of a restaurant and these letters on the umbrella—I thought, it seems I do have a sister. When it is written it has to be believed. And perhaps there is some sister or cousin. And religious people have always said

you should take every woman except your wife as your
mother or sister.'

When something is published—and in the scriptures . . .
Belief in the written word is very strong. When you tell
someone something, he asks where it was published. If you
say where, he will believe what you said. It is as if there is
some power in writing. Say how ancient it is—people will
accept it. It is as if truth is somehow related to age. Who
said it? Ashtavakra? Buddha? Mahavira? Then it must be
right.

From your side you haven't made any effort to wake
up—not a tiny bit. Someone said it, you believed it. And such
convenience—you have attained without doing anything!

Krishnamurti's followers have been listening for forty
years—exactly the same people more or less. They have
attained nothing. Sometimes one of them comes to me
saying, 'I know that everything is already attained, but why
hasn't it happened? I listen to Krishnamurti, so I understand
that everything is already attained.'

These people are greedy. They hoped that instead of
having to make any effort they should get it free. They have
not heard Krishnamurti nor understood Ashtavakra. They
have heard their greed. They have heard through their greed.
Then they interpret in their own way.

A friend has asked, 'Doing meditations seems irrelevant
now. Five meditations a day—and this lecture series on
Ashtavakra going on . . . It seems stupid.'

It is so easy to drop meditation—and so hard to do it.
What Ashtavakra attained was not attained through doing,
and yet he didn't attain by not doing anything.

Try to understand, this is a subtle point.

I have told you Buddha attained when he dropped all
doing. But first he did everything. Six years of untiring

effort, he gave everything to it. By giving everything, he experienced that nothing can be attained by doing. It wasn't by reading Ashtavakra . . . even though the Ashtavakra Gita was available in Buddha's time. He could have studied it—there was no need for these six years of effort. He persevered for six years, and in the midst of this effort he found out it is not attained by effort. He didn't leave a single stone unturned, proving to himself that it couldn't be attained by inner effort. There was no desire left inside. He did everything, and he saw that he didn't attain. His effort became so crystallized that, in this crystallization, doing dropped. Then it happened.

I say unto you, the state of non-doing will come when you have done everything. Don't hurry, otherwise what little meditation you are already doing will be lost, what little prayer you are doing will be lost. Ashtavakra remains far away, and the little progress you were making on the journey will stop too.

Before stopping, one needs to run totally. Though one does not attain by running, this knowing will be crystallized by it. One day effort will drop, but not from mere intellectual understanding. When every cell, every atom understands that it is useless—this is the moment it happens.

Ashtavakra is right in saying that practice is bondage.

But only one who practises will find out.

I am telling you this because I have practised and found it is a bondage. I am telling you this because I have practised sadhana and found that no sadhana leads one to the *sadhya*, to the goal. I meditated and found that no meditation brings one to samadhi.

When this becomes your deep experience, when this experience comes to a point of total intensity, when you have given everything—holding back nothing you have thrown yourself totally into the fire—the effort has become total, the inner fire is total, the sadhana is total; now existence cannot tell you that you have held anything back, all is given—that day, in that crystallization, in that state of ignited consciousness, suddenly everything is burnt to ash. All sadhana, all practices, all meditation, all renunciation—suddenly you wake up and find, 'Oh! What I was seeking was already there!'

But if it could happen just by reading Ashtavakra then it would be very convenient. Is it difficult to read Ashtavakra? The sutra is so clear and simple. Remember: to understand simple things is the most difficult thing in the world. And the difficulty comes from within you. You hope you won't have to do anything. It is very hard for people to accept the need to meditate.

This is the acid test—the Ashtavakra Gita. Those who hear Ashtavakra and continue meditating have understood. Those who hear Ashtavakra and stop meditating have not understood Ashtavakra, and they lose their meditation too.

Practise, and you will find out that practice is a dead end. This is the final phase of practising. Don't be in too much of a hurry.

'Through the study of texts like Vedanta and the Ashtavakra Gita, I have learned . . .' Has anyone ever known through study? Has anyone known through memorizing texts? Has anyone ever known through learning scriptures, learning words? This is not knowing, it is information; knowing *about*. You can say this information is known: 'What is worth attaining is already attained.' But when you realize it, everything is finished.

You were informed, you became excited, and it sprouted in greed! Your greed said, 'Look, I have been meaninglessly making efforts. Ashtavakra says, "without doing anything", so I will sit without doing anything.' So you sit, doing nothing. After a while you observe, 'The happening has not happened yet. Why this delay? And Ashtavakra said right now!' You sit looking at the clock, 'Five seconds have passed, five minutes have passed, an hour is almost over—and Ashtavakra said immediately! Right now! There is no need for even a second to pass!' You start thinking he was lying, your trust is broken.

This is not knowing, it is information. Always remember the difference between information and knowing. Information means it is borrowed. Someone else has known, and listening to him you have become informed. This is information. Knowing is an experience. No one else can know for you; it cannot be borrowed.

I have known—*your* knowing will not happen from this. My knowing will be mine, your knowing will be yours. Yes, if you collect my words it will be information. Through information one can become a scholar, but not a wise man. Knowledge about wisdom can be collected, but not the liberation of wisdom. A whole system of words can be created, but not the beauty of truth. The words will imprison you more, will enslave you more. So you will find scholars very constricted. Where is the open sky? Knowing that, 'What is worth attaining is already attained'—if you have known it then what is left to ask?

'Making efforts . . . is going astray. If you know this then what else is there to ask? I have deepened this trust.' Either there is trust or there is not; there is no way to deepen it. How can you deepen it? If there is trust there is trust; if there isn't, there isn't—how will you deepen it? What method is there for making trust deepen? Will you suppress your doubts? Will you sit on top of your doubts? What will you do? Will you falsify your doubts? When the mind raises questions will you ignore them?

Inside, the worm of doubt will be gnawing. It will say, 'Now listen, is anything attained without doing anything?

Has anything ever happened just by sitting? Things happen by doing; does anything happen by sitting idle? Can you get anything for free? What nonsense are you getting into? What illusion are you suffering from? Get up, move, run; otherwise life will run out—life is already running out! Don't waste time sitting here like an idiot.'

These doubts will certainly arise: what will you do with them? Will you try to suppress them? Will you falsify them? Will you say you don't want to hear about it? Will you throw them into the unconscious? Will you hide them inside, in your basement? Will you avoid looking them in the face?

What will you do to deepen your trust? You will do something like this—you will repress in some way. This trust will be false; disbelief will be smouldering beneath it. This trust is superficial. Above is a threadbare covering; underneath, the coals of mistrust, of doubt. Soon they will burn up your trust. This trust is of no use, you cannot deepen it. Trust is, or trust is not.

It is like someone drawing a circle. If he draws half a circle will you call it a circle? Can half a circle be called a circle? It is an arc, not a circle. It can be called a circle only if it is complete. An incomplete circle is not a circle. Incomplete trust is not trust, because incomplete trust means that distrust is also present. In the empty arc, what will happen? There will be doubt. Doubt and trust cannot move together. It would be like one foot going east, the other foot going west—you won't get anywhere. It would be like riding in two boats, one going to this shore and one going to that shore—where will you go?

The journeys of doubt and trust are quite separate. You are riding in two boats. What is the meaning of incomplete trust? Does half trust mean that half mistrust is also present? Trust exists in its completeness, or it doesn't exist.

And remember one important fact: whenever the higher is mixed with the lower, the lower does not lose anything, but the higher does. When you mix the higher with the lower there is no harm to the lower, but the higher is harmed.

A feast is prepared, fine foods are set out. Throw just a small handful of dirt on it. You could say it is a vast feast, what can a small handful of dirt do? But a small handful of dirt destroys the whole feast. Yet a whole feast cannot destroy even this small handful of dirt.

Throw a rock at a flower and nothing happens to the rock, but the flower will be destroyed. The rock is lower, lifeless. The flower is glorious, full of life. The flower is of the sky, the rock is of the earth. The flower is the poetry of life. When the flower and rock collide the flower is completely crushed, the rock completely unscratched.

One drop of poison is enough. Remember, doubt is lower. If the rock of doubt falls on the flower of trust, the flower will be crushed and die, the flower will be murdered. Do not think that trust will transform the rock. The rock will destroy the flower.

Either trust is or it is not—there are not two possibilities. When trust exists, it encompasses your whole life, it spreads into every cell. Trust is expansive. But such a trust does not come from the scriptures, it cannot come. Such a trust comes from life experience. It comes when you 'read' the scripture of life, not from reading Ashtavakra.

Understand Ashtavakra, but don't think this understanding is wisdom. Understand Ashtavakra, and preserve this inside yourself in some corner. You have received a touchstone. You didn't receive wisdom, but a touchstone. And when you do attain wisdom, you can easily test it with the touchstone of Ashtavakra.

The touchstone itself is not gold. When you go to a goldsmith you see he has a black testing-stone. This black stone is not gold. When he receives gold, the goldsmith rubs it on this black stone to find out if it is gold or not.

When you have an understanding of Ashtavakra's words preserve it as a touchstone, let it stay deep within you, and when your experience of life comes then you can test it. Then Ashtavakra's touchstone will be helpful. You will be able to know what has happened. You will have the language to understand it. You will have a method to understand it. Ashtavakra will be your witness.

This is the way I take the scriptures. The scriptures are witnesses. The path of truth is unknown. You need witnesses on that unknown path. When you first come face-to-face with truth, truth will be so vast that you will tremble, you will be unable to grasp it. You will shake to your very roots. There will be fear that you could go mad.

Imagine what will happen to a man who has been searching for a treasure for lifetimes and suddenly he finds that the treasure is buried where he is standing—won't he go mad? 'This seeking for many lives was a waste! The treasure is buried right under my feet!'

Just imagine. It will be a tremendous shock for this man: 'So many years I have wasted! This whole time has been a meaningless effort, a nightmare. What I have been seeking was waiting inside.' Won't a man go mad from such a shock? At that time Ashtavakra's sweet words will soothe you. At that time the Vedanta, the Upanishads, the Bible, the Koran and Buddha will stand as your witnesses. In that situation you will be unable to comprehend the new experiences that are happening to you. In aloneness it is very difficult.

I am speaking on the scriptures—not because by hearing the scriptures you will then become wise. I am speaking on them so that, as you move on the path of meditation, when the happening takes place—if not today, then tomorrow it will happen, it has to happen—it need not be that the gold is in front of you and that you cannot comprehend.

I am giving you a touchstone. Test your experiences on these touchstones.

Ashtavakra is the purest touchstone. You don't have to believe in Ashtavakra, you have to use Ashtavakra as a touchstone for your own experiences. Make Ashtavakra a witness.

Jesus said to his disciples, 'I will be your witness when you arrive.' But his disciples misunderstood. The disciples understood that when they died and came to God's heaven, then Jesus would bear witness that they were his disciples: 'Let them come in—these are mine, they are Christians. Be especially compassionate to them. Let more blessings shower on them.'

But what Jesus meant is something completely different. Jesus said, 'When you arrive I will be your witness'—this did not mean that Jesus would be standing there, but that what Jesus had said would be there as a touchstone. When your experience happens, immediately you can test it and unravel the knot. As it is, you have wandered around for so long in untruth your eyes have become used to it. The shock of truth should not break you apart, should not drive you insane.

Remember, many seekers of truth have gone mad. Many seekers of truth have gone mad just as they came near to the stage of becoming enlightened. They became deranged. This is because the happening is so vast, it is inconceivable, unbelievable. It is as if the whole sky has crashed on you.

Your water pot is small, and the infinite is pouring in it. You will be shattered—you won't be able to contain it. You are face-to-face with the sun—your eyes will be dazzled and then go dark. The sun is before you and all is darkness, your eyes will shut. At that moment you can use Ashtavakra's statements to understand the sun. At that time, the voice of Ashtavakra that has been lying in your unconscious will immediately speak. The sutras of the Upanishads will start resounding, the Gita will echo, the Koran will echo—its verses will come forth! Their fragrance will assure you that you have come home, there is nothing to freak out about; this vastness is you.

Ashtavakra says that you are expansiveness, you are vast. You are omnipresent. You are void of action, uncorrupted. You are the ultimate reality.

At that time these statements will have some meaning for you. Merely having faith in them, merely holding on to them, will lead you nowhere. And your greed is pushing you on from within, saying that self-realization has not happened.

A poet has said:

To control desire,
the snake charmer's pipe weaves a stream of music—
ah! in this itself
what a singularly deep passion quivers!

Listen to it again:

To control desire,
the snake charmer's pipe weaves a stream of music—
ah! in this itself
what a singularly deep passion quivers!
That's why the cobra's coil is motionless,
only the hood dances to and fro.

You want to become free of desire, but still you spread out a net of desire. You want to be completely clean and pure, but still you do it by means of greed, still desire goes on pulsating within you.

'See how a singularly deep desire quivers—the snake's coil is motionless, now only the hood dances to and fro.'

You have started out to attain the divine, but your way of attaining is the same as for attaining money. You go to seek the divine, but your desire, your passion is the same as the one who is after material things. Your madness is the same as the madness of one who wants to attain the world. The object of desire has changed, but the desire itself has not changed.

Listening to Ashtavakra your desire says: 'Wow, this is great! I never knew that what I am seeking is already attained. So now I will just sit.' Then you will wait: 'Has it happened yet? Has it happened yet ? Has it happened yet ?' Desire goes on quivering. 'Has it happened yet?' You haven't understood.

Listen to Ashtavakra again. Ashtavakra says it is already attained. But how can you hear it, how can you understand it? Your desire goes on quivering.

Until you have chased after your desires—until you have seen the worthlessness of chasing after them, run and fallen down and scraped yourself—you won't be able to understand. Only through the experience of desire does desire become worthless. Exhausted, it falls down broken— in this moment of desirelessness you will understand that what you have been seeking has already happened.

Otherwise you repeat like a parrot. It doesn't make the slightest difference if you are a Hindu parrot or a Mohammedan parrot or a Jaina, a Christian, a Buddhist—a parrot is a parrot. A parrot may recite the Bible, a parrot may recite the Koran. A parrot is a parrot, he will go on repeating.

Inside the temple all bathed and rubbed down,
in full voice, absorbed, open, in loud tones,

with clear and bold voices,
they go on singing the praises of the divine.
Inside, all are deaf, mute, meaningless prattlers,
without understanding; ignorant and small-minded.
But outside they are boastful, childish.

Look in the temples! 'Inside the temple, all bathed and rubbed down, in full voice, absorbed . . .' People seem so innocent in the temples. Look in the market at the same faces that you see in the temples. Their faces appeared different in the temples.

'In loud tones, with clear and bold voices, they go on singing the praises of the divine.' You must have seen people taking up a rosary and chanting. Wrapped in a shawl embossed with 'Rama, Rama', with sandalwood paste on the forehead—what a spotless, radiant image! When you meet the same man in the market, in the crowds, you won't be able to recognize him. People have different faces: they wear one face in the market, they wear another face in the temple.

'Absorbed, open, in loud tones, with clear and bold voices, they go on singing the praises of the divine. Inside, they are all deaf, mute, meaningless prattlers, without understanding; ignorant and small-minded. But outside they are boastful, childish.'

Information can make you a parrot, can give you a big mouth. It can give you the illusion of being religious, can give deceptions. But don't think it is wisdom. And on the basis of information the trust that you put forward will be sitting on doubt, riding on the shoulders of doubt. This trust cannot take you to the door of truth. Don't depend much on this trust—it is worthless.

Trust must come from your own experience. Trust must arise out of pure desirelessness and your meditation.

The second question:

> Osho,
>
> Yesterday, while out walking at dusk, I felt that suddenly your whole lecture of the morning began echoing in every cell of my body. I was looking as a spectator at the splendour of scenes going by, when the memory of the observer arose. This play of the observer went on for some time, then my legs began wobbling and to keep from falling I sat down at the side of the road. And then suddenly neither scene nor spectator remained, nor even the observer. Everything disappeared but still something was—sometimes darkness, sometimes light, playing hide-and-seek. But since then I have become more anxious as I could not understand all this.

This is just what I was saying. If a small glimpse of the truth comes to you, you will be upset, you won't be able to understand. Not understanding it, a deep uneasiness will take hold of you; madness too can overtake you.

This is why I speak on these scriptures. This is why I go on explaining every day, so that the information will remain in your unconscious, and when the happening takes place you can figure it out, you can clearly define what happened. Otherwise, how will you comprehend it? You won't have the language, the words; you will have no way to understand it; no measuring stick, no scales—how will you weigh it? You will have no touchstone. How can you appraise it?

You have said: 'Your whole lecture of the morning began echoing in every cell of my body. I was looking as a spectator at the splendour of scenes going by, when the memory of the observer arose. This play of the observer went on for some time, then my legs began wobbling and to keep from falling I sat down at the side of the road.'

Certainly this happens. When you first become aware of this observer, you wobble. Your whole life totters, because your whole life is set up without the observer. This new happening will shatter everything. It is like a blind man whose eyes suddenly open: do you think he will be able to walk down the road? He will stagger. Blind for forty, fifty years, he felt his way along with the help of his cane. In his blindness he gradually developed the ability to walk in the dark. He became skilful. He interpreted sounds around him. He got to know the turns in the roads. He had learned the art of seeing with his ears. For fifty years everything had been going well.

This life of the blind—which you cannot even imagine—bereft of light, colour, beauty, form, it depends only on the medium of sound. He has only one language: sound. He has created his whole life on this basis. If on the way to the market in the morning his eyes open suddenly, think of what will happen. His whole world will come crashing down. His world of sound will go completely topsy-turvy.

This event will be so strong—the eyes opening, seeing peoples' faces, seeing colours, the rays of the sun, sunlight and shadow, this crowd; so many people, buses, cars, bicycles—he will completely freak out! It will be such a great shock to his life. The small world he has created based on sound will disappear, be wiped out, die, it will be crushed. He will sit down on the spot trembling, he may stagger and fall. Perhaps he will not be able to make it home . . . maybe he will faint.

And this example is nothing. When the observer makes its entrance into your life, when just one ray of the observer comes, then this example is nothing—the event is so much bigger. The inner eye is opening. You have created your world without the inner eye, and when the inner eye suddenly opens it makes your whole world until now irrelevant. You will remain speechless in amazement.

You have asked rightly, and asked from experience. Consider the two types of questions. One is theoretical—it has no great value. But this question comes out of experience. If there were no experience this question could not have arisen. If these legs had not staggered, this question would not have arisen. This question is from direct experience.

'The memory of the observer arose.' Ashtavakra's words must have reverberated. An echo must have remained of what I had said in the morning. Its fragrance must have arisen in you, a few threads of what I said must have remained entangled in you.

'The memory of the observer arose. This play of the observer went on for some time . . .' Perhaps it was only a moment. A moment of the observer seems very long, because the observer is beyond time. Here only a second passes on your watch; there, as the observer, it seems centuries have passed. This watch is of no use there. This watch is not made for the inner eye.

'This play of the observer went on for some time, but then my legs began wobbling and I sat down at the side of the road to keep from falling.' This wobbling indicates that it happened. The questioner has not asked a question from his listening or reading—something transpired.

'And then neither scene nor spectator remained, nor even the observer.' In that wobbling everything dispersed, everything disappeared. In such moments insanity can arise if there has been no gradual preparation. If we are unable to assimilate it drop by drop, if it happens all of a sudden, there can be an explosion.

'Everything disappeared but still something was.' Certainly something was. Actually everything was for the first time. Everything of yours ended, your little house of straw fell down. The sky, the moon and stars—the ultimate remained. The boundaries, the lines you had drawn all disappeared—cloudless sky remained. Your conditioning of living in a confined shell was shaken. You were frightened by this wobbling and sat down by the roadside. Certainly something was. The experience makes one speechless. One cannot grasp: What was it, who was it?

Have you noticed: sometimes something will suddenly wake you up when you were deeply asleep. You were sound asleep at 5 a.m., at the hour of deepest sleep, and then something suddenly awakens you. Some noise, some firecracker goes off in the street, a car crashes into your door: some noise that immediately wakes you up. Instantly! You jump immediately from sleep to wakefulness. You come shooting like an arrow from the depths of sleep. Usually when we come out of deep sleep we come very slowly. First deep sleep drops away, then dreams gradually start floating, then we remain in dreams for a while.

You can remember your morning dreams, but you do not recall the night dreams, because the morning dreams are very light and exactly halfway between sleep and waking up. Then gradually dreams disappear. Then there is half-broken sleep. Then sun and shadow play a little hide-and-seek with your eyes: one moment you are awake, another moment asleep again; you roll over as if awake. In between you hear your wife making tea, a dish falls, the milkman comes, someone passes by on the street, the servant knocks, the kids are getting ready for school. Then you roll over again and start falling into the depths one more time. In this way you very gradually come to the surface. Then you open your eyes.

But if something happens suddenly, you come like an arrow from the depths straight to awakening. Your eyes open and you wonder: Where am I? Who am I? For a moment nothing is clear.

This must have happened to all of you at some time or other: you wonder, who am I? Even your name and address will be gone. Where am I? This too will be unclear. It is as if you have suddenly come to some alien world. It lasts only a moment, then you come back together, because this shock isn't such a great shock. And then too you are used to it—it happens every day. You get up every morning: you return from the world of dreams into the world of wakefulness. This routine is old, yet sometimes when it happens suddenly you are startled and frightened.

When the real awakening happens you will be completely speechless. You won't have any idea what is happening. Everything will become calm and silent.

But it was good. 'Neither scene nor spectator remained, not even the observer remained. Everything disappeared but still something was.' It is to help you to comprehend this 'something' that I speak on the scriptures—so you become capable of interpreting it. So you can give meaning to this 'something', you can identify it, you can define it. If not, it can drown you. You will be carried away in a flood, you won't have any place to stand. This is why I go on speaking about so many things.

'Everything disappeared but still something was. Sometimes dark, sometimes light playing hide-and-seek. But since then I have become more anxious and I cannot understand all this.'

Preserve it, keep what I say to you. Make a jewelled box for it. Don't take it as wisdom but only as information. Consciously make a box for it. Then gradually you will find, as experiences begin to happen, that my words arise from your unconscious, and make clear and comprehensible the experiences that happened. I will be your witness.

But if you argue with me as you listen I cannot become your witness—you listen and you are creating some kind of internal struggle against me, refuting me.

If you are not listening sympathetically, lovingly, but go on arguing, then I cannot be your witness, because then when you put something in your box it won't be mine, it will be yours.

Last night a psychologist from Australia took sannyas. I told him, 'You are welcome here even if you don't take sannyas. But then you will not become my guest. You are welcomed. But if you take sannyas you are welcome here and you will also become my guest.'

People ask me, 'Will your love for us be less if we don't take sannyas?' My love for you will remain total. You are welcome! But the moment you take sannyas you become my guest also. And there is a great difference. Without taking sannyas you listen from a distance. Taking sannyas you come close.

Without your taking sannyas your intellect goes on analysing, goes on choosing from whatever I say. Whatever fits with your mind you keep, whatever does not fit you throw out. And the possibility is that what doesn't fit with you is what will be useful for you. Whatever agrees with your mind cannot transform you. If it agrees with you it means that it is in harmony with your past. What doesn't fit with your past can spark a revolution within. What doesn't fit with you can transform. Whatever totally fits you will strengthen you as you are, not transform you. You go on selecting—you think you are intelligent.

Intelligent people sometimes do very idiotic things. They sit here selecting. They go on choosing. They hold on to things that fit with their prejudices, and make no connection with anything that is against their prejudices. But I repeat to you that what doesn't seem to fit you will some day be useful. Now you don't have any way to understand it, because you don't have any experience of it. But still I say unto you, keep it with you. When the experience comes some day, then suddenly it will arise from your unconscious and clarify everything. Then you will not remain speechless, the amazement will not break you apart, and you need not be frightened and uneasy.

A poet said:

High above what the wind sang, the cedars echoed,
what shone on the snow peaks,
what spilled over from the evening sky,
who received all this?
The one who extended his hands in prayer?
No, it just descended into my offered heart.
It poured into my welcomed tears.
It came unknown, unrecognized.
By means of all these, and me,
it brought itself to itself,
it entered itself.
Alone where it is resplendent,
eyes are helplessly lowered.
Not only the voice,
even the resonance of silence ceases there.

Hear me—with your deep tears. Hear me—with the heart. Hear me—with your love. Not with your intellect, not with your logic. This is the meaning of trust and faith.

'High above what the wind sang, the cedars echoed, what shone on the snow peaks, what spilled over from the evening sky, who received all this? The one who extended his hands in prayer?' No! Whenever the hand of desire is extended, it shrinks. The hand of desire can only contain alms, not an empire. A heart opened by love is needed to contain an empire. A begging, desiring bowl will not do.

'Who received all this? The one who extended his hands in prayer?' You can listen to me in such a way that you take what fits your prejudices and put it in your bag. Then you come to me extending your begging bowl. Desire is a beggar. You can take a little, but what you take are just scraps of bread fallen from the table. You could not become a guest. Sannyas will make you a guest.

'No, it just descended into my offered heart. It poured into my welcomed tears. It came unknown, unrecognized. By means of all these, and me, it brought itself to itself, it entered itself. Alone where it is resplendent, eyes are helplessly lowered.'

Where eyes bow down . . . 'Not only the voice, even the resonance of silence ceases there.' Get ready for this. Fill the heart with love for this. Learn to listen with sympathy. And keep in a treasure box what I am saying to you. Then you will not suffer. Then when the unacquainted, the unknown, descends, you can understand it. You will be able to understand its hidden music. You will not drown or be frightened by its silence, you will be liberated. Otherwise it seems like death.

If God comes without your understanding, if you have no means to understand him, it will feel like death, that you are finished! If you have a little understanding, some preparation, you have learned something from a master, have sat in his presence, then God is liberation; otherwise he seems to be death. And once you have freaked out, then you will stop going in that direction. Once you have been so frightened, then every cell of your body will tremble. You will go everywhere except there where there is such fear: where your arms and legs tremble, where you have to sit by the side of the road, where everything goes dark and all seems to be lost; something unknown remains and you are just freaked out—you won't go back there.

In one of Rabindranath Tagore's poems he says, 'I searched for God for many lives. Searched but never found. Sometimes I got a glimpse of him among the most distant stars. I kept hoping, kept looking. Then one day by a lucky accident I reached his door. There was a sign: "This is God's house." I climbed the steps—in one leap the journey of many lives was complete. Benediction! My hand was on the doorbell chain when a fear overcame me: "What if I meet him? Then? What will I do? My whole work has been to seek God. I live in this hope—it is my life's journey. So if I meet God it will be death. What will happen to my life, my journey? Then where will I go, what will I attain, what will I seek? Then nothing will remain." So in fright I let go of the chain, slowly let go of it so there would be no noise, so that he would not open the door. I took my shoes in my hand and fled, and since then I have been fleeing.'

'Still I go on seeking'—his poem continues—'even now I am seeking God, though I know where his house is. I seek him everywhere except there, because seeking is my life. I keep myself from going near it. I go anywhere except towards that house. I turn away from it. I ask everywhere else, "Where is God?"—and all along I know where God is.'

As I see it, many people have come close to that house many times in their endless seeking, but freaked out. Freaked out and forgot everything—only that fear they cannot forget. This is why people are not readily attracted to meditation. People are scared, and avoid even talking about things like meditation. They make formal use of the word 'God', but they never let themselves go in a deep search for him. They go to the temple, the mosque—it is a social formality, a convention, a custom. They go because they are supposed to, but they never let the temple and the mosque be established in their hearts. They won't take on such danger. They keep God far away. And there is a reason for it—somewhere hidden deep in their memory is an experience of fear, at some time they must have faltered in front of that door.

If the friend who has had this experience does not understand it correctly he will start being frightened. Sitting down freaked out in the street, all limbs trembling, heart pounding wildly, breath coming in gulps, everything every which way—it is better to stay away from such meditation! It is trouble. It is okay if you come back, but if you don't come back?

If you go on sitting by the roadside people will think you are crazy. It is okay for an hour or two; more, and the police will come. More, and the neighbours will take you away, or send you to the hospital to find out what happened. The medics will start giving injections, concerned you have lost consciousness, that there may be a brain injury.

A friend has written—a sannyasin—that he left here dancing, ecstatic. His family had never seen him dancing and ecstatic. When he arrived home dancing and blissed out, they thought he was insane. They came running, caught him, sat him down, and asked what happened. 'Wait,' he said, 'nothing has happened to me. I am very happy, in bliss.'

The more he spoke of spiritual truths the more his family were sure something was wrong. They took him from the house and forced him to enter a hospital.

A letter has come from him. He says, 'I am lying here in the hospital laughing. This is great fun. When I was sad no one thought of getting me any medical help. Now I am happy and people have brought me to the hospital. I am watching this drama. But they think I am insane. And the more they think I am mad the more I laugh! The more I laugh the more they think I am mad!'

It is good that you have asked. Don't be frightened. This experience will gradually quiet down. Witness it. This happening is natural.

The third question:

Osho,
We are part of God, and indestructible too. Please explain when, why and how this part became separated from the source. And is a reunion of the part to the source—an inseparable union—possible or not? If it is possible, then please unite this part to the source so that it doesn't have to be frightened coming in this tumultuous chaos again and again.

Do you see the difference? The last question came from experience. This question is academic.

'We are part of God and indestructible too.' Do you know this? You have heard it, you have read it—and, as it gives your ego satisfaction, you believed it. What could give the ego more satisfaction than saying we are part of God . . . we are God, we are the divine, we are indestructible? This is what you want. This is the search of the ego. This is your deepest desire—that you should become indestructible, a part of God, one who is Brahma, the lord of the whole universe.

'We are part of God and indestructible too.' Do you know this? If you know this, there is no need to ask. If you don't know, then writing it is meaningless: asking the question is enough.

'Please explain when, why and how this part became separated from the source.' This is a scholarly question. When? You want a date and time? What will you do with it? If I tell you the date, what difference can it make? If I give the year and time, that exactly at 6 a.m. on such-and-such a day, what change will that make? What transformation will it bring to your life? What will you attain?

'When, why and how this part became separated . . .'
If you know you are a part of God, then you know you
have never been separated. You have had a dream of
separation. You have never been separated—how can a part
be separated? The part exists only with the whole. You have
forgotten. You cannot be separated, but you can forget.
There is no way to be separate. We remain what we are; we
may forget it, we may remember it—the whole difference is
only of forgetting and remembering.

'When, why and how this part became separated from
the source.' If you were separate I could tell you when, why
and how. You are not separate. Asleep at night, you dream
you are a horse. In the morning you ask, 'Why, how, when
did I become a horse? It is very difficult—why did I become
a horse?' The first thing is that you never became a horse.
If you had, would there be anyone left to ask? Horses don't
ask questions. You were never a horse, you only dreamed
it. In the morning you wake up saying, 'What a dream I
had!' Remember, you were not a horse even when you were
seeing the dream. Though you may have been completely
absorbed in feeling you are a horse. This is Ashtavakra's
basic teaching.

Ashtavakra says that you become that with which you
identify your 'I'. Identifying with the body, you become
a body. You say you are a body and you are a body.
Identifying with the Brahman—say you are Brahman and
you are Brahman. You become that with which you identify
your 'I'. In a dream you identified with a horse, you became
a horse. Now you identify with a human body, you become
a man. But you never really do, you are always what you
are—just the same. There is never any change in your nature.

This kind of question has no meaning. Don't waste time
in asking such questions. And those who answer questions
like these are even more idiotic than you.

There is an anecdote about the Zen monk Bokuju . . .

One morning he woke up and immediately called his chief disciple, telling him, 'Listen, I have had a dream. Can you analyse it for me?'

The disciple said, 'Wait! I will bring a little water. First wash your face.'

He brought a pot full of water and helped the master wash his face and hands. While he was doing that, another disciple was passing by. The master said, 'Listen, I had this dream. Will you analyse it for me?'

He said, 'Just wait—I had better bring a cup of tea for you.' He brought a cup of tea.

The master had a good belly laugh. He said, 'If you had analysed my dream I would have beaten you and thrown you out!'

What analysis can a dream have? Now you have seen it, you are awake, now drop the whole circus!

The disciples gave the correct answer. It was a test, their examination—the moment of testing had come. One disciple brought water to wash the master's hands and face. 'The dream is gone, now be finished with it! What more analysis is needed? The dream was a dream, it is finished. What analysis? The truth can be analysed, but a dream? Can the false be analysed? Can what never happened be analysed? It is enough to know it was a dream; now wash your face. Now you've come back, just come out of it.' The other youth also did well, bringing a cup of tea: 'You've washed your face, but it seems there is still a little sleep left. Enjoy a cup of tea and you will be completely awake.'

This is what I am telling you: Wash your face, drink your tea! You were never separate—there is no way to be separate.

Then you ask, 'And is a reunion of the part to the source—an inseparable union—possible or not?' When you are not separate, to talk about union is nonsense. This is why Ashtavakra says practise for liberation prevents liberation. What is he saying? He is saying, 'You want a method to unite you with what you have never been separate from? Does madness have no limit? This very method will prevent union.'

Think a little. If you never left your house, then efforts to return home will prevent you from waking up.

A drunk returned home one night. He had drunk too much. He managed to knock on the door but didn't know that it was his own house. His mother opened the door. He said, 'Dear old woman, can you tell me where my house is?'

The old woman replied, 'You are my son, I am your mother, idiot! This is your home.'

He said, 'Don't try to fool me. Don't confuse me. I am sure my house is somewhere around here, but where?'

The neighbours gathered around and they tried to persuade him. But it is no use arguing with drunks. One who argues with drunkards is also drunk. They told him, 'This is your house!' They began proving it, showing him proof: 'Look at this', 'Look at that'. They didn't understand that this man was drunk—no proof could help. Who knows what he is seeing; it is something you cannot imagine. He is not seeing what you see; he is in some other world. He doesn't even recognize his own mother; how can he recognize his home? He does not recognize himself; how can he recognize anyone else?

Another drunk came along. He arrived with his bullock cart all hitched up. He said, 'Climb on, I will take you home.'

The drunk said, 'This man seems to be right. I've found my master! These others are all idiots: I ask them where my house is and they just go on repeating that this is my house. What am I, blind? This man is a perfect master.'

Remember, if you ask wrong questions you will fall into the snares of wrong masters. Once you ask a wrong question you will meet someone or other who will give you a wrong answer. This is the law of life. Ask, and someone is waiting to answer. The fact is that even if you don't ask, someone is ready to answer. They are looking for you. When you ask a question like this you only put yourself in trouble.

'And a reunion . . .' You were never separated, you never left—how can you be reunited? And you ask: 'Is it possible there is a union that cannot be separated?' What if union happens but somehow it separates again? These things all look real because we don't remember who we are. If God is separate, then all these things are true.

God is our nature, but we can forget our nature. This too is intrinsic to our nature, that we can forget our nature.

A friend has asked, 'If the soul is pure consciousness, freedom and infinite energy, supreme independence, then how was desire born?' This too is the independence of our being—that if it wants to desire it can desire. If our being could not desire it would be dependent. Think about it. This world is your freedom. You wanted it, so it happened. Your desire is free. If you wish, it ceases right now. If you wish, it is back immediately.

So I cannot say to you there is a union that cannot be broken. You have never been separated, but your being's ultimate freedom is that when it wants it can forget something and when it wants it can remember. If this possibility did not exist, the being would be confined, its freedom would be limited, something would be imposed on it, it would have characteristics.

There was a philosopher in the West, Diderot. He proved that God is not omnipotent, not all powerful. He gives arguments that seem to be right. For example, he says, 'Can God make two plus two equal five?' It seems difficult for even God to make two plus two equal five. So how could he be omnipotent? Two plus two equals four. 'Can God make a triangle a rectangle?' How can he do it? If he makes it a rectangle, it will no longer be a triangle. If it remains a triangle, then he couldn't make a rectangle out of it, so God is limited.

Diderot gave a shock to the Christian idea of God. But if Diderot knew of the Indian ideas he would have been in difficulty. They say that this is the whole trouble, that God has the freedom to make two plus two equal five, two plus two equal three. This is what we call maya, illusion—it can make two plus two equal five, two plus two equal three. When two plus two equals four, we are out of maya.

Here triangles look like rectangles. Here great deceptions go on. Here someone understands something, someone else understands something else. Only what actually is, that is unknown to anyone. This much is certain, that two plus two will be anything, but not four. This is what we call maya.

We have called maya the power of God. Have you ever thought what this means? We call maya the power of God. It means God has the power even to deceive himself. If not, he would be limited. What sort of God would he be if he couldn't dream? Then he would be limited, because he is incapable of dreaming.

No, the divine can see dreams. You are dreaming! You are the divine seeing dreams. You can wake up, you can dream—this ability is yours. Hence when you want you can dream, and when you want you can wake up. This is your choice: if you want to stay awake, you can remain awake. If you want to stay in dreams, you can continue dreaming.

Man's freedom is unrestrained.

The power of your being is unrestrained.

Truth and dream—they are the ultimate's two streams. Everything is contained in these two streams.

You ask is a reunion possible? First, don't say reunion. If you say 'remember', it will be the right word.

And you ask, 'an inseparable union.' I cannot guarantee it. Because it depends on you, it is your choice. If you want to renounce, to forget, then no one can stop you. If you want to remember, no one can stop you. And don't be troubled by this. Take it as a blessing that your freedom is so great that even when you want to forget God there is no objection. God does not harass you at all. If you want to oppose him, there is no objection. He still remains with you. When you want to go against, he still goes on giving you energy.

The Sufi fakir, Hassan, has written that, 'One night I asked God, "Who is the most religious person in the village?" God told me it is my next-door neighbour.'

Hassan had never even thought about him. He was a simple, straightforward man. No one thinks about simple folk. Thinking is about troublemakers. He was a simple fellow, living quietly. An ordinary man, in his own joy—nothing to do with anyone else. No one had given him any notice. Hassan said, '*This* man is the most virtuous?'

The next morning he inspected him carefully and found, 'What radiance the man has!' The next night he asked God, 'Now another question. It is good what you said. I will worship this man. I will bow down to him. He has become my guru. Now tell me one more thing, who is the worst man in this village? So I can avoid him.'

God said, 'The same neighbour.'

Hassan said, 'This is really confusing!'

God replied, 'What can I do? Last night he was in a beautiful mood, now he is in a bad mood. I cannot do anything. I cannot say what state he will be in by the morning. He could be in a good mood again.'

Your being is ultimate freedom. Nothing limits it. This ultimate freedom we call moksha, liberation. Moksha includes the freedom to forget. If you want to forget no one can stop you. What liberation would it be if you weren't free to come out of it when you want?

I have heard:

A Catholic priest died. When he reached heaven he was surprised to see many people bound in chains and irons. He said, 'What's going on? Chains and irons in heaven?'

He was told, 'They want to return—they are Americans, and they want to go back to America. They say it is more fun there. They had to be put in irons because it would be a scandal for heaven. They say, "We don't want to stay in heaven, we'd rather return to America. It is juicier there. We have better women than these heavenly damsels. Liquor? We have better liquor. Buildings? They are taller than this. What's with all these ancient buildings?"'

The buildings in heaven are old-fashioned now. They are completely out of date. The architects and engineers designed them many, many thousands of years ago and they're still standing.

'They say they want to return to America. We had to chain them, because if they run away and make it back to America it will be a great disgrace for heaven. How will anyone want to come here?'

But what heaven is this, where you can be put in irons? Hell would be better, at least there aren't chains. Remember this:

heaven is independence. Moksha is freedom. Liberation is where you are independent. And this is the ultimate experience. It is ultimate and unconditional. There can be no conditions on it.

If some liberated soul has the feeling to return to the world, no one can stop him. Liberated ones won't return, this is another matter. But if a liberated being wanted to return no one could stop him. And who would stop him? And if someone can stop a liberated being, then what liberation is this?

You start leaving heaven and someone says, 'Stop! You can't leave. This is heaven, where are you going?'—heaven is finished that very moment.

I am not saying that liberated beings return. I am saying that no one can stop them. Hence I cannot give you a guarantee. If you want to return, what can I do? If you want to avoid God, what can I do? I can only make a declaration of your total freedom.

'If it is possible, then please join this part to the source.' Your hope is very cheap. You are saying that you don't really want to be joined, someone else should take the trouble to do it. How can this be? Union can happen only if *you* want it. Only if it is your desire, your will, your yearning, your thirst . . . No one else can unite you. There is no way freedom can be forced—neither outer nor inner. You go by your own choice.

And if I manage somehow to join you to the source, you will still escape. Because a happening brought from outside cannot be connected with your being. It will be forced. It is not possible. Otherwise one enlightened person could enlighten the whole world. One enlightened one would be enough. He would liberate everyone, unite everyone with the divine. Are enlightened ones lacking in compassion? No, they are not lacking in compassion. But nothing can be done against your wish. And if you wish it can happen right now, this very moment. Be happy! Right now!

And this desire you have, that someone else should unite you with the divine, this is your means of returning to the world. Any desire for the other is a way of returning to the world. Someone else should make you happy, should love you, should respect you: now these old habits are saying someone should liberate you, should unite you with the divine—but someone else. How long are you going to remain weak, powerless, impotent? When will you awaken to your own power? When will you declare your virility? When will you stand on your own two feet? Sometimes you lean on your wife's shoulders, sometimes on the government's shoulders, sometimes on politicians' shoulders.

I have heard:

Near Delhi, some labourers were sent to do some work on the street. They arrived there only to find they had forgotten their picks, they hadn't brought their picks and shovels. They phoned the engineer to say they had come without their tools, and to send them right away.

He said, 'I'll send them, until then you'll have to manage by leaning on each other's shoulders.'

This is what labourers do. To rest they lean on their picks and shovels. The engineer said, 'I'll send them as fast as I can, but in the meantime you'll just have to lean on each other's shoulders.'

We are always leaning; we just go on changing shoulders. Then we drop all this and lean on the master's shoulders. Now some master should take us across, take us beyond.

When will you make your own declaration, your own, individual proclamation? With your declaration comes the potential for your own being to flower, to blossom. How long are you going to be dependent? How long are you going to insist on being a beggar? Are you going to attain God as alms too? Wake up from this sleep.

'So that it doesn't have to be frightened coming in this tumultuous chaos again and again.' You wanted to enter this chaos, so you entered. And the strange thing is, if you are put in solitude you will be frightened there too. Who is stopping you? Run away to the Himalayas, sit in isolation. There you will fear aloneness and come running back to this chaos. We remain in this chaos because we are afraid to remain alone, we cannot live alone. And we feel bad in the crowd. It's very difficult: we cannot live alone, we cannot live in the crowd.

Have you noticed what happens when you are left alone? What happens to you when you are alone in the forest on a dark night? What happens? Does bliss come? The chaos seems better. 'If I could only meet someone, talk to someone.' Alone you get very afraid of dying. Alone you feel death.

When you dissolve into the divine you will be completely alone. There are not two Gods here—there is only one. Dissolve and you are alone. Dissolving into God you don't remain you, God does not remain God—only one remains. This is why the preparation of meditation is needed, so you start enjoying the taste of being alone. Before entering into ultimate aloneness, let the joy of aloneness begin, let its melody play, its song resound. Start enjoying aloneness, then you can drop into ultimate aloneness. It is training for you to endure the experience of godliness.

If you ask me, I will say that meditation is not a method to attain God, God can be attained without meditation too. Meditation is a training to endure God. Meditation gives you the capacity to withstand. When you enter ultimate aloneness you will be completely alone. No radio, no television, no newspaper, no friend, no club, no society—nothing at all. You will be completely alone. Prepare for that aloneness.

I am ready to take you out of this chaos, but are you ready? When you sit alone your head starts creating this same chaos. The friends that renounce their homes start talking to themselves. In their head they start talking to the wife they left behind. The whole crowd is collected again. Webs of imagination are woven. You cannot remain alone. Hence you return again and again.

You do not return to the world without cause. You return of your own accord. You want this chaos, hence you return.

> The life of man is nothing at all.
> The matter is that nothing matters at all.

'The life of man is nothing at all.' Man's life is not life. Life belongs to the whole. 'The matter is that nothing matters at all.' Man is just meaningless. Yesterday, Mulla Nasruddin's falling off the bed—just meaningless. He was making space for a child that doesn't exist when he fell and broke his leg.

There was a case in court. Two men had been fighting. The judge asked what happened. Both of them hesitated. They said, 'What can we say? If we say what happened we will be very embarrassed. Just give us whatever punishment is needed.'

He said, 'I still want to know what the matter is: who should I punish?'

They looked at each other saying, 'You tell him.'

When the judge started getting angry—'Are you going to tell me or not?'—they were forced to.

One said, 'The matter is like this: we are friends. We were sitting in the sand on the riverbank. This friend said he was going to buy a buffalo. Then I said, "Don't buy a buffalo because I am buying a farm and if your buffalo comes into my farm then our lifelong friendship will be spoiled."

'Then he said, "Get lost! Because you are buying a farm, I shouldn't buy a buffalo? Then don't buy a farm! And a buffalo is a buffalo, if it gets in, it gets in. I'm not going to spend my whole day chasing after her. And what is the value of this friendship that just because my buffalo enters your farm you make such a fuss over it?"

'I too mounted my throne and said, "Good, so I bought my farm, just show me the buffalo you bought."

'Then I drew a field in the sand with a stick and this idiot made his stick buffalo enter. We quarrelled, we came to blows. What can we say to you? Just give us our punishment. We are embarrassed to say anything more.'

> The life of man is nothing at all.
> The matter is that nothing matters at all.
> You have given man everything,
> still man's person is nothing at all.
> The event of love is nothing at all,
> except this desire of the heart and liver.
> The world of beauty is everything,
> the world of love is nothing at all.
> Man only changes clothing:
> this life and death is nothing at all.

Man just goes on changing his clothes. Neither life as we know it is anything, nor is death anything important.

'Man only changes clothing: this life and death is nothing at all . . . The life of man is nothing at all. The matter is that nothing matters at all.' If you understand this, that you are a matter which doesn't matter, then you have understood everything.

The last question:

> Osho,
>   For ages I have wanted to ask: please will you tell
> me, what should I ask? Accept my pranam, my bowing
> salutation.

Dulari has asked this question. It is absolutely true: I have
known her for years, and she has never asked anything.
Very few people have never asked. This is the first time, and
still she doesn't ask anything: 'For ages I have wanted to
ask: please will you tell me, what should I ask?'

The real question of life is such that it cannot be asked.
A question you can ask is not worth asking. What you
cannot ask, that is worth asking. The real question of life
cannot be put into words. Life questions can only be said
with eyes thirsting for rain, eyes filled with longing to know.

I know Dulari. She has never asked, but I have heard
her question. And her question is not hers, because what
you are able to ask is yours. What you are unable to ask is
everyone's.

The same question is inside every one of us. And this
question is: all this is happening, all is going on, but still
nothing seems real. All this running around, this hubbub,
but nothing makes any sense. So much is attained and lost;
still nothing is attained, nothing is lost. This vast journey,
birth after birth, where no destination is visible. We are—
why? What is this being of ours? Where are we going, and
what is going on? What is our purpose? What is the meaning
of this music?

This existential question is inside everyone: What is the
purpose of existence? And in words there is no answer. A
question that cannot be asked in words, cannot have an
answer in words. That which is inside us—call it the witness,

observer, river of life, consciousness, call it whatever name you like. It is nameless, so give it any name you want— God, liberation, nirvana, being, non-being, whatever you like; fullness, emptiness, whatever; it is nameless within— submerge yourself in this. Just dropping into it, questions start gradually disappearing.

I am not saying you will find answers, the questions just dissolve. And when the questions dissolve your very consciousness becomes the answer. I am not saying you get an answer. When you become questionless, the joy of life, the great benediction and blessing comes raining down. You dance, you hum a melody, you sing. Samadhi has flowered. Then you don't ask anything. There is nothing to ask. Then life is not a question, life is a mystery. Not a problem to be solved but a mystery to be lived, to be danced, to be sung. A mystery to be celebrated.

Go in. Beyond the body, beyond the mind, beyond emotions—go in deeper and deeper!

> Lifelong I could not find out,
> What is affection? Where is love?
> Where do the flowers release their perfume?

A fragrance seems to be arising—where does it come from? Life is. Its shadow falls here, but where is its root? Reflections are shimmering, but where is the original? Echoes reverberate in the mountains, but where is the original sound?

> Lifelong I could not find out,
> What is affection? Where is love?
> Where do the flowers release their perfume?
> I met a bride of sighs
> I am given laughter of thorns.

Lifelong I could not find out:
What is fragrance? Where is the pollen?
And where do the clouds shower?

But the clouds are showering in your deepest interiority. Flowers are giving off their perfume in your innermost centre. The fragrance is in the musk deer's navel. This fragrance that surrounds you and has become a question—where does it arise? This fragrance is yours, it is no one else's. If you look for it outside it will become a mirage, it will spread the net of maya, taking you on an endless journey. The day you look within, the door of the temple opens. That day you will reach to your fragrant centre. Love is there, divinity is there.

The mind gets caught up outside. Mind says, 'I'll go inside, but a little later on.'

Sustained by some desire, I stand for a long time, silent,
alone on the bank of the river.
A pleasant dusk hour—a gathering of the joys.
This dusky twilight overwhelms my thinking.
I think my thinking too has reached its evening.
There is a great restlessness,
but in life, even in hopelessness hope is nourished.
O heart! Play your stubborn games a little longer.
Embrace the charmed twilight with a smile,
there is still time before night descends.

The mind goes on suggesting: just a little more, a little longer . . . just forget yourself in dreams . . . go on running after mirages. Such beautiful dreams! There is still plenty of time before death comes.

People think: we will take sannyas, we will pray, we will meditate—in old age, when death has come and stands at the door. When one foot is already in the grave we will lift the other foot for meditation.

'O heart! Play your stubborn games a little longer. Embrace the charmed twilight with a smile, there is still time before night falls.' We go on postponing. Night is drawing near. There isn't plenty of time, night has already fallen. Many times we have wasted this birth, this life. We are waiting for death—and death comes before meditation has come. One more life spoiled. One more chance wasted. Don't let it happen this time. This time don't postpone. This fragrance is your own. This life is hidden within you. The veil has to be opened within you.

Don't ask questions. No answer is going to come from there. Enter within, where the question arises from. Don't bother if the question is unclear. Enter this unclear half-light of questioning. Gradually enter inside this faint, dusky light. Seek that place where questions arise. Don't bother much about what the questions are—just watch where they are coming from. Find that place, that deep place within yourself where the seeds of questioning sprout, where questions take leaf. There is the root, there you will find the answer. 'Answer' does not mean you will find some fixed answer, some conclusion. Answer means you will experience blessedness, gratefulness, life. Where life is not a problem, where it becomes a celebration.

> The sleek, deep silence
> in which vociferous and burning desires
> ignite and dissolve.
> In it your soundless song pulsates,
> the truth is revealed.

'The sleek, deep silence in which vociferous and burning desires ignite and dissolve.' No, there is a silence within, a peace in which all the fire of desiring is gradually lost and becomes calm.

'In it your soundless song pulsates . . .' then no melody is heard, only the rhythm echoes—rhythm without words, without tone. Pure rhythm reverberates.

'In it your soundless song pulsates, the truth is revealed.' Here the truth of life manifests, becomes known.

> A black liquid night
> in which forms, statues, icons all melt down.
> All receive shelter into a sacred, deep sleep
> beyond dreams, beyond forms.
> From within it you extend your hand,
> suddenly draw me near and embrace me.

God is hidden within you. Go in a little. Leave your idols, your thoughts, icons, beliefs . . . soap bubbles of the mind! Enter the depths where there are no waves, no words; where silence is. Where ultimate silence takes voice. Where only silence resounds.

'In it your soundless song pulsates, the truth is revealed.' Enter there. 'From within it you extend your hand, suddenly draw me near and embrace me.' This is the meeting, the union.

What you seek is hidden within you. The question you are searching for, its answer is hidden within you. Wake up! Celebrate it right now! All of Ashtavakra's sutras give this one message: it is not to be attained, it is already attained. Wake up and celebrate.

Hari-om-tat-sat!

7

I Have Been Fooled!

Janak said: Amazing! I am pure, flawless, I am peace, I am awareness, I am beyond nature. Alas, I have been fooled by illusion all this time!

Just as I alone illumine this body, do I illumine the universe too. Either this whole universe is mine or nothing at all.

Amazing, having renounced the body and the world, now through the skill of your teaching I see only the divine.

Just as waves, foam and bubbles are not other than water, so this individual soul is not other than the universal soul.

Just as cloth when analysed is nothing but thread, this universe when analysed is nothing but the soul.

Just as sugar produced from sugar cane is wholly pervaded by it, the universe produced from me is permeated by me through and through.

From the ignorance of the soul this world then appears, from knowing the soul it does not appear. From the ignorance of the rope a snake appears, from knowing the rope it does not appear.

LIKE A SUDDEN flash of light in darkness, or like a blind man suddenly seeing—this is what happened to Janak. He saw what he had never seen before. He heard what he had never heard before. His heart was filled with a new rhythm, a new zest. His spirit had a new vision. Certainly, Janak was ready and available.

When it rains on the mountains, the mountains remain empty, as they are already full. When it rains on lakes, the empty lakes fill up.

One who is empty is available; the filled are unavailable.

Ego makes one stone-like. Egolessness gives one spaciousness, emptiness.

Janak must have been an empty vessel. Wonder, awe, immediately arose. He heard it and was awakened. The call was hardly given when he heard. The shadow of the whip was enough; there was no need to crack it, and no question at all of whipping.

Ashtavakra is very fortunate in having such a worthy listener as Janak. There is no master in all of human history who has been as fortunate as Ashtavakra. It is very rare to find a disciple like Janak, who awakens with just the slightest hint as if he was just waiting, as if a small puff of wind was enough to break his sleep. The sleep was not deep; not loaded with many dreams, just about to break. Predawn had arrived, dawn was fast approaching.

There is a story in the Buddhist Jataka tales that when Buddha was enlightened, he remained silent for seven days. Buddha thought: 'Those who can understand me will understand me even without my speaking, and those who cannot understand me will not understand, no matter how much I explain. So what's the use, why should I speak? Why uselessly exert myself? Anything can awaken those who are ready to awaken. For them, there is no need to call and shout. A bird will sing his song, a breeze will pass through the trees—it will be enough.'

And it has happened. Lao Tzu was sitting under a tree: a dry leaf fell from it and he attained enlightenment watching the dry leaf fall. The dry leaf became his master. He just watched everything—in that dry leaf he saw his birth, he saw his death. In the death of that dry leaf, everything died. One day he too would fall like a dry leaf. Everything was finished.

It was the same for Buddha. He was shocked when he saw a sick old man on the road. And when he saw a corpse, he asked, 'What has happened to this man?'

His chariot driver said, 'The same will happen to you and to everyone else. One day death will come.'

Buddha said, 'Then turn the chariot around and take me home. Now there is nowhere to go. If death is approaching, life has no meaning.'

You have seen corpses being carried down the road for burning. You have also been standing at the roadside and have felt sympathy for a moment. And you might have said, 'This poor guy has died—what a tragedy! He was still young, he left behind his young wife and kids. How tragic!' You had pity for the dead person—you didn't feel any pity for yourself.

The person dying brought the message of your death; today he goes carried on a stretcher, tomorrow or the next day you will be loaded up and carried away. Just as you are standing at the roadside feeling sympathy for him, other people will also be standing along the road feeling sympathy for you. You will be so helpless that you won't even be able to thank them. The dead body you see going down the road is yours.

If you have the eyes, the vision, the depth, a profound awareness, then when one man dies, the whole of humanity dies and life becomes meaningless. Buddha renounced everything and went away. But when he became enlightened, he thought that whoever was going to wake up would wake up anyway, without anyone awakening him. For that person any excuse would be enough.

It is said that a Zen nun was carrying water back from the well when her pole broke and the pots crashed. It was a full-moon night, and the moon was reflected in the water pots. Shouldering the pole with the pots suspended from it, she was returning to the ashram and watching the reflection of the moon in the pots. The pots fell. She stood there in shock. The pots fell, water flowed out—the moon too flowed out. It is said enlightenment occurred then and there; samadhi happened. She returned dancing. She had seen that this world is nothing more than a reflection.

Whatever we go on making here will break any moment. All these moons will vanish. All these beautiful poems will disappear. These charming faces will all vanish. They are all reflections on water. She saw this—all was finished.

Buddha thought: 'What's the use? Who will I speak to? Those who are going to wake up will wake up sooner or later without me; it is only a question of time. And those who don't want to wake up, even if I scream and shout they will just roll over and go back to sleep. If they open their eyes they will look angry and ask, "Why are you disturbing my sleep? Don't you have anything better to do? Can't you let those who want to sleep, sleep in peace? I was sleeping soundly and you come along to wake me up."'

You tell someone to wake you up early, and when he wakes you up, you are angry. You had told him, 'I have to catch a train: wake me up early, at four o'clock.' But when he wakes you up, you are ready to kill!

Immanuel Kant was a great German thinker. He would get up every day at three in the morning. He followed the clock, followed the very hands of the clock. It is said that when he went to the university to teach, people along the way set their watches by him—because for years, thirty years continuously, he would set out at exactly the same minute, the same second.

But when it was very cold, he would tell his servant, 'No matter what happens, you have to wake me up at three in the morning. Even if I hit you and fight back, don't pay any attention. You can even hit me, but wake me up.' This was such a big hassle that servants didn't last long with him. Awakened at three, he would be very angry. If he wasn't awakened, he would be angry when he got up. And it wasn't just that he was angry, they would actually come to blows. He had told the servant, 'Don't worry about it—you have to wake me up at three. Even if you have to drag me out of bed forcibly, you have to get me out of bed at three. Don't worry about what I do. Don't listen to what I say at that time, because I am asleep then. There is no need to listen to me.'

There are people like this too!

Buddha thought; 'What's the use? Those who want to sleep will go on sleeping in spite of my shouting. And those ready to wake up will wake up even without my shouting.'

He remained silent for seven days. Then the gods pleaded with him; 'What are you doing? Only rarely does anyone attain buddhahood. The earth is craving, thirsty people are yearning: the clouds have formed, now they have to rain. You are silent? Let the rain pour! The flower has bloomed; let the fragrance fly! Let the rivers of juice flow—many have been thirsting for lives.

'And we have listened to your argument. We have been continuously watching your mind these seven days. You say there are people who will wake up without your speaking, and there are people who will not wake up no matter how much you speak. This is why you remain silent? Still we approach you after thinking long about it: aren't there some who are standing between these two? You cannot neglect them. If someone awakens them, they will wake up. If no one awakens them, they will continue sleeping life after life. Consider these few. Ninety-nine per cent of people will be those you mention, but consider that 1 per cent who are standing exactly on the edge—if someone awakens them they will wake up, and if no one awakens them they will go on sleeping.'

Buddha could not refute their plea, so he had to speak. The gods convinced him—they were able to persuade him. Buddha's point was right, and the gods' idea was also right.

There are three types of listeners. The first that you try waking up again and again but you can't wake them up. This kind of people is the vast majority. They hear but they don't listen. They look but they don't see. They understand but make their own interpretations—patching up and whitewashing everything. They understand but still they hold on to their misunderstanding. They have a deep vested interest in misunderstanding. They are afraid to give up their old, familiar beliefs.

There is a second type of listener, in the middle. If someone makes an effort—a Buddha, an Ashtavakra, a Krishna—they will wake up. Arjuna was this kind of listener. Krishna had to work hard; he had to work long and hard on him. The Gita was born out of this effort. At the very end Arjuna felt, 'My illusions are far away, my doubts have fallen. I come to surrender at your feet. I have seen!' But this was after a great struggle had taken place—a great conflict.

And there is an even more superior listener—like Janak—who hears when it has hardly been spoken. Just as Ashtavakra started to speak, Janak started seeing. Today's sutras are Janak's words. Janak realized so quickly, so immediately, that what Ashtavakra was saying was absolutely right. The truth struck home.

So I say, rains fall, but sometimes the ground it rains on is stony. It is raining, but seeds will not sprout. And sometimes it rains on ground that is a bit rocky. Seeds sprout, but not so many as could sprout forth. And sometimes it rains on ground that is completely ready, that is fertile and has no rocks—there is a great harvest.

Janak is that type of soil. A hint was enough.

It is worth trying to understand Janak's state because you will be somewhere among these three. And it depends on you where you insist on placing yourself in these three. You can be just an ordinary person who insists on not listening, who has vowed to fight against the truth; who, listening, hears something else; who interprets as he listens; who, as he listens, goes on projecting other things he has heard on to it—colours it, distorts it, hears whatever he wants.

You do not hear what is being said. You hear what you want to hear.

I have heard that one day Mulla Nasruddin's wife came home in a rage and said to Mulla that beggars are big cheats.

'Why, what happened?' Nasruddin asked.

'Listen, a beggar had a sign hung around his neck which said "Blind from birth". I took pity on him and took ten paise from my purse and dropped it in his begging bowl. When he heard it, he said, "Oh beautiful woman, may God make you happy." Now you tell me: How could he know that I am beautiful?'

Mulla Nasruddin started to laugh and said, 'He is really blind and blind since birth.' Then Mulla added, 'I am not the only one who is blind, there is one more blind man. Otherwise, if he did have eyes, how could he say that you were beautiful?'

The wife says one thing, Mulla hears something else. Mulla hears what he wants to hear.

Remember, this goes on happening twenty-four hours a day. You go on hearing what you want to hear, never thinking whether what you hear is yours or if it was actually said.

Mulla was working somewhere and the boss told him, 'You are not doing good work, Nasruddin. I am forced to hire someone else now.'

Nasruddin said, 'You certainly should, boss, there is work here for two men.'

The boss is saying, 'I am going to sack you and hire another man.' Mulla is saying, 'There is enough work for two, you must hire someone else.'

Step back and think one more time about what you hear: is it what was said? If an individual becomes capable of hearing correctly he becomes the second type of listener; he rises above the third, the lowest type. The third adds his own interpretations to what he hears. The third type only hears himself, hears his own echoes. His vision is not clear, he distorts everything.

The second type of listener hears what is being said. The second type of listener will take a little time, because even after hearing what has been said, courage to translate it into action is still lacking. But if he has heard, courage will come because it is impossible to remain long in the fake after hearing the truth. Once truth is seen, then no matter how old a habit is, it will have to be dropped. When you find out that two plus two equals four, then no matter how old your conditioning is that two plus two equals five, it will have to be given up. Once you know where the door is, it is impossible to try getting out through the wall. Now it will not be possible to go on beating your head on the wall. When the truth is understood, sooner or later, enough courage will come so that one takes the jump and transforms oneself.

Then there is the first type of listener. If you have both understanding and courage, you will become the first type of listener. The first type of listener means that understanding and courage happen simultaneously— understanding arises and courage is ready. There is no gap between understanding and courage. It is not that today you understand and that tomorrow you have the courage, that you understand this lifetime and in the next life you find courage. You understand, and the courage is right here. You understand this very moment, and this very moment there is courage. Then a spontaneous happening occurs. Then the sun suddenly rises. Janak is the first type of listener.

One more thing related to this has to be understood. Janak is an emperor. He has everything. He has more than he needs. He has enjoyed the world. The revolution of consciousness happens easily in the life of a man who has experienced the world, because his life experience tells him, 'What I have known as life is meaningless.' Half the work is done by life; the life he knows is meaningless.

Questions began arising in his mind: Where is more life? Is there another life? Where is true life? But someone who has not enjoyed the world, who has only wanted to enjoy, who has only wanted to get but has not got anything—for him, there will be tremendous difficulties. So don't be surprised if all of India's great masters, all the great seers—whether Jaina or Buddhist or Hindu—if they were all princes, don't be shocked. It is not accidental. It is an indication that one becomes free of the world through enjoying it. An emperor can see that there is nothing in wealth, because he has a mass of wealth but inside there is nothingness, emptiness. He has a harem of beautiful women and nothing inside himself. He has beautiful palaces, yet inside all is desolation, a desert. When one has all, it starts to be clear that there is nothing in any of it. When one has nothing one lives in hopes.

It is difficult to get rid of hopes because there is no way that hopes can be checked against reality. The poor man thinks he will live happily if he gets money tomorrow. The rich man already has wealth; there is no way for him to hope. Hence when a society becomes prosperous it becomes religious. Don't be surprised if the winds of religion have begun to blow strongly in America. This has always happened. When India was wealthy—as it surely was in the days of Ashtavakra; it was wealthy in the days of Buddha; it was wealthy in the days of Mahavira—when India was at the peak of its prosperity, it reached the great heights of yoga. It took the ultimate flight into spirituality because then people saw that there is nothing in wealth; they had everything and still nothing had meaning. If a country is poor then it is very difficult to see this.

I am not saying that a poor man cannot become liberated; a poor man can achieve liberation. A poor man can become religious, but a poor society cannot become religious. An individual can be an exception but he will need great intensity.

Think about it. If you have money, you can see that money is worthless—it is very easy. If you don't have money it is difficult, very difficult, to see that money is worthless. How can you see the worthlessness of what you don't have? If you have gold in your hand, then you can test if it is real gold or fake. If you don't have gold in your hand, if it is only in your dream . . . but no test can be made of dream gold. Only real gold can be tested.

The poor man's religion cannot be real religion. When a poor man goes to the temple he asks for money, he asks for power, he asks for employment. If he is sick he prays to become well. If his son does not have a job he prays that he can find work. The temple remains just an employment exchange. No fragrance of love or prayer arises even in the temple. He needed to go to the hospital, instead he has come to the temple. He needed to go to the employment office, instead he has come to the temple.

The poor man goes on begging in the temple for what he doesn't get in his life. What we lack in our lives is what we ask for. But if you have everything or if you are intelligent enough, if there is such genius in you that you can awaken through understanding alone and can see that when you have everything, even then what have you got? Others have money; what happened to them? If you don't have it yourself then you need the intelligence to see. What has happened to those who live in palaces? Are there waves of joy in their eyes? Is there a dance in their feet? Is the fragrance of the divine around them? If it hasn't happened to them, how will it happen to you? But this understanding is quite difficult. Even when they do have it, most people cannot see that money is worthless, so to think of seeing it when one doesn't have money . . . It can happen, there is a possibility, but a remote possibility. It is easy for Buddha to be awakened. It is easy for Janak to be awakened. It is easy for Arjuna to be awakened too. But it is very difficult for Kabir. It is very difficult for Dadu, for Sahajo; it is very difficult for Jesus, for Mohammed, because they had nothing—and yet they woke up. The desire for what we don't have is all around us. This desire goes on catching us.

Last night I was reading a poem:

I want to live one life more—
so that in it I might meet a companion
who knows how to give love.
Who rises in the morning smiling at me,

who looks at me diving deep into my heart and soul.
Who, in the afternoons, in the midst of her various chores,
feels sad without me,
who passes her day in waiting.
Who, in the evening, gives such welcome,
which releases me from all desires and longings,
releases me from the cares of birth and death—
who brings me to timelessness.
I yearn for such a companion,
who adds the flame of faithful love to my happiness,
and who adds the colour of pearls of her warm tears
to my suffering;
who, when there is poverty at home,
won't be upset when the journey is difficult,
won't wrinkle her brow.
Perhaps in the next life I'll find such a companion
who knows how to give love.
For this, I want to live one life more.

What we don't get—someone didn't meet a lover, someone didn't find wealth, someone didn't become famous—we want to live in one more life. We have lived infinite lives, but every time something or other remains, some trivia or other remains incomplete, something or other—and for this another life, and yet another life . . .

Desires have no end. Needs are very few, desires have no limit. Man goes on living with the support of these hopes and desires.

Remember, money does not enslave you, the *desire* for money enslaves you. Position does not bind you, the *desire* for position binds you. Fame does not bind you, the *desire* for fame binds you.

Janak had everything, he had seen everything. It was as if he was just waiting for someone to give a hint and he would awaken. All hopes and dreams had become worthless; his sleep was about to be broken. So I say, Ashtavakra was blessed with a great disciple.

> Janak said: Amazing! I am pure, flawless, I am peace, I am awareness, I am beyond nature. Alas, I have been fooled by illusion all this time!

The rays of light started descending. *I am pure, flawless . . . How amazing!*

Hearing Ashtavakra say, 'You are pure, nothing sticks to you . . .' As soon as he heard it, the rays reached to his very depths, piercing straight like an arrow.

Amazing! I am pure, flawless, I am peace, I am awareness, I am beyond nature. 'Amazing—what are you saying? I am pure and flawless? I am peace? I am awareness? I am beyond nature? Amazing, that I have been fooled by illusion all this time!' Janak was shocked. What he heard, he had never heard before. What he saw in Ashtavakra, he had never seen before. His ears had not heard, his eyes had not seen—something unprecedented was revealed. Ashtavakra had become luminous. In his radiance, in his circle of radiance, in his aura, Janak was wonderstruck. 'Amazing, now I am becoming aware that nothing can stick to me!' He simply cannot believe it, cannot accept it.

Truth is so unbelievable, because we have believed the false for so many long lives. Think: when a blind man's eyes suddenly open, will he be able to believe that there is light, that there is colour, these thousands of colours, these rainbows, these flowers, these trees, this moon and stars?

Immediately when his eyes open, the blind man will say, 'It is amazing, I could not even think that all this is. And it is! I had never seen it, even in dreams!'

Forget about light, the blind man doesn't even know darkness. Ordinarily you think that a blind man lives in darkness, but you are mistaken. Eyes are needed to see darkness too. You see darkness when you close your eyes because you see light when your eyes are open. But one whose eyes have never opened doesn't know darkness either. Forget light, he is not even acquainted with darkness. There is no way a blind man can even dream of rainbows. But if he gains his eyesight and sees, this whole world seems incredible; he cannot believe it. Janak also experienced a shock. He was spellbound. He was filled with wonder and awe. He said, *Amazing! I am pure, flawless.*

We have always considered ourselves guilty, and the priests have always said that we are sinners. The pundits and priests have always preached that we should wash away our sins. No one has ever said that you are innocent, that your innocence is such that there is no way to destroy it, that a million sins cannot make you a sinner. All the sins you have done are only dreams you have seen—just wake up and they will be gone. Neither virtue nor sin is yours, the very doing is not yours, because you are not the doer—you are only the observer, the witness.

I am pure, flawless. In wonder, Janak said, *I am peace* . . . because he has known only turmoil.

Have you ever known peace? You will usually say yes. But if you look deeply, you will find that what you call peace is only a short gap between two periods of turmoil. The English expression 'cold war' is very good. Between two wars a cold war goes on; between two hot wars, a cold war—but war goes on. The First World War was over, then the Second World War began. Many years passed, some twenty years, but those twenty years were cold war. The conflict continued, war preparations continued. Yes, the conflict is not manifest now; it is internal, it is underground, kept beneath the surface.

There is a cold war right now in the world—war preparations are going on. Soldiers are training. Bombs are being made, rifles are being polished, swords are being sharpened. This is cold war. War continues. It will ignite any day, any day it can break out.

What you call peace is just 'cold turmoil'. Whenever it warms up it will be 'hot turmoil'. Between two periods of turmoil a little time passes which you call peace. It is not peace, it is only cold turmoil. The mercury hasn't risen much, the heat is not extreme—you can control this much. But you haven't known peace. Can peace exist between two periods of turmoil? Can peace exist between two wars?

For the one who knows peace, his turmoil is finished forever. You haven't known peace, you have only heard the word. Turmoil is your experience; peace is your aspiration, peace is your hope.

Janak says, *I am peace, I am awareness* . . . because he has known only unconsciousness. Whatever you are doing is done unaware, as if in sleep. If someone questions you thoroughly, you will not be able to answer a single thing. If someone asks you why you fell in love with this woman, you will say, 'I don't know, I just fell—it just happened like that.' Is this an answer? For something like love, is this the answer? That it happened, that it just happened? Love at first sight! Love happened just seeing the other! Do you know from where within you this love arose? How it came? You know nothing about it, still you want this love to bring happiness to you. You do not know where this love comes from, from which unconscious layer it arises, where its seed is, where it sprouts from; still you say your life will be made happy by this love! It doesn't give happiness; it gives unhappiness, conflict, enmity, jealousy. You suffer, then you say, 'What happened? This love turned out to be all false.' You were in a state of unconsciousness from the very beginning.

You are running—money must be earned. If someone asks you why, perhaps you can give some trivial answer. You say, 'How will one live without money?' But there are people who have plenty to live on and they continue running after money. You are certain that the day you have amassed that much you will be able to stop, but you won't; you will keep on running.

When Andrew Carnegie died he left behind a billion dollars, and he was earning even more at the time of his death. Two days before he died his secretary asked, 'Are you satisfied? A billion dollars!'

He replied, 'Satisfied? I am dying in great distress, because I had planned to earn ten billion dollars.'

For one who has planned to earn ten billion, one billion . . . it is a deficit of nine billion dollars. Look at his deficit! You are looking at one billion. One billion is not worth two cents for him, one billion has no value any more. You cannot eat one billion dollars, you cannot drink it—it is useless. But once this running has started, it goes on and on.

Ask yourself why you are running. You don't have any answer. You are unconscious: you don't know why you are running, you don't know where you are going, why you are going. If you don't go somewhere, what will you do? Stop—but how to stop? Stop—stop for what? You don't know anything about stopping either.

Man goes on living as if he is intoxicated, drugged. The various dimensions of our life are not in our hands. We are completely unconscious.

Gurdjieff used to say we are more or less sleepwalking. Our eyes are open, true, but our sleep is not broken. Our eyes are full of sleep. Something happens, we go on doing things, things continue—why?

We are afraid to ask why, because we have no answer. Raising such questions makes us uneasy.

Janak said, *Amazing! I am pure, flawless, I am peace, I am awareness.* 'And not only this, you are telling me, "You are beyond nature." Beyond nature! "You are not the body, you are not the mind. You are not that which is seen, you are not the observed. You are the observer, always beyond, beyond the external world. You are always transcendental."'

Understand it. This is Ashtavakra's basic device, his basic method, if it can be called method: Be beyond the world! Whatsoever I see is not me, whatsoever comes as experience is not me, because whatever I see, I am beyond this. I am the one who is seeing, I am not the one who is seen. Whatsoever becomes my experience I am beyond, because I am the observer of the experience—how can I be the experience? Hence I am not the body, not the mind, not emotion; not Hindu, not Mohammedan, not Christian, not Brahmin, not low caste; not a child, not a youth, not an old man; not beautiful, not ugly; not intelligent, not an idiot—I am not anyone at all. I transcend the whole of nature!

This ray of light entered into Janak's heart. He was filled with awe, he was surprised, shocked. His eyes opened for the first time. *Amazing! . . . I have been fooled by illusion all this time!* 'Whatever I had built, whatever I had loved, whatever beautiful dreams I had—it was all slumbering in ignorance. They were nothing but dreams! They were just ideas arising in sleep, with no reality whatsoever.'

Amazing! . . . I have been fooled by illusion all this time! 'You have shocked me, you have shaken me. All the palaces that I had built have fallen down, and this whole empire that I had created was all a projection of my ignorance.'

Try to understand: if you can listen, the same will happen. If you can listen, exactly the same will happen to you. All your doing and arranging will become meaningless. Success or failure, all will become meaningless.

Mulla Nasruddin was talking in his sleep. He opened his eyes and said to his wife, 'Quick! Bring my glasses!'

His wife said, 'What will you do with your glasses in bed in the middle of the night?'

He said, 'Don't waste time, bring my glasses quickly. I am looking at a beautiful woman in my dream. I want my glasses to see her more clearly. The dream is a little hazy, blurred.'

You go on trying to make your dreams true, to somehow let the dream come true! You don't want anyone to say your dream is a dream, you will get angry. We haven't poisoned mystics, haven't stoned them just for nothing. They made us very angry. We were seeing dreams and they started shaking us. We were in deep sleep and they started waking us up. Without asking us they started destroying our sleep, ringing the alarm. Naturally, we are angry. But if you listen you will be grateful, you will feel eternally grateful.

Remember, in Krishna's Gita, when Krishna is speaking, Arjuna goes on raising questions. In Ashtavakra's Gita, when Ashtavakra speaks, Janak didn't raise any question. Janak only expressed his gratefulness. Janak simply received what was said. Janak only said, 'You shocked me, you awakened me! There is nothing to ask.' Janak began to experience: *I am pure, flawless, I am peace, I am awareness, I am beyond nature*. It seems impossible to us, it happened so fast! It seems to us it should take some time. We are very surprised, it happened so quickly, with such suddenness.

There are many such accounts in the lives of Zen masters. Now books on Zen have begun to spread in the East, in the West, in every direction, and reading them people are very amazed, because there are thousands of stories where a monk awakens in a single moment and attains enlightenment. We don't believe it. We do great practices but enlightenment doesn't happen. We make efforts, but still meditation doesn't happen. We sit chanting, sit in torturous practices, but the mind remains restless. And this Janak has awakened in one moment!

Sometimes it does happen. It depends on your capacity of being receptive. The less your receptivity, the longer it takes. The delay is not because of enlightenment, it can happen right now. As Ashtavakra says again and again, 'Be happy, be happy right now! Be liberated! Be free right now, this very moment.'

It is happening right now; any delay is because of our receptivity. We have no capacity to receive. Whatever time it takes is to remove the stones that have come in between.

The spring can flow right now; the spring is ready, the spring is bubbling. The spring is waiting for the stones to be removed so it can be off, running to the sea! But it will depend on how many rocks lie in between, how many boulders lie in between. It takes no time for the spring to come out—its route is not closed, it is open, waiting. Sometimes the spring will burst forth, sometimes a little digging is needed somewhere. Sometimes there may be big boulders that need dynamite. But in all three cases— whether the spring bursts open now or after a while or after many lives—the spring was always present. The obstruction was not that the spring was not ready to burst forth, the obstruction was caused by the rocks lying over it.

There must have been no rocks at all on Janak's consciousness—thankfulness arose, gratefulness was proclaimed. He began to dance! He became ecstatic.

> Just as I alone illumine this body, do I illumine the universe
> too. Either this whole universe is mine or nothing at all.

This is trust. In the Bhagavadgita, Arjuna has no trust, he doubts. He raises question after question—he has a thousand doubts. He questions first from this angle, then from that. Janak did not ask anything. This is why I call this song the Mahagita, the great song. Arjuna's lack of trust is destroyed in the end; ultimately he returns home. Janak had no distrust. It is as if he was standing at the door of his home and someone shook him saying, 'Janak, you are already standing at your home, there is no place to go.'

And he said, *Oh! Just as I alone illumine this body, do I illumine the universe too.* Ashtavakra said your ultimate being—witnessing—is not only yours, it is not only your centre—it is the centre of the entire creation. On the surface we are separate, on the inside we are one. Outwardly we are separate, when we go in we are one—just as waves are separate on the surface of the ocean, but in the depths of the ocean all are one. On the surface one wave is small, another is big; one wave is beautiful, another is ugly; one wave is dirty, another is clean—on the surface they are very distinct, but in the depth of the ocean all are joined. One who remembers the centre loses his personality, he ceases to be a personality.

So Janak says, *Just as I alone illumine this body, do I illumine the universe too.* 'What are you saying? It is unbelievable!'

Last night a young man came to me and said, 'I don't believe what happened in meditation.' Right! When something happens, this is how it is—it is not believable. We put our faith in little things, in trivia. When the vast happens, how can we believe it? When the divine is standing before you, you will be filled with awe, stunned and speechless.

There was a great mystic in the West, Tertullian. Someone asked him, 'Is there any proof of God?'

He said, 'There is only one proof: God *is* because he is absurd. God *is* because he is unbelievable. God *is* because he is impossible.'

Tertullian is saying something very unique. 'God *is* because he is absurd! The world makes sense, God is absurd. The trivial is possible, the vast is impossible. But the impossible also happens,' Tertullian says. Accept the impossible and the impossible also happens. When it happens it is completely unbelievable. All of your roots will be ripped out; how can you believe it? When it happens you will not *be*, so who will believe it? When it happens you will be scattered to the winds. Until now you have existed as darkness. When the sun comes out, you will vanish.

Janak is saying, *Either this whole universe is mine or nothing at all.* These are the only two possibilities. Any position in between these is illusory. Either the whole universe is mine because I am a part of God, because I am God, because I am the centre of the whole universe, because my witness is the witness of the whole universe . . . so either the whole universe is mine—this is one possibility. Or I have nothing at all, because I don't even exist. In witnessing, I no longer exist, only witnessing remains. Who will make the claim that all is theirs when the claimant no longer exists?

So Janak says there are two possibilities—these are the two expressions of religion—either fullness or emptiness. Krishna chose fullness, the Upanishads chose fullness: Everything comes out of that whole, but that whole remains the whole. Everything merges into that fullness, but that fullness neither increases nor decreases. The Upanishads, Krishna, Hindus and Sufis all chose fullness. Buddha chose emptiness.

The statement Janak has made says, 'Either everything is mine—I am the perfect fullness, I am the absolute Brahman—or nothing at all is mine, I am the ultimate emptiness, I am the void!' The truth is both of these together.

Buddha's statement is incomplete; Krishna's statement is also incomplete. The whole truth is included in Janak's statement. Janak says both can be said. Why? Because if I am the centre of the entire universe, the entire universe is mine. But when I am the centre of the entire universe, then I am no longer *I*. My I-ness has dropped away long ago. It is left behind like a cloud of dust. The traveller moves ahead, the dust remains behind. Then what can be mine? Then nothing is mine.

> Either this whole universe is mine or nothing at all.
>   Amazing, having renounced the body and the world, now through the skill of your teaching I see only the divine.

Amazing, having renounced the body and the world . . . 'It is a wonder, my body has gone and with the body the whole world has gone.' Let-go happened! Renunciation is not to be done, renunciation is a state of consciousness. Let-go is not a doing. If someone says he has renounced, it is no renunciation. He has made let-go into another worldly experience. If someone says, 'I am a renunciate,' he doesn't know anything about renunciation, because as long as there is an 'I', how can there be renunciation?

Let-go does not mean abandoning things. Let-go means waking up and seeing; 'Nothing is mine—how can I drop it?

What to drop? If I had a hold of it, I could let go. If I had it, I could let go.'

When you get up in the morning you don't say, 'Okay, now I'm going to renounce my dreams.' Waking up in the morning you don't say, 'At night I dreamed I was an emperor. There were great gold palaces, diamond-studded ornaments; my kingdom spread far and wide, and I had beautiful sons and a queen.' Waking up in the morning you don't say, 'Now I renounce all these.' If you say it you will look insane. If you get up in the morning and march through the village beating a drum proclaiming, 'I have renounced all—my kingdom, money, luxury, queen, princes: I leave everything'—people will be startled.

They will say, 'What kingdom? We never knew that you had a kingdom.'

You will reply, 'At night I dreamed . . .'

People will laugh and say you have gone mad. A dream kingdom need not be renounced.

So the key to realization is this: When you see that the world is nothing, what need is there to renounce? But there are people who keep track of how much they have renounced.

A friend came to see me. His wife was also with him. This friend was known for his charity. His wife said, 'Perhaps you aren't acquainted with my husband, he is very charitable, he has given one hundred thousand to charity.'

Immediately, the husband put his hand on his wife's saying, 'Not one hundred, but one hundred and ten thousand.'

This is not charity, this is calculation. This is trade. Every cent is kept track of. If he should ever meet God, he will grab him by the throat saying, 'I have given one hundred and ten thousand; tell me what you are giving in exchange.' He gave it because the scriptures say if you give one here, there you will receive a millionfold. Who is going to pass up such a deal? A millionfold! Did you hear the interest rate? Have you seen business like this? Even gamblers are not such great gamblers! Gambling, you don't get a millionfold. It is pure gambling. Give one hundred thousand in the hope that it will be returned a millionfold. This is just an extension of your greed.

And calculating one hundred thousand . . . the value of these rupees is not yet gone. Before, the rupees were kept in the safe; now in place of the safe, a record is kept of how much has been renounced. But the dream is not broken.

There is a very ancient Chinese story:

An emperor had only one son and that son was on his deathbed. The physicians had given up, saying, 'We cannot do anything to save him. He will not survive. It is not possible to save him.' There was no cure for the disease. It was a matter of just one or two days; 'He will die any moment.'

The father stayed awake all night at his bedside. It was time to say goodbye. Tears were flowing from his eyes. Sitting and sitting, at about three in the morning the father began to doze. While he slept he dreamt of a great empire which he was lord of. He had twelve sons—all very handsome, young, talented, intelligent . . . great fighters, warriors! There was no one comparable in the whole world. He had a vast horde of wealth, unlimited. He was a world ruler—his rule extending over the whole earth.

He was having this dream when the son breathed his last. His wife screamed and started crying. He opened his eyes. He was completely shocked. He sat there, dumbfounded, because just a moment before there was another kingdom, twelve sons, great wealth—it was all gone. And here this son had died! He was completely bewildered. His wife worried whether his mind was damaged, because he had had great affection for his son, and not a single tear was coming to his eyes. When the son was living he had cried over him; now the son has died and the father was not crying? His wife shook him and said, 'Has something happened to you? Why don't you cry?'

He said, 'Who should I cry for? There were twelve sons, they died. There was a great empire, it has gone. Should I cry for them or should I cry for this one? I wonder who should I cry for? Just as twelve sons have gone, thirteen have gone. Everything is finished. That was a dream and this too is a dream. When I was seeing that dream, I had completely forgotten this son, this kingdom . . . everything was forgotten. When that dream broke I remembered you all. Tonight I will sleep and again, I will forget you all.

'So it comes and goes, now it is, now it is not; and now both dreams are gone. Now I have awakened from dreaming. Now I won't be roaming about in dreams. It is enough, the time has come. The fruit has ripened, it is time for it to fall!'

Janak says, *Amazing, having renounced the body and the world* . . . Let-go happened! He has not moved even an inch, he is where he is, in that same palace to where he had invited Ashtavakra, seated him on the throne—he is sitting there in front of Ashtavakra. He hasn't gone anywhere, the kingdom goes on, the wealth of the court is there, the guards are at the door, the servants are keeping the fans moving. Everything is continuing just exactly as it was, the treasury is in its place. But Janak says, 'Amazing, let-go happened!'

Renunciation is of the inner being. Renunciation happens through understanding.

Amazing, having renounced the body and the world, now through the skill of your teaching . . . 'And by what skill is it that hardly a leaf is shaken and the transformation has happened? That not even a tiny incision is made and the surgery is complete! What expertise! What is this teaching of yours? Now I am seeing the divine, the world is no longer to be seen. My whole vision is transformed!'

It is a tremendously significant sutra: you stay right where you are, you remain just as you are—the transformation can happen. There is no need to flee to the Himalayas. Sannyas is not escaping, not running away. Everything remains just as it was—the wife, the children, house and home. No one has heard a single word about it—and the revolution happens. It is an inner matter. You will be surprised—what is this that has happened? Now the wife will not seem to be yours, the son won't seem to be yours, the house will not seem to be yours. You will still live there, but now you will live like a guest. The home is the same but it has become a place for an overnight stay. All is the same—you will work, you go to your shop, your office; you will work, but now no worry catches hold of you.

Once you see that everything here is just a play, a great drama, the revolution happens.

An actor was asking me, 'Tell me how I can become more skilful in acting.'

So I said: There is only one rule. Those people who want to be skilful in life, for them the rule is they should take life as acting. And those who want to be skilful in acting, for them the rule is to take acting as real life. There is no other key. If an actor takes his acting as real life, he becomes skilful. Then he takes the drama as real life.

You will be impressed by an actor whose skill has become so deep that for him the unreal is the real. If an actor is not able to see the make-believe as the real he cannot be a great actor. He will remain outside, he will not be able to get into his part—he will be performing very superficially.

But you will find that his spirit has not entered it, he has not disappeared into it.

An actor completely forgets himself in his acting. When he plays Rama, he completely forgets and he becomes Rama. When his Sita is stolen away, he doesn't think, 'What has this got to do with me anyway? This whole play will be over in a little while, we'll each go home; why cry for nothing? Why ask the trees where my Sita has gone? Why scream and shout? What's the use? Do I have any Sita? And there is no Sita here, another man is playing Sita. I have nothing to do with him.' If he does not lose himself in it, he cannot be a great actor. Skill in acting is taking the acting as life, taking it as completely real. His very own Sita is lost. Those tears are not false, they are real. He cries as if he has lost his beloved—he fights the same way. His acting is real life.

If you want to live skilfully, take your life as acting. This too is a drama. Sooner or later, the curtain will fall. Sooner or later, everyone will depart. The stage may be vast, but it is still a stage no matter how vast. Don't make your home here. Stay here just as in a caravanserai. It is a waiting room. All are in a queue here. Death comes here and people go on departing. You are going to depart. There is no need to sink roots down here: one who does will suffer.

The person who does not sink roots in this world is a sannyasin. One who doesn't get rooted here, whose feet don't become planted, is a sannyasin. One who is always ready to move on . . . One is a sannyasin if he is a nomad, a gypsy, a *khana-badosh*.

This word 'khana-badosh' is very good. It means one who carries his house on his shoulders. 'Khana' means house, 'badosh' means on the shoulders—one whose house is on his shoulders. The khana-badosh is a sannyasin. At most pitch a tent, don't make a house here. A tent can be struck at any time, without a moment's delay. A caravanserai!

It is told about the Sufi, Ibrahim . . .

Earlier he had been the emperor of Balkh. One night while he was sleeping in his palace he heard someone walking on the roof. He asked, 'What ill-mannered fool is walking on the roof in the middle of the night? Who are you?'

A voice answered, 'I am not ill-mannered, my camel is lost. I am looking for her.'

Ibrahim started to laugh. He said, 'Madman! You are mad! Can a lost camel be found on the roof? Think about it: how will a camel get up on the roof?'

A voice came from above: 'Before calling others ill-mannered and mad, think about yourself. Is happiness found in wealth, or luxury, or wine and song? If happiness is found in wealth, in luxury, in wine and song, then camels can also be found on the roof.'

Ibrahim was startled. It was the middle of the night but he got up and immediately sent his men to catch the man: that fellow seems to know something. But by then the man had slipped away. Ibrahim sent men around the capital to find out who the fellow was—he seemed to be an enlightened fakir. What did he say? For what purpose did he say it?

Ibrahim could not sleep the rest of the night. While he was holding court the next morning, he was in a melancholy mood. The words had struck him hard.

He must have been someone like Janak: he was hit by the truth of what had been said. 'If this man is mad, am I intelligent? Who has found happiness in this world? I am also searching for it. Happiness is not found in this world, and if it is, a camel can also be found on the roof. Then the impossible does happen, there is no problem. But who is that fellow? How did he get up on the roof? How did he escape, where did he go?' He sat lost in thought. He was holding court—the court was open, business was being discussed—but today his mind was not there. His mind had flown away somewhere. The bird of his mind had already flown off to some other world . . . as if let-go had already happened. Just a small incident—as if Ashtavakra himself had climbed up on his roof and spoken.

Just then he noticed there was trouble at the door. A man wanted to come in and was telling the guard he wanted to stay in this caravanserai. And the guard was saying, 'You are mad—this is not a serai, this is the palace of the emperor. There are many serais in the city—go and stay there.'

But the man was saying, 'I will stay right here—I have stayed here before. It is a serai. Tell someone else this nonsense—you can't fool me.'

Suddenly, hearing his voice, Ibrahim realized that this is the same voice and this is the same man. He said, 'Bring him in—don't chase him away.'

He was brought in. Ibrahim asked, 'What are you saying? What kind of arrogance is this? This is my palace. You call it a serai? This is an insult.'

The man said, 'Whether it is insult or praise, I ask one thing: I have come here before, but then someone else was sitting on this throne. Who was he?'

Ibrahim replied, 'That was my father.'

The fakir said, 'And before that also I came here; another man was here.'

The king replied, 'That was my father's father.'

So the fakir said, 'This is why I call it a serai. People sit here then depart, they come and go. How long will you sit here? When I come again I will find someone else sitting here. Hence I call it a serai. This is not a home. A home is a place where once you stay, you stay . . . where no one can drive you away, where it is not possible to be driven out.'

Ibrahim, it is said, descended from the throne and said to that fakir, 'I bow down to you. This is a serai. You stay here, I am going. What's the use of staying in a serai?'

Ibrahim left the palace. He must have been capable, ready.

Janak says, 'In one moment I saw that I renounced this world and the body. I became a sannyasin. With what skill did you do this? What is this teaching you gave? What skilfulness you have! What art you have!'

Amazing, having renounced the body and the world, now through the skill of your teaching . . . 'What skill! What a master I have met.'

I see only the divine. 'Now I see only the divine. I don't see anything else. Now all this appears only as manifestations of the divine, just his waves.'

> Just as waves, foam and bubbles are not other than water,
> so this individual soul is not other than the universal soul.

'Just as waves arise in water, bubbles form, foam appears— and they are not separate from the water. They arise from it, they disappear back into it. In the same way there is nothing here that is separate from the divine. All are his bubbles, all are his foam, all are his waves. They arise in him, they dissolve back into him . . . *Just as waves, foam and bubbles are not other than water* . . . we are just like this. I start to see this, lord.'

Janak is saying to Ashtavakra that he is seeing it directly. This is not a statement of a philosopher. This is an experience, an expression arising from a deep experience that he is having.

You also take a look! It is just a matter of a small change of vision, what in the West is called a change of gestalt. The word 'gestalt' is very meaningful. Sometime you must have seen a picture published in children's books . . . a single picture in which, if you look carefully, sometimes you will see an old woman, sometimes you will see a young woman. As you go on watching, it begins alternating: sometimes the old woman appears, sometimes the young woman appears. They are made from the same lines. But one thing—you will be surprised, it is something you might never have thought about—you cannot see both of them at the same time.

Even though you have seen them both—in that picture you have seen the old woman, and you have seen the young woman; you know now that both are in that picture—still you cannot see them simultaneously. When you see the young woman, the old woman disappears. When you see the old woman, the young woman disappears . . . because the same lines are being used for both. In German this is called gestalt. The meaning of gestalt is: by looking in one way it has one appearance, by looking in another way it has another appearance. It is the same thing, but the way you look changes the whole meaning.

The world is the same. When the ignorant looks at it he sees an infinite variety of things: one gestalt, one way to see. And when a wise man looks at it, the infinite variety disappears—the myriad forms disappear. A single vast expanse is seen.

Janak says: *I see only the divine.* 'I see the ultimate reality.' These green trees are the greenery of the divine. In these flowers, it is the divine flowering in colour. In the fragrance of the flowers it is it frolicking with the wind. It is it in the gathering clouds in the sky. Inside you it is it who is asleep, and inside Ashtavakra and Buddha it is it who is awake.

It is it who is in the denseness of the stone in a deep sleep. In man it is it who is a little alert, a little awakening has begun: but it is it.

All forms are its forms. Upside down, it is it, right side up, it is it. From the human viewpoint trees are upside down. A few days ago I was reading a book on plant life. I was surprised, but it seemed to be right. This scientist had written that the heads of trees are buried in the ground. Because the trees take their food from the ground, their mouths are in the earth. They eat and drink water from the earth, so their mouths are in the earth. And their feet are in the sky—they are doing headstands. They seem to be very ancient yogis.

Scientists are attempting to prove that we can slowly understand the whole evolution of man on this basis. There are earthworms, there are fish—they are level. They are horizontal, parallel to the earth. Their tails and mouths make a straight horizontal line. They have evolved somewhat beyond trees. Then there are dogs, cats, lions, cheetahs— their heads are a little raised. There is a little change from the horizontal, the head is raised a little; the angle has changed. Then there are monkeys—they can sit. They more or less make a ninety-degree angle with the earth, but they cannot stand. They are sitting men; trees are men doing headstands. Then there is man: he stands up straight, he makes a right angle—completely the reverse of trees. The head is on top, the feet are below.

I loved this idea: all are the play of the one. Sometimes the one is standing upside down, sometimes it is standing right side up, sometimes it is lying down; sometimes sleeping, sometimes awake. Sometimes it is lost in misery, sometimes lost in happiness. Sometimes it is in turmoil, sometimes at peace—but the waves are all of the one.

Just as waves, foam and bubbles are not other than water . . . in the same way there is nothing separate from the soul. All are one inseparable whole.

See it, don't just listen! It is a question of changing the gestalt. It can be seen in one glance. It can be so in a single glimpse. If you look deeply you will find that everything slowly merges into one and disappears. A vast ocean is putting forth waves. This experience will not last long, because for it to last your capacity needs to be developed. But if it can be seen even for a moment that this vastness is putting forth waves, and we are all his waves; that one sun is radiating, and we are all its rays; that one music is sounding here, and we are all its notes—then transformation happens. Gradually, that experience of one moment will permeate your being forever.

You can catch hold of it if you want, or you can miss it. Janak caught hold of it.

> I woke up in the night.
> It seemed I suddenly heard the whisperings of the deep stillness
> coming from behind the curtain of darkness—
> as a soft, mysteriously melodious, ultimate song.
> And that song said to me:
> Invincible one! Oh, haven't you woken up yet?
> And this light, from an unbound source, floods.
> Oh, unfortunate one,
> how many times has your cup been filled
> and, unnoticed, been tipped over and emptied.

This is not the first time you hear these words. You have already heard them many times. You are very ancient. It could well be that you have heard them from Ashtavakra. There are certainly some among you who have heard him. Some have heard Buddha, some Krishna, some Jesus, some Mohammed, some Lao Tzu, some Zarathustra. On this earth there have continuously been such men; you have passed near all of them and gathered here. So many lamps have been lit, it is impossible that the light of some lamp has not come to your eyes. Your cup has been filled many times.

'Oh unfortunate one, how many times has your cup been filled and, unnoticed, been tipped over and emptied?' Your cup goes on being filled but still it remains empty. You are unable to contain it.

'And that song said to me: Invincible one! Oh, haven't you woken up yet? And this light, from an unbound source, floods.' And morning is approaching. Many mornings have come and many suns have come out, but you go on sitting, holding tight to your darkness. If you let go of your poverty, it will be gone.

Janak says, 'I see only one. I have been dissolved into that one. That one has dissolved in me.'

> The Vedas say:
> the one who renounces all, is a sannyasin,
> is greater than the Vedas.
> His brilliance outshines the world.
> He resides in the lord of the universe,
> the lord of the universe resides in him.

'The Vedas say: the one who renounces all, is a sannyasin, is greater than the Vedas'—he is higher even than the Vedas, because—'He resides in the lord of the universe, the lord of the universe resides in him.'

In that moment Janak's consciousness was not separate from the universal soul, it became one. He himself was startled.

> Just as cloth when analysed is nothing but thread, this universe when analysed is nothing but the soul.

Looking wakefully, discriminately, looking consciously . . . If you look carefully at cloth what will you find? You will find only woven threads—one thread going this way, one thread going that way. Cloth is made by weaving them like this again and again—cloth is a mesh of threads. But the strange thing is that although you can't wear threads, you can wear cloth. If you collect a heap of thread, you can't put it on. Although cloth too is nothing but a collection of threads, it is only a difference of the arrangement. By weaving threads across each other, cloth is made; then you can cover yourself with cloth. But what is the difference? It is still thread. What difference does it make how you arrange them?

Janak is saying that existence sometimes becomes green in a tree, sometimes becomes red in a rose, sometimes it is water, sometimes it is hills and mountains, sometimes moon and stars. These are all different manifestations of consciousness. Cloth is woven from thread, and you can weave many kinds of cloth from it—fine, thin cloth to wear in hot weather, thick to wear in the cold. You can weave all kinds of cloth from it: beautiful and ugly, for the rich and for the poor. You can create thousands of types of cloth from it.

Scientists say that the whole universe is made of one energy. Their name for energy is electricity. What difference does the name make? But one thing scientists agree with is that the whole universe is made of one thing. It is the myriad forms of that one thing. It is just as various gold ornaments are all made of gold. If they are melted down, only gold will be left. The forms are various, but what the form is made of is identical.

Just as cloth when analysed is nothing but thread, this universe when analysed is nothing but the soul. Just as cloth is only thread, in exactly the same way this existence is woven from being. And certainly it is better to say 'being' than to say 'electricity'—because electricity is also a part of matter, and there is no possibility that consciousness can come from electricity. And if it is possible for consciousness to come from electricity, then it is meaningless to call electricity the source, because what can come from it must be hidden within it. Consciousness is visible, consciousness has become manifest. And what is manifest must also be hidden in the original, otherwise how did it appear? You planted a mango seed, a mango tree appeared. Mangoes grew on it. You planted a neem seed, and a neem tree appeared. Tiny neem pods started growing on it. That which appears, the fruit that is born, was already in the seed.

Consciousness is visible in the world, so consciousness does appear, various forms of consciousness appear—so consciousness must be hidden in the basic stuff of existence. Hence to say 'electricity' is not right, it is more appropriate to say 'being'. Say 'being-electricity', but consciousness must be included in it. Whatsoever we see all around us must be hidden in the root.

> Just as cloth when analysed is nothing but thread, this universe when analysed is nothing but the soul.
>
> Just as sugar produced from sugar cane is wholly pervaded by it, the universe produced from me is permeated by me through and through.

Just as when you extract sugar from sugar cane, the sugar-cane juice permeates the sugar, in the same way the divine permeates all consciousness, the divine permeates me, the divine permeates you, and you permeate the divine.

> From the ignorance of the soul this world then appears . . .

Try to understand this. It is very significant.

> From the ignorance of the soul the world appears, from knowing the soul it does not appear.

The gestalt changes, the way of seeing changes.

> From the ignorance of the rope a snake appears, from knowing the rope it does not appear.

In the darkness of night you see a rope and become afraid thinking it is a snake. You run away. You bring sticks and start to beat it. Then someone brings a lamp and the sticks fall from your hands, the fear vanishes: in the light you see it is not a snake, it is just a rope. The snake existed only because you could not see the rope as a rope. There was no snake—it was only a projection.

The world exists only because being is not seen as being. When one knows himself, his world disappears. This does not mean that doors and walls, mountains and rocks disappear. No, these will be there but they will all be merged into the one. These will all be various waves, foam, bubbles of the one.

The world is finished for the one who knows himself. The world cannot be finished for the one who does not know himself. You will not be able to know yourself by dropping the world. But by knowing yourself, the world drops.

There are two approaches to renunciation. One approach says that by renouncing the world you can know yourself. The other approach says, know yourself and the world has already dropped. The first approach is wrong. By abandoning the world you cannot know yourself. Because, in abandoning the world you go on creating the illusion of the world.

Try to understand a little. A rope is lying on the ground but you see a snake. If someone meets you and says, 'Just drop the idea of a snake and you will see the rope,' you will say, 'How can the idea of a snake be dropped? I see a snake, I don't see a rope.' If you take courage by chanting 'Rama, Rama' and somehow stand straight, saying, 'Okay, it is not a snake, it is a rope, it is a rope, it is a rope,' still you will know inside yourself, 'It is a snake, who is fooling who? Don't go near it, to avoid any trouble.' You will escape. You will say, 'It is a rope. I believe it is a rope, but why go close to it?'

The one who escapes from the world—he says the world is maya, but still he escapes—question him a little: 'If it is maya, then why are you escaping? If it doesn't exist, then why are you escaping? What is it you drop and leave behind?

He says money is just dirt. Then why is he so afraid of money? Then why be frightened? If money is dirt and he is not afraid of dirt, then why is he afraid of money? It is dirt, if he sees only dirt, it is okay. If money is lying there, okay; if not, okay. Sometimes dirt is needed, so man uses dirt too. If money is needed, use money. But now it is all dreamlike, like play money.

The second approach is deeper and nearer to the truth— that if you light a lamp and see the rope as a rope then the world is gone, the snake is gone. *From the ignorance of the soul this world then appears, from knowing the soul it does not appear.*

If you look at the being, the world is not visible. Look at the world, and the being is not visible. Of the two only one is seen, both cannot be seen simultaneously. If you see the world, then you don't see your being. When you start seeing your being, then the world is not visible. There is no way whatsoever that both can be seen simultaneously.

It is as if you are sitting in a room and you see nothing but darkness. Then you bring light to look more closely at the darkness, so you can see it more clearly; then you won't see it. When you bring light, darkness is not visible. If you want to see darkness, then don't make the mistake of bringing light. If you don't want to see darkness then bring light—because darkness and light cannot be seen simultaneously. Why can't they be seen simultaneously? Because darkness is the absence of light. When light is present, how can its absence also be there?

This world is the absence of knowing your being. When the dawn of knowing your being comes, the world disappears. Everything stays just as it is and still nothing remains as it is. Everything is just as it is—and everything is transformed.

People ask me, 'You give sannyas but you don't tell people to leave the home, leave the wife, leave the children.'

I answer, 'I don't tell them to leave anything, I tell them to be centred, be centred in their being, so that they can see what is. What is, cannot be dropped. What is not, need not be dropped.'

We see what we want to see.

A case was being heard in court. The judge asked Mulla Nasruddin, 'How did you recognize your own buffalo from among these hundreds of identical-looking water buffaloes?'

Nasruddin replied, 'What is so difficult about it, your honour? In your court, hundreds of lawyers in black coats are standing around, but still I can recognize my own lawyer, can't I?'

He is saying that we can recognize what we want to recognize. A man recognizes his own buffalo, although buffaloes look alike—just like lawyers.

What we want to know, we come to know. What we want to recognize, we come to recognize. Our intention becomes the reality of our life. If you want to awaken from this world, don't fight with it. If you want to awaken from this world, just make efforts within to wake up.

Mulla Nasruddin and his wife took their lively young baby along with them to see a dance programme. The doorman warned them saying, 'Nasruddin, if the child cries during the programme you will have to leave the hall. If you want we can return the cost of your tickets, but you will not be allowed to return to the programme, so be aware.'

About halfway through the programme Nasruddin asked his wife, 'How do you like the dance?'

'It's absolutely lousy!' his wife answered.

So he said, 'Then what are you waiting for?—give the baby a good pinch.'

When you know the world is absolutely useless, then don't wait. Give yourself a good pinch. Shake yourself inside, awaken yourself. Your awakening is all that is needed. Awakening is the great mantra—the only mantra.

Hari-om-tat-sat!

8

The Gift of Existence

Osho,

It feels to me that my body is like a cage or bottle, in which a very powerful lion is imprisoned and he has been sleeping there for many lives, but now he has been awakened by your harassment. He is hungry and very impatient to be freed from the cage. Many times during the day he becomes enraged and roars, he leaps up roaring. Every cell of my body trembles from this roaring and leaping up, and the forehead and upper part of my head begin to burst with energy. After this I fall deep into an extraordinary intoxication and ecstasy. Then the lion becomes a little quiet, goes on wriggling within, paces up and down and keeps on growling. And then in kirtan, or in remembering you, he dances ecstatically too. Please explain what is going on.

Yoga Chinmaya has asked this question.

What is happening is good. It is happening just as it should. Don't be frightened by it—let it happen. Help it in every way. A unique process has begun, whose final crescendo is liberation.

We are certainly imprisoned in the body—a lion locked up in a cage, confined for such a long time that he has forgotten his own roar, confined for such a long time that he has started thinking the cage is his home. Not only this, he has started thinking, 'I am the cage. I am the body!'

A hit is needed. That's why you are with me, so I can hit—and you wake up. These words that I say to you are not mere words. Think of them as arrows. They will pierce you. Sometimes you will be angry with me too . . . because everything was moving along peacefully, comfortably, and suddenly there is confusion. But there is no other way to wake you up—you will have to pass through pain.

When energy rises within, the body will not be able to bear it. The body has not been made to endure it. The capacity of the body is very small. The energy is vast . . . as if one wants to enclose the whole sky in a small courtyard. So when the energy awakens many disturbances will arise in the body. The head will be splitting with pain.

And sometimes it happens that even after enlightenment disturbances continue in the body. It is completely natural before enlightenment, because the body is not ready. It is as if you put one thousand candlepower of electricity into a line that only has the capacity to carry one hundred candlepower—it will be overloaded and catch fire!

It is just the same when the energy which had been sound asleep within you awakens—it manifests and your body is not ready for it. Your body is ready to accept your being a beggar, it cannot accept your being an emperor. The body has limits, you have no limits. It will be jolted, storms will arise. Before enlightenment happens, before samadhi, these shocks are completely natural. And sometimes it happens that samadhi happens and the shocks continue, the storms continue, because the body was not able to get ready.

This is what has happened in Krishnamurti's case. The process has continued for forty years after attaining the ultimate. The body could not absorb the shock. Krishnamurti will wake up in the middle of the night shouting and screaming. He will start to growl—really growling. And for forty years he has had a headache that doesn't go away; it comes and goes but it never totally leaves him. Sometimes the pain is so strong that it feels as if his head will burst.

From the standpoint of the body, these last forty years have been years of great difficulty for Krishnamurti. Sometimes it happens this way. Usually, the body becomes ready as samadhi happens. But with Krishnamurti, the body could not adjust because samadhi had been forced. The thinkers that brought Krishnamurti up, those theosophists, worked hard, made untiring efforts to bring on samadhi. Their aspiration was to give birth to a world teacher. The world needs it—if a buddha can be incarnated . . .

If Krishnamurti had worked only by his own efforts, perhaps then he would have needed one or two more births. But then this problem would not have arisen. The work was forced: what needed two lifetimes to happen, happened instantly. It happened, but the body could not get ready. It happened suddenly, when the body was not ready. So there have been forty years of physical suffering. Even now Krishnamurti growls at night and wakes up again and again from his sleep. The energy won't let him sleep. He screams!

It seems amazing that a person who has achieved the ultimate should scream at night. But the cause is clear. An enlightenment that should have taken two lifetimes to happen was forced too quickly. Because of this, the body was not ready and the process continues.

Samadhi has happened, but this process continues. He has reached home, but the body remains behind, still being dragged along. The being has reached home, the body has not. The pain and suffering of this dragging continues.

Don't be frightened by what is happening. These are the first indications of samadhi, the first steps of samadhi. Take them as auspicious, accept them happily. If you are ready to accept them as blessings, then very soon they will slowly become quiet. And as soon as the body begins to accept, begins to cooperate, its readiness and capacity increase. You have called out to the infinite, so you will have to become infinite. You have challenged the vastness, so you will have to become vast.

There is a very unique story in the Old Testament—the story of Jacob. Jacob was seeking God. He distributed all his wealth. He sent away all his beloved friends, his wife, his children, his servants—he sent them all far away. He was waiting for God on the deserted bank of a river. God arrived.

But it was very strange—Jacob started wrestling with God. Does anyone wrestle with God? But Jacob started struggling with God. It is said that they fought the whole night. As morning approached, as dawn was about to come, Jacob was defeated. When God was about to leave him, Jacob fell at his feet and said, 'Please give me your blessing.'

God said, 'What is your name?' Jacob told him his name. God said, 'Today, you have become Israel'—the name that the Jews are known by. 'From today onwards you are Israel. Now you are no longer Jacob, Jacob has died'—just as I change your name when I give you sannyas initiation. The old is gone. God told Jacob: 'Jacob has died, from now on you are Israel.'

This story is from the Old Testament. There is no other story of someone fighting with God, but there is a great truth in this story. When that ultimate energy descends, what happens is almost like a fight. And when the ultimate experience happens and you are defeated by the divine and the body is vanquished and you accept defeat—then your final initiation happens. In that moment divine blessings shower on you. Then you are new. That is when you taste the nectar of the eternal for the first time.

Yoga Chinmaya is almost there where Jacob must have been. It is difficult to say how long the night may be. It is hard to say how long the struggle will last. No prediction can be made. But this struggle is auspicious.

Cooperate with this energy. This lion inside that wants freedom—it is you. This energy that wants to rise towards the head, that wants to go from the sex centre to the crown chakra, that wants to create a path—it is you. For many lives it has been subdued and lying coiled up; now it is starting to raise its hood. You are fortunate, you are lucky. With this you are approaching the final blessing. Your real transformation will happen.

Krishnamurti has written in his notebook, 'Whenever my head is splitting, when at night I cannot sleep and the screaming and shouting come and something inside me growls—after all this is over, a unique experience comes. After this a great peace descends. Blessings shower in every direction. Everywhere lotuses and more lotuses are blooming.'

Exactly this is starting to happen to Chinmaya. It is good. 'After this I fall deep into an extraordinary intoxication and ecstasy.' When the energy arises after it has had its struggle, and the body becomes a little ready, then a new ecstasy will come: there is growth. You have come up a little, you have transcended a little. You have come out of the prison a little, you have found open sky. You will be fulfilled. You will dance, you will dance for joy.

'Then the lion becomes a little quiet, goes on wriggling within, paces up and down and keeps on growling. And then in kirtan, or in remembering you, he dances ecstatically.'

The lion wants to dance. There isn't enough room to dance in the body. More space is needed for dancing—what space is available in the body? Dance can only happen outside of the body. This is why if you dance totally you will find you no longer remain a body. In the ultimate grace of dance, at the ultimate height, you are out of the body. The body goes on turning, goes on moving rhythmically, but you are outside, you are no longer inside.

This is why I have invariably included dance in my methods of meditation, because there is nothing more miraculous for meditation than dancing. If you dance fully, if you dance totally, then in that dance your being comes out of the body. The body will go on moving in rhythm but you will experience that you are out of the body. And then your real dance begins: below, the body will go on dancing; above, you will dance. The body on the earth, you in the sky. The body in the earthly, you in the celestial. The body will dance the dance of matter, you will dance the dance of consciousness. You will become Nataraj, the king of dancing.

You ask, 'Please explain what is going on.'

The unprecedented is happening, the wondrous is happening, the rare is happening! What is happening is not to be explained, it is to be experienced. Whatever I say will not help you understand this experience, at the most it can help you become capable of accepting it more easily. Accept it with joy. Don't repress it.

Naturally the idea will come to suppress it; you will think, 'What madness is this? I am growling like a lion. What is this roaring? People will think I am mad!' So naturally the idea will come to suppress it, to hide it—not to let anyone know. What will they say?

Don't worry. Don't bother about what anyone says. If people say you are mad, then go mad! Has anyone become enlightened without going mad? Give your attention to your interiority. If bliss is coming from this, if ecstasy is coming, if wine is raining, then don't worry. This world has nothing as valuable as this to give to you. So don't make any compromise with the world. Don't sell one iota of your being, even if in exchange you receive the whole of the universe as your kingdom. Jesus has said, 'What use is it if you gain the whole world but lose your own soul?' If you save your soul, even if you lose the whole world, you have everything.

Have courage, be daring. Let your trust, your faith in yourself, grow. Soon, your body will start gradually accepting it. Then the roaring will disappear. Then only dance will remain. Then the lion will not suffer, because the lion will have found a path: when he wants to go out, he can go out; when he wants to come in, he can come in. Then this body is no longer a jail, then this body becomes a place to relax. When you want to come in, come inside; when you want to go out, go outside.

When you can go out and in as easily as you come and go from your house . . . It is cool, you feel cold; you go outside and sit in the sunshine. Then the sunshine increases, the sun climbs high, it starts getting hot, you start sweating; you get up and come in. It is just as you come and go from your house: then the house is not a prison. If you are sitting in prison, you don't have the possibility to come out or go in whenever your heart feels like it. In jail you are a prisoner; at home you are a master.

When your lion can dance outside, can fly in the sky, can play with the moon and stars—then there is no problem. Then there is no fight with the body. Then the body is a place for relaxation. When you get tired, you can return inside and rest. Then there is no enmity with the body either. Then the body is a temple.

The second question:

> Osho,
>   Yesterday you said that you are always with us, and
> when we take sannyas we also start being with you. I do
> not remember any moment when I took sannyas: neither
> when nor where. You just gave it. Even now, have I come
> near you? I didn't know anything about sannyas then, nor
> do I know anything now. Master, how can I become a real
> sannyasin? How can I come closer to you? Where is that
> worthiness in me? Where is that trust and surrender in me?

It has happened many times that I have given initiation to
people who have no idea about sannyas. I have given sannyas
to those who had not come to take sannyas. I have initiated
those who had never thought of sannyas even in their wildest
dreams . . . because I don't look only at your mind, I look at
the many things repressed in your unconscious.

Last night, a young woman came to see me and I didn't
even ask her. I said to her, 'Close your eyes and take sannyas.'
I didn't even ask if she wanted to take sannyas. She closed
her eyes and accepted initiation. Ordinarily, one would be
surprised if asked to take sannyas, and would want to think
it over. Some people think of taking sannyas for months, for
years. Some have kept on thinking about it and died before
taking it. She graciously received it. On a conscious level,
she doesn't know anything about it.

But we are not new here—we are very ancient! This
girl has been seeking for many lives. She carries treasures of
meditation. Just seeing this treasure I said, 'Close your eyes
and go inside.' I told her, 'I am not going to ask you whether
you want to take sannyas or not. There is no need to ask.'

I gave Dayal sannyas in the same way. This question is
from Dayal. I didn't ask Dayal—Dayal also didn't know.

What do you know about yourself? You don't know where you came from. You don't know about the treasures you have gathered. You don't know what you have been doing these many, many lives. You don't know what you have found in your search and what remains incomplete. Every time death has come and rubbed out everything that you have done. There are many among you who have taken sannyas many times: every time death came and erased everything, and you don't have the ability to recall it.

Understand it like this: you had been creating something—you had been painting a picture when death came, and it remained incomplete. Death came and you forgot. You were born again. Then even if you get a message about that incomplete painting, even if that incomplete painting is put in front of you, you won't remember, because in this life you have never even thought of yourself as a painter. And if I tell you, 'Finish the painting—it has been left incomplete. You had made it with great hopes, you had created it with a very deep thirst. Now just go ahead and finish it. Death had come in between and it was left incomplete.' You will say, 'I don't know anything. You can have me take up the brush, but I don't know how to hold it. You can put the colours in front of me and I will paint, but I don't know anything about how to paint.' Still, I tell you to start, and just by starting, the memory will come. Just take the brush in your hand and perhaps you will be reminded.

It happened in the Second World War, a soldier was wounded and fell, and he lost his memory. He had received a blow to the head and his memory cells got messed up. He forgot everything. He forgot even his own name, he forgot who he was. He was unconscious when he was taken from the battlefield. His identification had fallen off somewhere, his number too had fallen off.

It was a great problem: when he came to his senses he didn't know his number, he didn't know his name, he didn't know his rank. The psychologists worked hard; they tried in every way to remind him but couldn't find out anything. The man had gone completely blank . . . as if all connection with his memory had suddenly broken off. Someone suggested that now there was only one way: have him taken all around England. He was a soldier in the British army, and if he was taken around England, perhaps when he came near his own village he would remember.

So he was taken around England on the trains—two men took him around. The train stopped at every station and they brought him down and he stood and stared around. England is a small country, so it wasn't very difficult to take him everywhere. In the end, at a very small station where the train didn't usually stop, but for some reason it did this time, the man got off, read the sign on the station and said, 'This is my village!'

He began to run. He forgot that there were two men with him. The two men began running after him. He ran out of the station and into the village. He remembered everything. He remembered the lanes and paths. He didn't even ask anyone. He passed through the streets and bypaths and arrived in front of his house. He said, 'Oh! This is my house . . . this is my name . . . this is my nameplate hanging here.' He remembered everything. Just a click, and his whole memory came back again. Forgetfulness disappeared, the memory system fell back together again.

So sometimes I give sannyas as I gave it to Dayal in the hope that if I send you around in orange clothes, perhaps you will remember that you have previously worn orange clothes. If I say, 'Dance!' perhaps one day while you are dancing you will arrive at that psychological space where you remember your dancing of past lives. I say, 'Meditate.' While you are meditating perhaps some door in the unconscious will open and a flood of memories will come.

This is why I go on speaking—sometimes on the Gita, sometimes on Ashtavakra, sometimes on Zarathustra, sometimes on Buddha, sometimes on Jesus, sometimes on Krishna: who knows which words will stir your heart? Who knows which words will become a key to your inner depths? Who knows which words will awaken you from your slumber? I go on trying everything. My effort is simply to create a continuity, a harmony, a connection with that which deaths have broken and scattered. With this continuity your destiny will start unfolding in front of you. Many times you have made the house—it was abandoned again and again.

Hence Dayal is right: 'I do not remember any moment when I took sannyas.' He didn't take it, I gave it.

'Neither when nor where. You just gave it. Even now, have I come near you?' You will come near me, when you reach yourself. There is no other way to come near me. Reach yourself and you have reached me. Know yourself and you have known me. You don't need to make any outer pilgrimage towards me—descend deeper and deeper within.

'I didn't know anything about sannyas then, nor do I know anything now.' It will happen soon—soon you will know. 'I didn't know anything then, nor do I know anything now.' This is true. But this attitude is good where you think, where you know, that you don't know. Unfortunate are those who don't know but think they know. You are in the right state. This is the attitude of the innocent mind: 'I don't know.' You are empty, you can be filled. There are some who don't know anything—and their number is vast—but they think they know. Through this wrong idea they miss even what they could have known.

Knowledge prevents—prevents you from real knowing. If you know that you are ignorant, then you are moving in the right direction. The ultimate happens only in such innocence of mind. To know that 'I don't know' is the first step towards knowing.

'Where is that worthiness within me? Where is that trust and surrender within me?' This feeling arises in a worthy person's heart: 'Where is that worthiness in me?' The unworthy think, 'Who is as worthy as I am?'

This feeling of humility itself is worthiness, of 'What do I deserve? What surrender, what trust do I have?' This is the indication of trust. The seed is present, one just needs to wait: at the appropriate time, in the appropriate season, it will sprout, transformation will happen.

And this journey is a rare journey. This journey is a journey of the unknown, of the unknowable.

A poet says:

This secrecy of the perpetual silence.
It is useless knowing this secret.
I lost my peace in my madness for you.
I have become a flame filled with joy in my pain for you.
At the hands of time I have become so bent
I who was once an arrow, am now the bow.
No companion, no guide for this journey.
What path is this I have set out on?
I find great joy in this ecstasy.
Having disappeared, I have become
a beacon for the destination.

This goal is such that it is reached by losing yourself. As long as you exist, you will not arrive; when you disappear, you attain.

'I find great joy in this ecstasy.' When you are not, when your ego has disappeared, when ecstasy arrives, 'I find great joy in this ecstasy. Having disappeared, I have become a beacon for the destination.'

'As I have disappeared, I have arrived.' This path is one of losing yourself. So if you feel, 'Where is my worthiness to surrender?' you have started to disappear, the ecstasy is arising. If you feel, 'Where is that trust in me?' then you have started disappearing, you have started losing yourself. Sannyas means for you to disappear, so the divine can be.

'No companion, no guide for this journey.' This is a journey of great aloneness. 'No companion, no guide for this journey.' There isn't any companion, no one to guide you on the path. Finally, the master too has to be dropped, because there is no space. Kabir says:

> The path of love is very narrow.
> There two cannot walk!

Where is the space for three to exist? Not even two can exist. The disciple, the master, the divine—they are three! There, not even two can exist. There, the master is dropped, you also are dropped. There, only the divine remains.

'No companion, no guide for this journey. What is this path I have set out on?' Sannyas is an unknown journey. A journey of great courage, of great daring! Those who are ready to accept the risk of going into the unknown—it is for them. It is not for the clever, those who calculate everything. It is not mathematics, it is a leap of love.

The third question:

Osho,
    You said, 'You are liberated here and now, this very moment.' But how can I get free of this 'I'?

If you ask 'how', you have missed. You didn't get it. This is Ashtavakra's whole message: practising; 'how' means practising. 'How' means by what method, by which rites and rituals. If you ask 'how', you have missed. Then you cannot understand Ashtavakra. Then you should go knock on Patanjali's door: he will tell you 'how'. If you are insistent upon this 'how', then Patanjali will be your path. He will tell you to do outer discipline, inner discipline, control, breath control, turning inward, concentration, meditation, samadhi. He will make it so extensive that even you will say, 'O lord, make it a little less. Tell me some easy method. This is too long, it will take many lives.'

Most yogis are only practising outer discipline; they never even reach to inner discipline. Most yogis die still trying to master asanas—yoga postures. Concentration is far away, meditation is far away. There are so many yoga postures it seems impossible to ever complete the training in them. At the very most, those who seek deeply reach the state of concentration—and the real happening can occur only in samadhi. And even samadhi Patanjali divides into two: samadhi with seed—with mind, and seedless samadhi—with no mind. He goes on dividing, he goes on making more and more steps. He makes steps all the way from the earth to the sky.

If 'how', if practising appeals to you, then ask Patanjali . . . even though, in the end, Patanjali also says to drop everything, enough of this 'doing'. But there are some people that cannot stop doing, so they will have to do.

Think of it like this: there is a child in the house making noise and causing mischief. You tell him, 'Sit quietly,' but even if he does, he will be bubbling over. His hands and feet will wriggle, his head will shake—he wants to do something, he is bursting with energy. This is no way to get him to sit still. It is dangerous—there can be an explosion. This way he is going to do something or other. It is better that you tell him, 'Go and run around the house seven times.' Then he will come back huffing and puffing and sit quietly on his own; you won't even have to say 'Be quiet.' He will sit quietly on the very chair that he could not sit quietly on before.

Patanjali is for those who cannot become quiet directly. He says, 'Run seven circuits. Run long and hard. Distort and twist your body; stand on your head; do this, do that.'

Doing all these practices, finally one day you will say, 'O lord, I am tired of this doing!'

He will say, 'You should have said so in the very beginning, then both of us would have been saved from all this bother. Now go and sit quietly!'

Man wants to do, because it just doesn't fit your logic that anything can happen without doing. Ashtavakra is beyond your logic. Ashtavakra says you are liberated! But you still misunderstand. Your question is, 'You said, "You are liberated here and now, this very moment." But how can I get free of this "I"?'

Ashtavakra says that 'how' exists only when one thinks he is not free. First, you have accepted that you are bound. Now, you say, 'How can I get free?' Ashtavakra says there is no bondage—only the illusion of bondage.

But you will still say, 'How can I get free of this illusion?' You still don't get it. Illusion means that which is not: so get free of what? Just watching, just being wakeful, you are free. If you get involved in methods, you will be in great difficulty.

> Every method proved false,
> Finally life itself proved too short.

If you get stuck in methods, you will find that not just this life but many lives will not be enough. Methods are many—

and for life after life you have gone on practising them. You put faith in doing because doing inflates your ego.

Ashtavakra is asking you not to do anything. The whole is the only doer. What is happening is happening—just become one with it. Don't even ask, 'How to get free of this "I"?' If this 'I' is happening, let it happen. Who are you to try to get free of it? You can also accept it: good, if this is happening, then this is what is happening. You didn't create it. Do you remember having it? You didn't give shape to it. You didn't bring it. How will you drop what you didn't bring? How will you destroy what you didn't create? You ask, 'What can we do?' You have two eyes and a nose; you also have an ego. You have received all of these. Nothing is in your hands.

Whatever exists is good. If 'I' exists, that too is good. Don't complain even a little about it. In this attitude of no complaint, in this total acceptance, you will suddenly find the 'I' is gone . . . because the 'I' is created from doing. When you do something, the 'I' is created.

Now you are asking something new: 'How can I destroy this "I"?' The one who destroys will become the 'I'. You will not be able to escape. This is why a humble man also has an ego—and sometimes it is bigger than an egoist's.

Have you seen the ego of the humble? The humble man says, 'I am just the dust at your feet.' But look into his eyes—what is it that he is saying? If you say, 'You are absolutely right, I knew already that you were just the dust at my feet', then he will start fighting. He is not saying it for you to agree. He is saying it so you will say, 'You are such a humble man . . . I am very fortunate to have met you.' He is saying it so you will refute it: 'You are dust at my feet? No, you are pure gold. You are the very spire of the temple.' The more highly you talk of him, the more he will say no, he is just dust. But when he says he is only dust, if you agree,

'You are absolutely right, everyone thinks that you are just dust at their feet', then he will never even look at you again. It was not humility; it was ego in a new colour, ego dressed in new clothes, ego dressed in humility.

So if you try to drop the 'I', the one who is dropping it will create a new 'I'. Man goes on changing costumes. The clothes change but you remain the same.

Try to understand what Ashtavakra is saying. Don't be too quick to ask what to do, how to get rid of this ego. Don't be in a hurry to do. Relax and take a little time to understand. Ashtavakra is saying, 'Understand how this "I" is created'—it is created by doing, it is created from striving and effort, it is created from success. So wherever you make an effort, it will be created. Then one thing becomes clear: if you want to be free of ego, then don't make any effort, don't try. Accept whatever is, just like it is. In this acceptance you will find the ego has disappeared as if it had never existed, because the element that was giving it energy has slipped out, the foundation has fallen down so the house cannot stand for long.

And if the feeling of being the doer falls away, then all of life's diseases fall away; otherwise there are many traps in life. Running after money is also the running of the doer. Running after power is also the running of the doer. Running after fame is also the running of the doer. You want to show something to the world.

Many people come to me saying, 'Tell us a way to show something to this world.' What is it you want to show? They say, 'No, it's just that we want to make a name for ourselves. We will be gone, but our name should remain behind!' What is the use of your name remaining? No one else is interested in your name. When you yourself are gone, who is going to bother? When you couldn't be saved from death, will your name be saved from dying? You cannot be kept alive; how can this name which is only an indication be saved? Who bothers about your name? So what if your name does remain? It will be hidden away in some old books, it will be grieving there. Alexander's name is there, Napoleon's name is there—so what?

But no, we have been taught these diseases since childhood. Since childhood we have been told, 'Do something before you die. Don't die without doing anything. If you can, do something good; if not, do something bad—but make a name for yourself.' People say, 'So what if you get a bad name?—at least your name is known. If you don't find the right way, then do something crazy, but make a name for yourself!'

People are so crazy that when they go to the mountains they inscribe their names in stone. When they go and visit an ancient castle they scribble their name on the walls. And the man writing his name doesn't see that he is rubbing out another name to write his: someone else will come and rub his out and write over it. You have erased someone else's, you are writing over others' writing—and in big letters. If someone else comes they will write in even bigger letters. What madness have you fallen into?

Beautiful longings have woven many webs of dream,
many trampled feelings have arisen with a brilliance.
The intoxication of beauty, the drunkenness of love,
the fame of name, the pride of wealth,
many are the spread out snares of illusion for man.
Each to his own destiny and each to his own nature,
many are there trampled by happiness,
many are there affluently rich with sorrow.
There is famine of humans, hard are the times for the
world,
many are the famines that have passed,

but when have such hard times come.
The wealth of the heart is rarely found,
though wealth is found aplenty,
many are the wealthy I saw whose hearts were paupers.
How many scenes are latent in the depths of
unconsciousness—
the world of consciousness is one,
the nether worlds of unconsciousness are many.

'How many scenes are latent in the depths of unconsciousness
. . .' This is our unconscious: in it so many scenes are
hidden—scene after scene, curtain behind curtain, stories
within stories! This is our unconscious: there are so many
hells hidden in it—of wealth, of power, of fame, of dreams
. . . the snares are set!

'How many scenes are latent in the depths of
unconsciousness—the world of consciousness is one, the
nether worlds of unconsciousness are many.' But one who
becomes aware—his world is one, his nature is one, his
being is one, his flavour is one. Buddha has said, 'Wherever
you taste the ocean, it is salty—likewise, if you taste me,
I am fully conscious all over. I have only one flavour:
consciousness.'

This is also the flavour of Ashtavakra. Not the doer, not
the one who enjoys and suffers—but the witness.

So don't ask 'How?' . . . because with 'how' the doer
comes in, the enjoyer comes in—then you miss, you miss
Ashtavakra's message. Ashtavakra is saying, 'Whatever
is, observe it. Be a witness. Just watch. If there is ego then
watch ego. What else to do? Only watch—and by watching,
transformation happens.'

Do you understand? It is a little subtle, but not so
subtle that you can't understand it. It is straightforward
also. Ashtavakra is saying to just observe; when you

observe, the doer disappears, only the witness remains. With the doer gone, everything that got energy from the doer, got strength from it, will fall away. Without the doer, how can one run after money, run after power? Without the doer, where is the ego? These will all fall away by themselves.

Master just one thing—the witness. There is nothing else to be done. Everything else happens by itself. Everything else goes on and on, always. Why should you uselessly get in the way?

I have heard:

An elephant was crossing over a bridge. The bridge started shaking under his weight. A fly was sitting on his trunk. When they both got to the other side, the fly said, 'Son! We really shook that bridge.'

The elephant said, 'Lady, until you spoke I didn't even realize you were here.'

You think you are shaking the bridge, but it is not you who is shaking the bridge, it is life energy. You are like a fly that sits on top of life energy and says, 'Son! Look how I have shaken it!'

This ego is just sitting on top of you. Everything is happening from your limitless energy. It is the energy of existence—you don't have anything to do with it. This same energy breathes in you, awakens in you, sleeps in you. And in between all this you stand there conceitedly. This much is certain: it doesn't take objection to your pride. At least the elephant objected. The elephant said, 'Lady, I didn't even realize you were sitting on top of me.' At least the elephant said this much. Existence doesn't even say this—it is silent. If you are conceited, it lets you be. If you lay claim to its work, it lets you. If you say you are doing something when in fact you have not done it, then too it doesn't intrude and say, 'No, I am doing it.' It has no 'I'; how can it tell you 'I am doing it'? So your illusion goes on and on.

But look closely, open your eyes a little and see. You are not doing anything. Everything is happening by itself.

This is the incomparable concept of destiny, the unparalleled concept of fate: everything is happening by itself. People have given it incorrect meanings, that is their fault. If you understand the idea of fate rightly, you will remain a witness and there will be nothing else to do. But people don't become a witness, they become lazy. They don't become non-doers, they become lazybones.

There is a difference between non-doing and idleness. Idleness is lazy, indolent, dead. Non-doing is full of energy—one doesn't think, 'I am doing,' but, 'Existence is doing, I am only watching. This play is going on, I am observing.'

Man is very tricky. He uses even the most beautiful truths in the ugliest way. Fate is a very beautiful truth. It means that everything goes on by itself, you are not doing anything. All is destined: what will be, will be; what is to be, is; what was to happen, has happened. You can sit quietly on the side and watch the play. There is no need for you to jump into the middle of it. Your running back and forth doesn't make any difference. What is to happen is happening; what will be, will be. Then you become a witness.

The idea of fate was devised to lead you to witnessing. But people have not moved into witnessing; they have become lazy. They say, 'When what is to be is happening, then good, why should we do anything? Fate means we have no power to do; why should we do?' Before, they said they will show the world; now they say there is nothing in doing! But the feeling of the doer hasn't gone; it remains standing in the same place.

If you understand Ashtavakra, then there is no method, there is no practice: Ashtavakra says practice is bondage, methods are bondage, doing itself is bondage.

The fourth question:

Osho,
    Through your grace I can see the sky. I experience light and become one with the inner current also. But when sex overtakes me, I want to drown in that just as much as in meditation. Please explain this condition of mine.

The first thing: be a witness of sex too. Don't be the controller of it, don't try to forcibly bring it under control; remain a witness of it too. Just as you are a witness of everything else, remain a witness of sex too.

It is difficult, because you have been taught for centuries that sex is sin. That concept of sin has been fixed in your mind. Sin does not exist in this universe—there is only godliness. Drop that idea. In this universe there is only one—it pervades all—it is godliness. It is in the tiniest of the tiny, in the most vast of the vast. It is in the lowest, in the highest. It is in sex, it is in samadhi too. There is no sin here.

This does not mean that I am suggesting that you remain stuck in sex. I am only saying: understand it too as a form of godliness. There are other forms. Perhaps the first level of its forms is sex. And there is a small taste of samadhi reflected in sexual experience, hence so much attraction. When greater samadhis start to happen, the attraction will disappear by itself.

The friend has said, getting absorbed in meditation, 'I become one with the flow within. But when sex overtakes me, I want to drown in that just as much.' Drown! There is no need to stop. Just remain a witness as you go on drowning. Go on observing that you are going under. Go on observing that sex has encircled you.

In fact the word 'sex' brings condemnation into the mind. Think of it this way: a kind of godliness has encircled you, this divine energy has encircled you, this divine nature has encircled you, the divine maya has encircled you. But don't use the word 'sex'. The old associations connected with the word are wrong; they make it appear like sin. Then it will be difficult to remain a witness—either you will become unconscious or you will control. To be a witness is neither to go unconscious nor to control—it is to stand firm between these two. On this side you fall in a ditch, on the other you fall in the well—remain in between; master this . . . then samadhi.

Both are easy: it is perfectly easy to go unconscious in sex, to completely forget what is going on. To get intoxicated is easy. To control sex, to force it to stop, to prevent yourself is also easy. But in both you miss. The one who indulges misses; the celibate misses too. The real brahmacharya happens when you stand in the middle, between these two— then you are only watching. Then you will find that sex arises in the body and reverberates in the body; in the mind a shadow briefly falls and departs. You remain standing far away. How can sexual desire be in you? How can any desire be in you? You are nothing but the observer.

And it usually happens that when meditation starts going well your sexual desire becomes stronger. Understand this, because it happens to most people. When meditation is going well, when you start relaxing into the rhythm of your life, tension is less. Then the suppression you have been forcing on sex for many lives will be gone. Then the repressed desire will arise like a volcano. So if sexual desire increases with meditation, don't worry; it is a good sign, indicating that meditation is progressing well. The meditation is doing good work. The meditation is getting rid of your tensions, removing your control, getting rid of your repressions. Meditation is taking you towards your naturalness.

First, meditation will make you natural, and then it will bring you to godliness . . . because it is impossible to bring what is not yet natural to its deeper nature. What is not yet natural cannot reach the divine. So meditation first brings you to nature, then brings you to the divine. Nature is the divine's outer covering. If you are not in tune with it, how can you be in tune with the innermost godliness? Nature is the steps of the temple. If you don't climb the steps, then how will you enter into the inner sanctum of the temple?

If you can understand what I am saying, then don't suppress any more. Now quietly accept it. What this existence shows to you will be good. Existence is presenting it, so it must be good. Neither control nor become the one who decides, nor stand back saying, 'This is good and that is bad'; 'I want to do this and don't want to do that.' Simply observe.

> Age is descending,
> the candle of desire is melting away,
> slowly, slowly the fire is burning out.
> Longings are settling,
> the flood of passions are ebbing,
> pleasures are ebbing,
> the colour of silence is deepening,
> the fire is burning out.

It is going well. But before the fire goes out, it will flare up one last time. You can ask the physicians—before dying a person becomes completely healthy for a little while. All symptoms disappear. One who was lying on the bed like a corpse sits up, opens his eyes and looks invigorated. Just before dying, all symptoms disappear, because life is making its last leap—the life energy arises once more.

You have seen when a clay lamp is going out it flares up one last time. As the last of the oil burns out, it drinks the last drop of oil and flares up. It is its last burst of flame. You have seen how dark the night is before dawn. It is the last burst of darkness.

It is the same when you go deep in meditation: you will find that when the fire is about to go out the last burst of flame . . . sex energy arises. 'Age is descending, the candle of desire is melting away.' The lamp of desire is melting, life is going out . . .

'Slowly, slowly the fire is burning out. Longings are settling, the flood of passions are ebbing.' The flow of life is stopping . . .

'Pleasures are ebbing, the colour of silence is deepening.' The juiciness of meditation is increasing. The juiciness of silence is deepening.

'The colour of silence is deepening, the fire is burning out.' In this state a burst of flame will flare up at any moment. Such a blaze is flaring up in you—observe it. Do not suppress it, otherwise it will move into you again. You are very close to getting free of it; don't suppress it, otherwise the bondage will start again. What has been suppressed will flare up again and again. Whatever you have forced down will come again and again. Let it go, let it come out, let it flow out. However high it flares up, you go on watching peacefully. It will not interfere with your meditation. You continue witnessing.

The fifth question:

Osho,
    You said don't fall into any bondage, be at peace and be happy. Is not sannyas also bondage? And are

not methods, devices and practice also bondage? Please
explain.

If you have understood, then don't ask. If you ask, then
you have not understood. If you have understood not to
get into any bondage and to be at peace and be happy, then
just by this understanding you will become happy and be
at peace. Then where did this question come from? Do
serene and happy people ask questions? All questions arise
from disease, from suffering, from misery. If you are still
asking questions then you are not yet at peace; you will need
sannyas initiation. If you become serene, then what need is
there of sannyas? You have become a sannyasin!

But don't deceive yourself. If you don't have the courage
to take sannyas, don't use Ashtavakra as an excuse. Yes,
if you have attained peace there is no need for sannyas. It
is in search of peace that one takes sannyas. If you have
become happy, if you think you have become happy, if you
have become as worthy as Janak, then the matter is finished.
But then this question would not have arisen. Janak did not
ask questions, Janak said, 'Amazing, master! Then I am
liberated! It is surprising how I have been under the spell
of maya until right now!' If you are ready like Janak you
would say, 'I am blessed! I am liberated! I have been under
the spell of maya until right now!' You wouldn't be asking
this question.

The truth is, in your mind, you have the desire to take
sannyas, but you don't have the courage. While listening to
Ashtavakra you thought, 'It is good to know that sannyas is
bondage; now there is no need to get into it.' Will you drop
your other bondages, or only the bondage of sannyas? And
you are not yet a sannyasin—there is no way to drop what
you don't even have. What other enslavements will you
drop? Will you leave your wife? Your home? Your money?

Your power? Your mind? The doer? Will you drop your ego? Of what you have, what else will you drop?

Certainly it is only possible for you to drop what you have. Let sannyasins ask this question, those that have become sannyasins. You have not yet taken sannyas. It would be understandable if a sannyasin asked if now he should drop sannyas. He has sannyas, you don't. How will you drop what you don't have? Ask about what you do have. Ask whether you should renounce your house and home.

Hearing everything that Ashtavakra has been saying, is this all you could understand, that sannyas initiation is bondage? Is nothing else bondage?

Man is cunning. The mind is deceptive, the mind is very calculating: 'If I can extract the meaning I want, then it is very good, then I can avoid trouble. I was very hesitant about taking sannyas; it is good I have met Ashtavakra on the way. He has explained well, he has put me right; now there is no need to make the mistake of taking sannyas.'

Will you learn anything else from Ashtavakra?

People come to me saying, 'Shall we drop meditation now? Because Ashtavakra says there is bondage in meditation.' Will you drop wealth, will you drop power? Or only meditation? And meditation hasn't happened yet—but you will drop it? If meditation has happened and you ask, 'Shall I drop it?' I will say, 'Drop it.'

But one who is meditating will never ask about dropping, he is beyond dropping and holding on to. He will understand Ashtavakra, he will be blissful, filled with joy. He will say, 'Great, it is absolutely true: in meditation, meditation itself is dropping away. In sannyas, bondages are dropping by themselves. Sannyas is no bondage. It is only a device for dropping all bondage. In the end, it too will drop.'

Understand it like this: you get a thorn in your foot, then you use another thorn as a needle to take the first one out. The second thorn is also a thorn, but it is useful in removing the first thorn. Then you throw both of them away. You don't keep the second thorn thinking it has done a great kindness in removing the first thorn. Or, thinking how very loving it is, you don't put the second thorn back into the same place where the first thorn was stuck.

Sannyas is a needle. The thorn of the world is stuck in you—this is a way to take it out. If you can pull it out without a needle, that's even better. What could be more of a blessing than your understanding Ashtavakra? Then there would be no need for sannyas. But make sure you aren't deceiving yourself! If it is deception, then be courageous and jump into sannyas. And that moment will also come when you will be worthy of dropping sannyas too.

But what is there to drop? When you understand, then there is nothing to drop—everything has fallen away. This is what Janak has said, 'O lord, this body has also dropped.' Janak is still in the body, the body hasn't fallen away, but Janak says, 'This body has also dropped! This whole world has dropped. Everything has dropped. I am completely unattached, beyond emotions. What great skill there is in your teaching. What an art. Nothing has happened, I have not left the palace, not left the world, not left the body—and yet I have left everything!'

The day you understand it, there is nothing to drop—not the world and not sannyas. The very idea of dropping comes only to the man who thinks there is something to hold on to.

Renunciation is just the shadow of indulgence. The renunciate is a worldly person standing on his head. When the world goes, renunciation also goes. These two live together and leave together. This is why you see the worldly at the feet of the renunciate—they are together. The renunciate does half the job, the worldly does the other half—they are joined together. The worldly cannot live without the renunciate; the renunciate cannot live without the worldly. Have you seen this conspiracy?

A man came to me, saying, 'I want to learn to meditate.'

He was a sannyasin, an old-fashioned sannyasin. So I said, 'Good—come to the morning meditation.'

He said, 'That is a little difficult.'

I said, 'Why, what's difficult about it?'

He said, 'The difficulty is, I cannot come without this man who has come with me, because he keeps the money, I don't touch money. He has to go somewhere else in the morning, so I won't be able to come tomorrow morning.'

This is just hilarious! If you need money, what difference does it make whether it is in your pocket or in someone else's? And this becomes another bondage—the one who keeps the money in his pocket is better off than you, at least he can go wherever he wants. It is a peculiar situation: unless this man comes along, you cannot come because you need to have money for the taxi—but you don't touch money! So you are having this man sin for you? Commit your own sins! This is great fun—you will ride in the taxi and he will go to hell for it! Have a little compassion for him. This is the great connection of the worldly and the renunciate!

All your renunciates live bound to worldly people. And your worldly people also live bound to the renunciate, because they touch the feet of the renunciate thinking, 'Today I am not a renunciate, but at least I can touch the feet of one. I can get the satisfaction of having done something! If not today, then tomorrow I too will become a renunciate. But right now I can worship him.'

If you ask Jainas where they are going, they say they are going to serve the sadhu. Serving him, they think, is a gain—earning some merit. There the sadhu sits, looking down the road to see when the worldly person is coming. Here the worldly are looking to see when the sadhu will come to town. The worldly and the sadhus—two sides of the same coin.

Think a little: if the worldly people stop going to the sadhus, how many sadhus will remain? They will all start running away. Who will organize things, who will make all the arrangements? They will all go. But the worldly go on taking care of the sadhus, and the sadhus go on taking care of the worldly—it is mutual.

The really wise man is neither a renunciate nor indulgent. He only knows, 'I am the witness.' Now what difference does it make whether the money is in his pocket or in someone else's pocket? He is the witness. If it is, he is a witness; if it is not, he is a witness. Poor, he is a witness; rich he is a witness. In witnessing, what difference is there between poverty and wealth? Do you think that if a beggar becomes a witness his witnessing will be a little less, and if an emperor becomes a witness his witnessing will be a little more? Can witnessing ever be less or more? Poor or rich, healthy or unhealthy, well-read or illiterate, beautiful or ugly, famous or infamous—it makes no difference.

Witnessing is a treasure that is in equal measure inside everyone, there is no less or more to it.

We can be a witness of every circumstance—success, failure; respect, disrespect.

Be a witness, this is all Ashtavakra is saying.

But if you find it is difficult to be a witness and you want to use some method, then use a method, don't be afraid. Continuing to use the method helps you to become the witness of the method too. This is why I say, meditate, and don't worry about it . . . because I know that if you don't meditate you will never come to witnessing, by not meditating you will only continue thinking. So the choice is not between meditation and witnessing, the choice is between thinking and meditation.

Do you understand what I am saying? If you don't meditate . . . You have heard Ashtavakra, Ashtavakra said that meditation and methods are bondage. And he is absolutely right, 100 per cent correct! So you stop meditating. What will it do? Will you now become a witness? No, you will just go on repeating the same old rotten thoughts. It is so hilarious: because of Ashtavakra you have fallen deeper into the world. This ladder is for you to climb up! You have started using it to descend! The same steps!

I tell you to meditate because the alternatives before you are meditation and thinking: right now witnessing is not an alternative for you. Yes, if you continue to meditate your thoughts will be finished, then a new choice will present itself. Now you can choose: witnessing or meditating? Then you can choose witnessing, and meditating can be dropped.

But if you decide not to take sannyas you will remain indulgent. Now the choice is between sannyas and the world. I say, take sannyas now, and one day the moment will come when the choice is no longer between the world and sannyas. The world is gone; sannyas remains. Then the choice is between ultimate sannyas and sannyas. Then I will tell you: forget about sannyas, now merge yourself into ultimate sannyas. Yes, if you can go immediately, like Janak, then I am not going to object. Be joyous! Be happy! If you can't, then no one else can decide for you. If you are not able to be happy, you will have to decide what you need to do.

You can turn truth into untruth, and you can even turn flowers into thorns—it all depends on you.

> Don't run with closed eyes in the light,
> my naive heart!
> The routes are all unknown.
> On the path you encounter thorns and rocks.
> Just smelling a delicate fragrance,
> don't believe there are only flowers.

Remember, take your steps carefully. The step you take shouldn't be chosen just by the sweetness of a delicate fragrance.

'On the path, you encounter thorns and rocks. Just smelling a delicate fragrance, don't believe there are only flowers.' When a delicate fragrance comes to you, be careful that it is not just your projection, that it is not just your greed, that it is not just your fear, that it is not just your weakness that you are projecting. And don't be led astray by that sweet, soft smell.

It appears very easy—not to do anything. It seems easy when you hear it, but when you come to not doing anything, then there is nothing harder. Hearing about witnessing it seems so simple—that there is nothing to do, you only have to watch. When you come to do it you will find, 'Oh! This is tremendously hard!'

Try this: sit down with your watch in front of you. The second hand makes its round in one minute. Look at the second hand, witness its movement and try to go on witnessing it. You will find it moves two to four seconds— and the witness is gone! Some other thought has come. You forgot. You will be shocked that the second hand has slipped on ahead. Then you will be a witness for two to four seconds, and forget again. In completing one minute you will lose it two, four or ten times. You cannot remain a witness for even one minute.

So right now there is no question of the witness. Now you can choose thinking or meditation. Then, eventually, choosing between meditation and witnessing will become possible.

You ask about sannyas. Sannyas is only a gesture that you want to be with me. It is not a commitment—you are not bound to me. I do not give you any discipline. I give no rules of conduct. I don't tell you when to get up, what to eat, what to drink, what to do, what not to do. I only tell you to be a witness. I only tell you my hand is available, take my hand in yours. Perhaps taking a few steps with me, you will also catch my disease. This disease is contagious. Walk a little with Buddha and you will be dyed a little by his colour. You won't be able to prevent it. Some of his fragrance will begin to emanate from you too. If you pass through a garden, the fragrance of the flowers gets into your clothes—even if you didn't touch the flowers!

Sannyas is just showing a little courage to move with me, an expression of wanting to be with me. It is falling in love with me. The whole idea behind this love is that I am making arrangements for you to be free. Move with me—I want to give you the fragrance of liberation.

I am a puppet of the breath.
I am tied to old age.
And to death I am given over.
But there is this thing called love, you know!
By it, I have been liberated.
This weapon of time eternal, a weight impossible to bear,
is balanced by one miraculous childlike moment.

What are you? 'I am a puppet of the breath. I am tied to old age. And to death I am given over.' Birth and death, this is all that you are. Breath comes in and goes out, and in between there is a brief tale, a short drama. If there is anything here that can take you beyond death and birth . . .

'But there is this thing called love, you know! By it, I have been liberated.' If love happens between life and death . . .

Sannyas means to fall in love with me, nothing more than this. This is enough, this is the definition. If you are in love with me and are ready to move with me a little way, then moving that little way will take you a great distance.

And everything else is superficial: changing the colour of your clothes, wearing the mala. These are only to awaken courage and to help you remember your being. These are only outer beginnings, then much happens inside. Those you are seeing in these dyed orange clothes, don't look only at their clothes, take a look into their hearts too—you will find a new stream of love beginning to arise.

'But there is this thing called love, you know! By it, I have been liberated.' Let me rain over you. Even if you are stone right now, don't worry: this stream of water will cut through your rock.

> When the ray of light showered on me,
> I said—
> 'I am as hard as diamond, a stone eternal.'
> The ray said, 'Is it so?
> You are the very one I have been searching for.
> I will sculpt a temple out of you.
> From your interiority I will carve a statue of light.'
> I was speechless,
> the ray cradled me in her deep love.

'When the ray of light showered on me, I said, "I am as hard as diamond, a stone eternal."' You also say this to me,

'No, you cannot change us. We are stone, very ancient—we have taken a vow not to be transformed.'

But I say unto you:

'The ray said, "Is it so? You are the very one I have been searching for. I will sculpt a temple out of you. From your interiority I will carve a statue of light." I was speechless, the ray cradled me in her deep love.'

These orange clothes are only an indication of my love—of your love towards me, of my love towards you. This is a love tie.

The last question:

> Osho,
>
> O sweet beloved, accept my gratitude. Give these tears their destination. You have filled this begging bowl, but still I am as empty as ever, blank, unwritten. Oh sweet beloved, our friend, this head, like the fruit for offering, is at your feet.

Jaya has asked this. She has been close to me for many years. She has a heart exactly like that of Meera. In her heart a song just like Meera's is waiting. In her heart a dance just like Meera's is hidden. When it appears, she will manifest her greatness; then another Meera will appear. Just waiting for the right moment . . . any time the ray of light will descend and chase away the darkness. And she is courageous—this is why a prediction can be made that it will happen.

> But is not this very mist the ongoing gift
> in which your cloud-like compassion
> is showering day and night.
> The shadow that peeps in once in a while

is the ultimate language, the only possible name—
O, abode of compassion.
This is the seed mantra,
this is the essence of essences,
this is the only scale for measure of depth,
this is our grateful bowing down.
How deep is thy mist-covered well—
how tiny our hands.

Facing the divine our hands always appear small! The cup of our palms is so small.

'How deep is thy mist-covered well—how tiny our hands.' Whoever has love in their heart, they always feel how small their hands are.

Jaya has asked: 'O sweet beloved, accept my gratitude. Give these tears their destination. You have filled this begging bowl, but still I am as empty as ever—blank, unwritten.'

This is the kind of filling that makes one become more and more empty. This is a filling of emptiness. This is filling up with emptiness. My effort is to make you blank. If you have become blank then I have succeeded. If you remain full then I have failed. When you become absolutely blank and nothing more remains inside of you—no trace, no word, no rubbish—in this emptiness the divine manifests.

I want to say to Jaya:

Go, O soul go,
virgin girl, become a bride,
his companion.
Now that great void is thy only path.
Your destination: protector of grains and water.
The bridegroom: the nature of light.
It alone will make you joyous, thrilled.
O, soul! You are chosen.

O united one.
O wedded one,
thy wedding with the great void is celebrated.

'Thy wedding with the great void is celebrated.' This being empty, this being blank, is to celebrate your wedding with the great void. Dancing, letting that great ecstasy manifest, singing, ecstatic—you have to lose yourself!

There is only one way of being—disappearing more and more.

The moment you become totally empty, immediately the divine descends in its totality. You are the only barrier. So don't be afraid. When you become blank, you have achieved all.

A story from Maharashtra:

Once Eknath wrote a letter to Nivrittinath. He sent blank paper, nothing written on it. Nivrittinath read it very thoroughly—a blank sheet of paper with nothing to read on it. He really got into it, reading it again and again and again.

Muktabai was sitting nearby, and he gave it to her and she read it. Her tears started flowing . . . she was completely gone! Other people were present, and they started saying, 'This is sheer madness! First, Eknath is mad sending a blank sheet of paper. A letter means that something is written! Then this Nivrittinath is mad to be reading it, not just once but time and again. Then strangest of all, this Muktabai, she is completely gone and her tears start flowing!'

All scriptures are blank paper, and if you learn how to read blank paper, then you know how to read all the scriptures—the Vedas, the Koran, the Guru Granth, the Gita, the Upanishads, the Bible, the Dhammapada.

One who can read blank paper achieves everything.

My whole effort here is that you become like blank sheets. I am trying to obliterate you, because *you* are the only barrier.

> Go, O soul go,
> young girl naive and virgin,
> thy wedding with the great void is celebrated.

Hari-om-tat-sat!

9

I Bow Down to Myself

Janak said: Light is my self-nature. I am not other than that. When the universe is illuminated, it is illuminated by my light.

Amazing that through ignorance the imaginary world appears in me, just as silver appears in mother-of-pearl, a snake in a rope, or a mirage in the rays of the sun.

The universe which has emanated from me will dissolve into me, just as a pot dissolves into clay, a wave into water, or a bracelet into gold.

Amazing am I, I bow down to myself. When the whole world shall perish, from Brahma down to the very blade of grass, I shall not perish. I am eternal.

Amazing am I, I bow down to myself. Although embodied, I am the non-dual. I neither go anywhere nor come from anywhere; I just exist, I pervade the universe.

Amazing am I, I bow down to myself. None here is as capable as I, who have been maintaining the universe for an eternity without even touching it with the body.

Amazing am I, I bow down to myself. I have nothing at all, or I have all that can be encompassed by speech or thought.

RELIGION IS EXPERIENCE, not thinking. Thought cannot be even the shadow of religion. And one who is entangled in thoughts will always remain far away from religion. No one is further away from religion than a thinker.

Just as love is an experience, godliness is also an experience. And if you want to experience it, it is possible only through one's totality.

The process of thinking is only a small fragment of man, and a very superficial one. It has no depth. It is not part of man's interiority, not of the centre, it is on the periphery. Even if thinking stops, man can live. And now, thinking machines have been developed. They make it very clear that a machine too can think—it is no special glory of man.

Aristotle and thinkers like him have called man the thinking animal, the rational animal. This definition should be changed, because now computers can think—and with greater efficiency, with greater skill, than man. Man makes mistakes, but with computers there is no possibility of error. Man's greatness is not in his thinking. Man's greatness is in his ability to experience.

Just as when you taste something, the taste is not just a thought—it happens, it happens in your very cells. You are immersed in the joy of tasting. When you drink wine, the effects of drinking are not only in your thoughts; your legs begin wobbling.

Have you seen a drunkard walking? The wine has reached his very cells. It is visible in his stride, in his eyes; it is visible in every move. It doesn't just show in his thoughts but encompasses his totality.

Religion is like wine—one who drinks it will know. One who drinks it and becomes delighted will experience it.

Janak's words were uttered in a moment when he was filled with this wine. If you consider them without tasting, there is a possibility of misunderstanding and his meaning will seem something quite different. Then you will add your own interpretations.

For example, when Krishna says in the Gita, 'Drop everything, Arjuna, and surrender at my feet,' when you read it, you will feel this declaration is very egotistical: 'Drop everything, Arjuna, and come to my feet.' To *my* feet!

The meaning you give to this 'my' is your meaning, not Krishna's. In Krishna, no 'I' remains—it is just a reference, it is only a symbol. For you the symbol is much more. In your state of illusion, the symbol has become the truth. For Krishna it is merely practical, not indicating anything more.

You have seen: if someone spits on the national flag it will cause a fight, it will result in bloodshed, it can cause a war. 'He spat on the national flag!' But have you ever thought that the national flag is a symbol of the nation and you spit on the nation every day, but nobody starts fighting? Nobody starts a fight if you spit on the earth. Whenever you spit you are spitting on the nation—wherever you spit. Nobody starts a fight if you spit on the nation. The symbol of the nation, merely an indication, just an ordinary piece of cloth . . . but if someone spits on it then even war can happen.

Man gives great importance to symbols—more importance than they have. In his blindness man lives in symbols.

When Krishna uses the word 'I' it is only practical. He has to speak so he uses it. He wants to communicate so he uses it. But after speaking there is no 'I'. If you look into Krishna's eyes you will not find any 'I', there is only ultimate silence, only emptiness. The 'I' has disappeared. This is why Krishna can easily say, 'Come, come to my feet!' When he says to come to his feet, we feel it is very egotistical, because we interpret 'I' as we know it.

These words of Janak will surprise you even more. These statements are unique on this earth. Krishna had at least said, 'Come to my feet.' These assertions of Janak are such that you will not believe them.

Janak says in them, 'Amazing, my nature! Amazing, my light! Surprising! What am I? I go to my own feet! I bow down to myself!' It will shock you.

In these statements Janak bows down to himself; the other no longer remains. He says again and again, *Amazing am I, I bow down to myself. I am eternal.* 'I am so filled with awe, I myself am in wonder. I bow down to myself, because all will perish, but still I will remain. From Brahma to the smallest atoms, all will be destroyed, but still I will remain. I bow down to myself. Who is as capable as me? I am in the world and yet unattached' . . . in the water like a lotus leaf. 'I bow down to myself.'

Mankind has never heard such a declaration: 'I bow down to my very self.' You will think, 'This is the ultimate egotism. It would be all right if he said it to others, but he is touching his own feet!'

It is said that an artist came and painted Ramakrishna's portrait. When he brought the completed portrait, the devotees of Ramakrishna felt very strange because Ramakrishna looked at the picture and started to touch the feet in it. It was his own picture, and he began to bow down to it. A devotee said, 'Paramahansa, are you going mad? This is your own picture.'

Ramakrishna said, 'It's good you reminded me—I was seeing a picture of samadhi. It must have been painted while I was in samadhi. It's good you remind me, otherwise people will think I am crazy. I was just starting to pay my respects to samadhi. This is a picture of samadhi, not of me.' But those who saw it must have thought that the man had gone mad. Touching the feet of his own picture! Bowing his head to his own picture! What can be more insane? 'This is the last word in egotism, there can be no heights of ego beyond this.'

Janak is making these statements in ecstasy. The taste has arisen and he has become oblivious to everything else. If he could dance, he would dance like Meera. If he could sing, he would sing like Chaitanya. If he could play the flute, he would play on his flute like Krishna. Each individual has his own unique possibilities of expression. Janak was an emperor, a cultured man, a well-educated person, he was brilliant, the essence of brilliance—his statements are worthy of being written in gold letters in the history of man. To understand these words, put aside your own interpretations.

A poet says:

For some days I'm going sightseeing in this world,
the life of man is a window for seeing.
What kind of thing is this intellect
which stops my joyful heart in every activity,
which interferes with everything.
Creating beauty with meaning is the inspiration of a poet.
Getting entangled in words
is the art of the mere rhymester.
What kind of thing is this intellect
which stops my joyful heart in every activity,
which interferes with everything.

Whenever waves arise in the heart, the intellect immediately stops them. Whenever some feeling goes deep, the intellect immediately starts meddling.

'What kind of thing is this intellect which stops my joyful heart in every activity, which interferes with everything.' Put this intellect aside a little—just for a little while, just for a moment. In these moments, the clouds will scatter and the sun will be seen. If you cannot put this intellect aside, it will go on interfering. It is in the habit of questioning. Its nature is to interfere, its juice is in meddling. And religion comes through the heart—those heart waves will be spoiled. The mind will influence them and they will be lost. Your understanding will be completely wrong.

'Creating beauty with meaning is the inspiration of the poet.' A real poet, a seer, a sage, they give all their attention to meaning: 'Creating beauty with meaning is the inspiration of a poet'—in his imagination the flowers of meaning blossom, the fragrance of meaning arises.

'Getting entangled in words is the art of the mere rhymester.' But one who is just rhyming verses gets entangled in words—he is not a poet. The rhyme-maker just goes on joining words to words. He has no use for meaning—getting words to fit together is enough.

Intellect is a rhyme-maker, a rhymester. The secret of meaning, the mystery of meaning is hidden in the heart. You will be able to listen only when you put aside the mind.

I have heard that Mulla Nasruddin went into a cloth shop and asked about a particular cloth, 'Brother, what is the price of this cloth?'

The shopkeeper said, 'Mulla, it's five rupees per metre.'

Mulla said, 'Will you give it to me for four and a half rupees?'

The shopkeeper said, 'Sir, it would cost me four and a half rupees if I took it home.'

So Mulla said, 'Good, that's fine. I'll just take it home.'

Man goes on putting his own interpretations on things.

A patient asked a dentist, 'Can you pull a tooth without pain?'

The dentist said, 'Not always. Just yesterday I dislocated my wrist while pulling out someone's tooth.'

The dentist has his own pain. The one who came to have a tooth pulled has other worries, his own pain.

Mulla Nasruddin was given a job somewhere. The boss said, 'When you were given this job, you said that you never got tired—and now you are sleeping with your feet stretched out on the desk.'

Mulla said, 'Boss, this is the secret of my not getting tired.'

We go on interpreting our own way. And as long as we go on interpreting, the meaning of the sutras will not be apparent. A special art is needed to read sutras. To read sutras, a mind free of projections is needed, a mind emptied of projections. Reading sutras, don't be in a hurry to interpret: the capacity of listening, of tasting, of relishing joyfully and patiently is needed.

Listen to these sutras:

Light is my self-nature. I am not other than that. When the universe is illuminated, it is illuminated by my light.

Janak says this whole universe is illuminated by 'my light'. Certainly this light Janak is talking about cannot be the light of the 'I'. This light can only be a light void of 'I'. So don't look at the language, don't be a rhyme-maker, don't let the intellect meddle. The meaning is plain and simple; don't twist and distort it.

Light is my self-nature. If one is to speak, one has to speak this way, because language belongs to the ignorant. The enlightened have no language. If two enlightened ones meet, they remain silent. What is there to say? There is neither language nor anything to say; neither any subject to speak on nor the language to say it in.

It is said that when Farid and Kabir met, they remained silent for two days. They took each other's hands in their own, they embraced each other, tears flowed in streams, they began swaying in great ecstasy. Their disciples freaked out. The disciples had a great expectation: 'If they speak together, it will shower on us too. If they say something, we can also hear it. If we catch even a single word, it will give meaning to life.'

But they didn't speak. Two days passed . . . those two days became very long. The disciples were waiting while Kabir and Farid sat silently. Finally, when they had left, when Kabir had seen Farid off, Farid's disciples asked, 'What happened? Why didn't you speak? Ordinarily you are always speaking. If we ask anything, you speak. And we had brought you together with Kabir in the hope that there would be some talk between you, some juice would flow, so that we unfortunate ones could also drink a little of it. We brought the two riverbanks together so that if the Ganges flowed we could bathe in it, but the Ganges didn't flow. What happened?'

Farid explained: 'There was nothing to be said between Kabir and me, nor any language to say it in. Neither anything to ask, nor anything to say. Much was present there, a current was flowing, the Ganges flowed but not in words—in silence.'

Kabir's disciples asked him the same thing: 'What happened? Why did you become silent? It seemed as if you were a deaf mute!'

Kabir said, 'Idiots! If I speak in front of Farid, I prove myself ignorant. Whoever speaks proves himself ignorant. Where not speaking will do, there is no question of speaking. Where a needle can do the job, only a madman raises a sword. It was already happening without speaking. An immense stream was flowing. Didn't you see how the tears were flowing, what ecstasy there was?'

Words are not needed between two enlightened ones. Between two unenlightened ones there are words heaped upon words, but without any meaning. Between two enlightened ones there are meanings within meanings, but without any words. Between an enlightened one and an unenlightened one there are both words and meaning. For dialogue, an enlightened one and an unenlightened one are needed.

Between two unenlightened people there will be argument. Dialogue is not possible, conversation is not possible; only a clashing of minds is possible.

Between two enlightened ones there is no verbal conversation. In some deeper world, their centres are meeting. Union is happening, what need is there for conversation? Without speaking it is communicated; without talking about it, they both see it.

The possibility of dialogue exists between an unenlightened and an enlightened person. If the enlightened one is ready to speak and the unenlightened is ready to listen, then dialogue is possible.

In one sense, the meaning of scriptures is always paradoxical . . . because what the scripture says cannot be said; it is an attempt to say the unsayable. It is a great kindness that innumerable enlightened ones have tried to say that which cannot be said. They have wanted us to lift our eyes to where we have long forgotten to lift them. They have given us a glimpse of the sky. We crawl and wriggle along the ground—we have stopped raising our heads.

It is said that when Mansoor was captured and tied up he began to laugh. A crowd of one hundred thousand had gathered and someone asked, 'Mansoor, why are you laughing?'

Mansoor said, 'I am laughing because, yes, it is good that I have been tied up here—at least you have raised your eyes a little bit!'

He was hung up so high that people had to lift their faces to see him. So Mansoor said, 'At least now you had to raise your eyes towards the sky, even though my death is the excuse. So I am happy—this persecution is right. Perhaps when looking up at me you will see what it is hidden within me. Perhaps in this moment of death, from the impact of this death, your thought processes will stop, and for a moment the sky will open and you will have a glimpse of that one that I am.'

Light is my self-nature. I am not other than that. 'I am not separate from this light.' This inner source of light is achieved when the 'I' has gone. But how can one say it? When it is to be described, then the 'I' has to be brought in again.

'When the universe is illuminated it is illuminated by my light only.' Certainly Janak is not talking here about the person named Janak. That person has disappeared, that individual wave is gone—only the ocean remains. This ocean is everyone's. This declaration of Janak's is not only about himself, it is also about you. It is about everyone who has ever been, it is about everyone who will ever be. This proclamation is for the whole existence.

Learn to be obliterated, then the taste of this will start coming. And when the taste comes, declarations like this will arise from you too. It is difficult to stop them.

Mansoor knew that if he makes this sort of statement— 'Ana'l haq—I am the truth, I am the divine existence'—then he will be killed. The Mohammedan crowd will not be able to tolerate him. This crowd of blind people will not be able to see him. Still he proclaimed it. His friends told him not to make such claims, these proclamations would be dangerous. Mansoor also knew that it would be dangerous, but he could not stop giving such declarations.

When a flower blossoms, its fragrance will have to be shared. When a lamp is lit, its light will have to spread. Then whatever happens happens.

One of Rahim's sayings is: 'The juice of the betel nut, blood, coughing, joy, enmity, love, drunkenness: Rahim says these cannot be hidden, the whole world will know.'

There are some things that cannot be suppressed. In drinking ordinary wine how can you suppress its effects? It usually happens that the more a drinker tries to hide his drunkenness, the more it shows. Have you ever noticed a drunkard trying hard to prevent anyone from knowing? He speaks very cautiously, and this caution gives him away. He tries to walk with great care, and this is what makes him stagger. He wants to show his alertness so no one will know.

Mulla Nasruddin came home drunk one night. As he was returning, he thought hard how to keep his wife from knowing. What should he do? He thought, 'Let me read the Koran. Has anyone heard of a drunk reading from the Koran? If I read the Koran, then it will be clear that I am not drunk. Have drunkards ever read the Koran?'

He got home, lit a lamp and sat reading the Koran. Finally his wife came and gave him a good jerk, saying 'Stop this nonsense! What are you doing, sitting here with this suitcase open?'

How can a drunkard find the Koran? He had taken the suitcase, opened it and had started reading!

It is impossible to conceal it. And when ordinary wine cannot be hidden, how can divine wine be hidden? Ecstasy will be reflected in the eyes, the eyes will become intoxicated. The flavour of another world will colour one's speech. The speech will become rainbow-like, spreading over all seven colours. Speaking, ordinary prose becomes pure poetry. Talk, and it sounds just like a song. Move, and it feels like a dance. No, it cannot be hidden, it goes on being revealed. Truth is always revealed, it is its nature. As soon as truth happens within you, your declaration starts unknowingly being disclosed.

Janak did not say these words after thinking it over: he would have hesitated to say them if he had thought about it. He had just brought Ashtavakra there, Ashtavakra said a few things and Janak's enlightenment happened!

He would have held back if he considered it intellectually, thinking, 'What will Ashtavakra think: an ignorant man like me saying such things? This is appropriate only to realized ones. Does it ever happen so quickly? Just by hearing about it, can it happen? Has it ever happened this way? It takes time, it takes many lives, it is a very arduous journey. It is like walking on the edge of a sword.' He would have remembered all this and thought to himself, 'Don't make such a far-reaching declaration!'

But I want to remind you that this declaration is happening by itself. It is not right to say that Janak is speaking, it will be more correct to say it is being said through Janak.

Amazing that through ignorance the imaginary world appears in me, just as silver appears in mother-of-pearl, a snake in a rope, or a mirage in the rays of the sun.

Just like the illusion of silver appearing in mother-of-pearl, like the projection in the dark of a snake on a rope and like the illusion of an oasis appearing in a desert because of the sun's rays—like this, mirages are born.

Amazing! The happening happened so suddenly, it happened so forcefully—his enlightenment happened so quickly that Janak could not contain it. He was filled with awe . . . as if a small child had entered into the world of fairies. Everything captivates him and everything is beyond belief.

Tertullian has said: 'As long as I had not seen God, there was disbelief. And when I saw God, then too there was disbelief.'

His disciples said: 'We don't understand. We have heard that when one sees God then faith comes.'

Tertullian said, 'As long as one has not seen, there is disbelief: How can God exist? Impossible! How can there be faith without experience? And when the experience of God happens, then one cannot believe that so much bliss is possible. So much light, so much nectar—it still seems impossible.

When it hasn't happened, it seems impossible, and when it happens, it seems even more absurd.'

Janak is in exactly the same state: 'Amazing! Everything is just imagined. Only I am true, only the witness is true. All else is illusory, everything else is maya.'

> The universe which has emanated from me will dissolve into me, just as a pot dissolves into clay, a wave into water, or a bracelet into gold.

Do you see the transformation? Janak's human form is disappearing and his divine form is manifesting.

Swami Ramateertha went to America. Someone asked him who created the universe. Ramateertha was an ecstatic person, and he must have been in ecstasy, it must have been a moment of samadhi: he said, 'I did.' In America no one is going to listen to such a thing. Here it is all right, in India it is accepted, even this kind of expression is accepted. It became a great sensation there.

People asked, 'Are you in your senses? You made the moon and stars?'

Ramateertha said, 'I made them. I set them in motion, and they have been moving ever since.'

To understand this statement is difficult. And it is not surprising that his American listeners couldn't understand. It is natural. This statement is not Ramateertha's, or if it is, it is the real Rama's—not Ramateertha's. At this moment Ramateertha is not speaking as a wave, he is speaking as the ocean. He is speaking as the eternal, the immortal; not speaking as the momentary; not speaking as a man limited and defined by body and mind—speaking as the one beyond body and mind, indefinable, unknown. It is Rama speaking through Ramateertha, not Ramateertha himself. This declaration is from existence itself. But it is very difficult, very hard to accept it.

Ramateertha returned to India and went on a pilgrimage to the source of the Ganges. He had been bathing in the Ganges, and then he climbed a mountain and jumped to his death into the river. He left behind a short note that said, 'Now Ramateertha goes to meet his original form. The call has come—now I cannot stay in this body. The universe has called me!'

The newspapers printed the news that he had committed suicide. It is true, the newspapers were also right. He jumped into the river and committed suicide. But if anyone could ask Ramateertha, he would say, 'You say I committed suicide? I only dissolved the boundaries and became one with the universe. I removed the barrier in between. I have not died. I was as if dead; now I have become alive, now I am one with the universe. Now that small stream of life has become the ocean. I let go of the limitation, not of life itself. Now I have achieved real life, by letting go of the limitation.'

So it is necessary always to remember this, that when samadhi becomes stronger inside you, when the clouds of samadhi gather within you, the rain is not of your ego, your 'I'-ness. That rain is coming from beyond you, it transcends you.

In this moment Janak's personality is dissolving. The universe which has emanated from me will dissolve into me, just as a pot dissolves into clay, a wave into water, or a bracelet into gold.

> When nothing was, God was.
> Had nothing been created, God would still be.
> It is my own existence that has drowned me.
> Had I not been, what would I have been?

'It is my own existence that has drowned me.' We will say Ramateertha committed suicide. Ramateertha will say, 'It is my own existence that had kept me drowned . . . it was when I drowned in the Ganges that for the first time I began to exist. As long as 'I' was, I was drowned.'

As Ghalib says: 'When nothing was, God was. Had nothing been created, God would still be. It is my own existence that has drowned me. Had I not been, what would I have been?' God would have been! Existence would have been!

This 'I', this limitation of being—when someone removes it as if taking off his clothes, he sees the truth. Like a snake sloughing off its old skin as it slides along—this is exactly how it happened to Janak. Ashtavakra was there as a catalyst.

Scientists have discovered catalytic agents. They say that some substances don't take an active part in certain reactions, but without their presence the reaction will not take place.

You have seen lightning flash in the monsoon rains. Scientists say that water is made by the combination of oxygen and hydrogen, but they will combine only when electricity is present. If electricity is not present, the reaction does not take place. Still electricity does not take any direct part in it, electricity does not get involved in bringing hydrogen and oxygen together—only its presence does. Scientists call this kind of presence a catalytic agent.

The master is a catalytic agent. He doesn't do anything, but without his presence nothing will happen. In his presence, something happens, although he doesn't do anything—just his presence. Understand it like this: his energy surrounds you. Engulfed in this energy field, strength arises in you— the strength is yours. Songs start exploding—the songs are yours. Declarations start to happen—the declarations are yours. But without the presence of the master perhaps they would not have happened.

The presence of Ashtavakra worked as a catalytic agent. Seeing Ashtavakra's serene, silent, highest state, Janak must have been reminded of his forgotten home. Looking deep into those eyes, seeing that infinite expanse, he must have recalled his own lost and forgotten potential. Hearing Ashtavakra's words—soaked in truth, soaked in experience—his own sense of taste must have been aroused.

I have heard about a man who raised a lion as a pet. He brought it home as a tiny cub whose eyes had not yet opened. The lion had never eaten meat, had never tasted blood. He was a vegetarian lion—he ate vegetables and bread. He didn't have any idea, he had no reason to know.

But one day the man was sitting in his chair when he scratched his leg and a little blood oozed out. The lion was sitting nearby. Sitting there he licked up the blood with his tongue. And that was enough! In one moment, he changed: the lion roared. There was violence in that roar. Until then he was a perfect Jaina—suddenly he became a lion. Until then he was a vegetarian, and he made only the sounds of a pure vegetarian. Although he still had not eaten any meat—only tasted a few drops of blood—he was reminded. The dormant capacity of being a lion that had been sleeping in every cell awoke. Something woke up, something started stretching its limbs. The one who was asleep opened his eyes. He stood up growling, and soon he started attacking. It became impossible to keep him at home; he had to be set loose in the jungle. He had been asleep for so long—that was the first time he remembered who he was.

Under Ashtavakra's influence Janak remembered who he was. If Janak had thought about the words beforehand, he would not have spoken, he would have hesitated. Is this something easy to say: *The universe which has emanated from me will dissolve into me, just as a pot dissolves into clay, a wave into water, or a bracelet into gold?*

Under Ashtavakra's influence, in Ashtavakra's presence, he awoke. The lion, that had been sleeping for lives, began to roar! He remembered his own nature, he remembered his being. This is the meaning of satsang.

Great importance has been given to satsang in the East. In western languages there is no equivalent word, because the West does not understand the significance of satsang. The meaning of satsang is, simply sitting near one who has known, and the taste becomes infectious. Becoming absorbed in the waves of someone who has known, the forgotten waves sleeping within you are activated, they begin vibrating.

The meaning of 'satsang' is that by simply seeing one who has gone beyond you, seeing that he has gone ahead, a challenge is provoked within you. You also have to go! Then it is difficult to stop.

The meaning of 'satsang' is not so much listening to the master's words as it is drinking the presence of the master, letting the master come deep inside you. It is vibrating in one rhythm with the master.

The master is living in a certain vibration. When you are near the master, his vibration provokes the same kind of vibration in you. And even if only for a short while, you too enter into another world, the gestalt changes. Your way of looking at things changes. For a little while you look through the eyes of the master, hear through the ears of the master.

I want to make it clear to you that although Janak said these words, still these words are Ashtavakra's. It says 'Janak said', but I want to remind you it is really 'Ashtavakra said'. The presence of Ashtavakra and what Ashtavakra had said to him became so strong that Janak was gone, Janak was washed away in the flood. His abode was gone without a trace, the house had collapsed. Someone else had started speaking: *The universe which has emanated from me will dissolve into me, just as a pot dissolves into clay, a wave into water, or a bracelet into gold.*

I am that lost and wandering traveller,
who is his own destination.
What can I receive from existence?
I myself am the ultimate reward of existence.

'I am that lost and wandering traveller.' I am a pilgrim gone astray, a traveller who has lost the way . . . 'who is his own destination.' I don't know it, but I am my own destination. The destination is not somewhere outside. I have gone astray because I have not looked inside; otherwise there is no need to wander. I have gone astray because I have not closed my eyes and looked inside. I have gone astray because I have not made any effort to know myself. And where I am searching for the goal, the goal cannot be possible.'

'That lost and wandering traveller, who is his own destination.' This is the reason for straying: the goal is inside and we are looking outside. The lamp is burning within, but the light falls without. Seeing the light that falls without, we start running, thinking that the source of light is also outside. The light that falls outside is our own. The fragrance that comes outside is the fragrance that we have given off, it is reflected, it is an echo. We are running after this echo.

There is a Greek story, about Narcissus, a very beautiful young man. He got into great difficulty. He was sitting on the shore of a lake—a calm, beautiful lake without any waves—and he saw his reflection in it. He became infatuated with his own reflection, he fell in love with it. He became so mad that he never left that place. He forgot hunger and thirst. He became a Majnu and took his own reflection to be his beloved Laila. The reflection was beautiful—again and again he went into the lake to catch hold of it. But when he went in the water, the lake was disturbed, waves arose and the reflection disappeared. Again he would sit on the bank. When the lake became calm, it would appear again. It is said he went mad. He died on the shore of that lake.

You must have seen the narcissus plant. It is a western plant, found on the banks of rivers. It has been named in memory of Narcissus. It grows on the bank of a river and looks at its reflection, goes on looking at its own flowers in the water.

Each of us is a Narcissus.

What we are seeking is within us. But where we are searching there are only reflections, only echoes. There is no way to find anything in echoes. We must turn towards the original source.

'I am that lost and wandering traveller, who is his own destination. What can I receive from existence?' 'What have I got to do with life?'

'I myself am the ultimate reward of existence.' 'I myself am the conclusion of life. I don't have anything to get from or give to life. I am not searching for some meaning in life. I myself am the meaning of life. I am the conclusion of life, the epitome of life. I am its ultimate flower, its final stage, its highest peak.'

But one who is searching for meaning in life continuously experiences meaninglessness. This has happened in the modern world—meaning has disappeared. People say, 'What meaning is there in living?' Such a disaster has never happened before. It is not that there were no intelligent people before—there were very intelligent people, it is difficult to find anyone to compare them with. There were people like Buddha, Zarathustra, Lao Tzu, Ashtavakra: what greater peak of intelligence can there be? What greater brilliance can there be? But none of them ever said there is no meaning in life.

Intelligent people in the modern age—whether it is Sartre or Camus or Kafka—say there is no meaning in life. Meaningless, perverse, 'a tale told by an idiot' . . . the meaningless babble of an idiot, incoherent prattle. 'A tale told by an idiot full of sound and fury signifying nothing!' No meaning, no substance, just useless nonsense—this is life!

What happened? Why has life suddenly become meaningless? Could it be that we are looking for meaning in the wrong direction? . . . Because Krishna says that life is immensely meaningful. Krishna says that life is filled with ultimate meaning and splendour. And Buddha says that ultimate peace, ultimate bliss are hidden in life. Ashtavakra says that life is pure godliness. There must be some mistake, we must be missing something. Somehow we are searching in the wrong direction. 'What can I receive from existence? I am the reward of existence.'

When we search outside, our life seems meaningless. When we search within, our life becomes full of meaning: we ourselves are the meaning of life.

> Amazing am I, I bow down to myself. When the whole world shall perish, from Brahma down to the very blade of grass I shall not perish. I am eternal.

Such a wonderful statement had never been uttered before, nor has it been said since. Do you see how wonderful this statement is: *I bow down to myself*? Certainly, this is not Janak's statement; this is an expression of the ultimate happening that has taken place. This is the voice of one in samadhi, this is the music of samadhi.

I bow down to myself. When the whole world shall perish, from Brahma down to the very blade of grass I shall not perish. 'All shall be destroyed, I will not be destroyed. All are born, all die—I am not born, I will not die. I am amazed. I myself am in awe.'

I bow down to myself. When the whole world shall perish, from Brahma down to the very blade of grass . . . 'Their time comes and goes. They are all events, just waves happening in time. I am the witness! I watch them being created and I watch them being destroyed. They are enacting a play, this drama is happening before my very eyes. They are illuminated by the light of my eyes and absorbed back into the same ultimate reality.'

Brahma too! Those whom you worship in the temple—Brahma, Vishnu, Shiva—they come and go. There is only one thing in the universe that does not come and go. It is you—you freed from yourself. And when you are free from yourself, you find you have bowed down to your own feet. You find godliness totally revealed within you. You find that what you were searching for had always been present inside of you, waiting. *Amazing am I, I bow down to myself . . .*

> Amazing am I, I bow down to myself. Although embodied,
> I am the non-dual.

'Two appear, but still I am non-dual.' This appearance of two is only on the outside, like seeing the branches of a tree. If you count the branches, there are many. If you come down the tree to the trunk, they all become one. It is just the same in the world: many are seen, but coming back to the source, they become one. It is the expanse of the one.

> Amazing am I, I bow down to myself. Although embodied,
> I am non-dual. I neither go anywhere nor come from
> anywhere; I just exist, I pervade the universe.

Listen! Janak is saying that he pervades the world, he encompasses the world. He is the definition of the world. He is unlimited . . . the world is inside him. Usually we see ourselves as inside the world. This is an unparalleled transformation—the whole gestalt has changed.

Janak says the world exists inside of him. Like clouds arising in the sky and disappearing, whole ages arise and dissolve in him. He is formless, he is the witness, he is only the observer: he encompasses all.

Understand it like this: when you were a child, one form was contained in your sky—childhood. Then you became a young man, and that form disappeared and another cloud surrounded you. You assumed a new form, you became a young man. When you were a child, you didn't have any idea of sex. Even if someone explained, you would not be able to understand. When you became a young man, new desires arose. Desire put on new clothes, new colours flowered, and your life took on a new style.

Then you started getting old. Your youth also left. The noise and clamour of your youth also went, desires too washed away. Now you are surprised how you could have got lost in those desires. Now you are shocked to think that you were such an idiot, that you were so foolish.

One day or other, every old man—if he has really succeeded in seeing life a little—is filled with surprise: 'What kinds of things I was running after—money, power, infatuations, women or men, running after all sorts of things. What was I chasing after? I really chased around like that? I cannot believe that I could have been in such dreams.'

In Arabia there is a saying that if a young man cannot cry, he is not truly young, and if an old man cannot laugh, he is not truly old. A young man who cannot cry is not truly young, because one who cannot cry, who cannot let tears flow—his feelings are blunted. There are no waves of feeling, no enjoyment. One who cannot suffer in misery is not young, he is stony-hearted. His heart has not flowered, it has still not flowered. And an old man who cannot laugh—at this whole life and at himself, seeing what idiocy, what foolishness!—is not truly old. An old man is one who can laugh at all this idiocy, his own and everyone else's, and say, 'What great foolishness!' People are running like mad after things which have no significance. Now he can see there is no real value.

Sometimes you are young, sometimes you are old. Sometimes clouds take one form, then another, and yet another. But have you ever thought that inside you are one? The one who had seen childhood is the same one who saw youth. The one who saw youth is the same one who saw old age. You are the observer: the one who stands back and sees is exactly the same.

When you sleep at night your observer watches dreams. When there are no dreams, only deep sleep, dreamless sleep— then your observer watches dreamless sleep, what a good deep sleep . . . ! This is why, sometimes when you wake up in the morning, you say what a deep sleep you had. Who observed it? If you were totally asleep, no seer left inside of you, then who saw it? Who knew? Who found out? Who is saying it?

Getting up in the morning, who says, 'Last night I slept very deeply'? If you were sound asleep, then who is the one who knows? Certainly someone remains awake inside of you, in some corner a lamp goes on burning and seeing that sleep is deep, very restful, very delightful, very peaceful, without a wave of dreaming, no tension, no thought. Someone goes on seeing. In the morning, the seer says, 'Last night my sleep was very deep.' If the night was full of dreams, then you say in the morning, 'I spent the night dreaming; who knows how many bad dreams I had.' Certainly the seer was not lost in dreams. Certainly the seer did not become a dream. The seer remained standing apart.

Then in the day you see the world with open eyes. At your work you are a businessman. With your friend you are a friend, with your enemy you are an enemy. Then you come home—with your wife you are a husband, with your son you are a father, and with your father you are a son. Thousands and thousands of forms!

You see all of this, but you are the seer who is beyond all these. Sometimes you see success, sometimes failure; sometimes illness, sometimes health; sometimes good days, sometimes bad days—but one thing is fixed, these come and go: you neither come nor go.

Amazing am I, I bow down to myself. Although embodied, I am non-dual. I neither go anywhere nor come from anywhere . . . Neither going nor coming, just being. This just being is your nature. *I just exist, I pervade the universe.* 'And I encompass the universe.' This is your world. This world is inside you, you are not inside it. You are the master of it, you are not its slave. The very moment you decide to, you can spread your wings and fly away! If you are inside it, it is of your own choice, no one has forced you. If you remember this much then there is no problem. Then if you accept any limitation of your own free will, bondage is no longer a bondage. Then whatever you choose, whatever you want to do you can do. But never forget one thing, that you are not the doer, the doer is again a form. You are not the enjoyer, the enjoyer is a form. You are the witness. This is your very immortality.

In the East, the goal of our greatest seeking has been to find that which is beyond time, not bound by time. What is created and falls, what deteriorates in the flow of time is a reflection. Only what stands beyond time as a witness is true.

Amazing am I, I bow down to myself. None here is as capable as I . . .

Do you hear? Janak is saying no one is as capable as he is!

. . . who have been maintaining the universe for an eternity without even touching it with the body.

This is art, skilfulness. 'Who is as skilful as I? As capable as I? I haven't touched the body, I have never touched it!' There is no way to touch it because your nature and the nature of the body are so different that touching is not possible, touching cannot happen. You are simply the witness, you can only see. The body is the observed, it can only be seen. You and the body cannot meet. You exist in the body, the body exists in you—but without touching—as if at an infinite distance. Their natures are so different that you cannot mix them.

You can mix milk with water, but you cannot mix water with oil. Their natures are different. Water will mix with milk because milk is water in the first place, more than 90 per cent water. So water will mix with milk—but you cannot mix water with oil, they just won't mix. They cannot mix, their natures are different. Still it can be that perhaps scientists will find some method of mixing oil and water, because no matter how different they are, both are matter.

But there is no way to mix consciousness and the inert, because the inert is matter and consciousness is not. There is no way to mix the observer and the observed. The observer remains the observer, and the observed remains the observed.

So Janak says, 'I am filled with wonder, I have become wonder itself! What is this capacity of mine? I have done so many things and still I am unattached. I have enjoyed so much but still no trace of attachment pulls on me!'

As if you are writing on water, you go on writing and nothing is written—with the witness, you go on doing things, enjoying things, but nothing is written, everything disappears like lines on water. You don't manage to finish writing and already they have disappeared. *None here is as capable as I, who have been maintaining the universe for an eternity without even touching it with the body.*

He resides in thy heart,
He is not separate from thy heart.
No matter how much he appears to be separate,
He is not separate.

We can go on telling ourselves we are one with the body, but we cannot be. And we can go on telling ourselves we are separate from the divine, but we cannot be. And we can understand only when we understand both of these together. As long as you think you are one with the body, on the other side, you will also think you do not have a connection with the divine.

The day you know you are joined to the divine, that day you will know: 'Oh, wonder of wonders! I had never been united with the body!'

'He resides in thy heart, He is not separate from thy heart.' That ultimate reality resides in your heart.

'He resides in thy heart.' He has built his house there . . .

'He is not separate from thy heart. No matter how much he appears to be separate, He is not separate.' Why? Because there is no way to be separate. There is no possibility of being separate from the divine and there is no way to be one with the world. We have been trying to manage this life after life, although it is not possible.

The day you wake up—and you will certainly awaken one day, because if one is asleep, how long can one go on sleeping? Because awakening is the nature of a sleeper—that's what falling asleep means. Sleep gives the indication that one can wake up, that awakening is one's potential. How can one who cannot awaken fall asleep? Only one who can awaken can fall asleep.

You will wake up one day or another. When you wake up you too will feel: *None here is as capable as I, who have been maintaining the universe for an eternity without even touching it with the body.* 'I have upheld this universe, no one else is supporting it. I have not touched it and still I am supporting it.'

Zen masters say: 'Cross the river but remember the water cannot touch you.' They are saying that if you understand what witnessing is, then you will cross the river but the water will touch the body, it cannot touch you. You will go on witnessing.

Learn to be a witness in ordinary life. Make a little effort. Sometimes when you are walking, walk in such a way that you are not walking, only the body is walking. You 'neither go anywhere nor come from anywhere'. Watch yourself walking on the road and be a witness. While eating at the dinner table, watch yourself eating. The body is eating, the hand picks up a spoonful, brings it to the mouth: you stand silently watching. Watch yourself making love, watch yourself being angry. In happiness, watch; in suffering, watch.

Slowly, slowly you help and support the witness. One day the declaration will happen within you too, the ultimate rain will come, nectar will shower. It is your right, it is your birthright, the right of your inherent nature. You can declare it whenever you want.

> Amazing am I, I bow down to myself. I have nothing at all, or I have all that can be encompassed by speech or thought.

Janak is saying in one sense nothing is his because he is not. He no longer exists, how can 'his' exist? So in one sense nothing is his and in another sense everything is his. As 'he' no longer is, only existence remains in him; godliness remains, and everything belongs to it. This paradox has happened, where it seems nothing is his and everything is his.

Amazing am I, I bow down to myself. I have nothing at all, or I have all that can be encompassed by speech or thought. Whatever is visible to the eyes, whatever experience comes through the senses is not his, because he is the observer. But as soon as he becomes the observer he finds out that all is his, because he is the centre of the whole existence.

The observer is not your individual form, the observer is your universal form. As the enjoyer we are all separate, as the doer we are all separate—but as the observer we are one. My observer and your observer are not separate, my observer and your observer are one. Your observer and Ashtavakra's observer are not separate, your observer and Ashtavakra's are one. Your observer and Buddha's observer are not separate.

The day you become an observer is the day you become Buddha, Ashtavakra, Krishna . . . that day you become all. When you become an observer you become the centre of the universe. You disappear from this side, you are fulfilled from that side. You lose this small 'I', this small droplet— and gain the infinite ocean.

These sutras are the sutras for worshipping your own being. These sutras are saying that you yourself are the devotee, you yourself are the divine. These sutras say you are the one worthy of adoration and you are the adorer. These sutras are saying that both are present inside you: allow them to meet! These sutras are saying something very unique: bend down to your own feet, lose yourself within yourself, drown inside yourself! Your devotee and your God are inside you. Let the union happen there, let the fusion happen.

The revolution will happen when inside you your devotee and your godliness meet and become one. Neither

God nor devotee will remain. Something will remain—without form, without attributes, beyond limit, beyond death, beyond time, beyond space. Duality will disappear, non-duality will remain.

The first glimpses of these non-dual moments are what we call meditation. When these non-dual moments start becoming stable, it is what we call 'samadhi with seed'. And when this non-dual moment becomes permanent, becomes so stable there is no way it can be dismissed—this is what we call 'seedless samadhi, with no-mind'.

This can happen in two ways—either just by awareness, as it happened to Janak, merely through understanding . . . But great intelligence is needed, sharp intelligence is needed, great intensity is needed—a very sharp-edged awareness is needed within you. It can happen immediately! If you find this happening, good. If you find this is not happening, then don't sit repeating these sutras. It will not happen from repeating them. These sutras are such that if it happens while listening to them, then it happens; if while listening you miss, then even if you repeat them a million times it won't happen, because it does not happen through repetition. The sharpness of your brain does not come through repetition; through repetition, its edge is lost.

One way is if it happens when you hear these sutras. If it happens it happens, you cannot do anything. If it doesn't happen, then slowly, slowly you will have to start with meditation, from meditation to samadhi with mind, from samadhi with mind to samadhi with no-mind—you will have to make the journey. If the leap happens, then good; if not you will have to go down the steps. If the leap happens, it happens. It can happen to some. Every miracle is possible, because you are a miracle of miracles. Nothing is impossible in it. Sitting here listening to me the leap can happen to someone. If *you* don't come in between; if you keep your 'I' separate; if you put away your intellect like taking off your shoes and clothes and putting them away; if you become a pure, naked consciousness before me, this leap can happen. It can happen to you as it happened to Janak. If it happens, good. Then there is no method in it. You won't be able to prepare for it to happen.

If you ask about preparations it doesn't happen. Then there is another way. Then Patanjali is your path, or Mahavira or Buddha. Ashtavakra is not your path. This is why the Ashtavakra Gita goes on lying in darkness. Such urgency, such intensity, such brilliance is rare. This can happen with one who has prepared himself for many lives. But it happens! Only to one or two in a hundred, but it happens. There are many historical accounts of some insignificant event transforming someone.

I have heard of a sadhu in Bengal. He was a clerk at the court, the head clerk, then he retired. Rajababu was his name. He was Bengali, so of course he was a petty official, a babu. He was over sixty. One morning he went out walking. It was early morning, the sun had not yet risen. Behind closed doors some woman in her hut was waking somebody. It must have been her son or brother—she was waking somebody up. She said, 'Rajababu wake up, it is very late!'

Rajababu was just going out with his walking stick in hand, going for his morning walk. Suddenly, in this predawn moment, the sun was just about to rise, pink was spreading across the sky, the birds were starting to sing, the whole of nature was full of wakefulness—it happened!

The woman was waking up someone else, she hadn't even said anything to this Rajababu. She didn't even know that this Rajababu was passing by. He was going out walking and she was saying to someone inside, 'Rajababu, wake up, it is morning, it is very late. Get up, will you? How long are you going to go on sleeping?'

He heard—and it happened. He didn't return home, he kept going and he reached the forest. His family found out: they came looking for him and found him in the forest. They asked, 'What happened?'

He started laughing. He said, 'It is enough! Rajababu woke up, now you can go!'

They said, 'What do you mean? What are you saying?'

He said, 'Now there is nothing to say, nothing to hear. It is already too late—a lot of time has already been lost. Now I have understood. It was dawn, all of nature was awakening—and in this awakening I also woke up at last. A woman was saying, "Wake up, it is very late." Her words struck home.'

This woman was not Ashtavakra, she herself was not awakened. Sometimes it happens: if your intelligence is crystallized, if your fruit has ripened, then one puff of wind . . . or, if no wind is blowing, sometimes ripe fruit falls by itself. If it happens, it happens! But if it doesn't, don't be disheartened, don't be sad. If it is not sudden, then it can be step by step. Sometimes it does happen suddenly—as an exception. So Ashtavakra's Gita is an exception. There is no method in it, there is no path.

In Japan there are two schools of Zen. One school is of sudden enlightenment. What they say is the same as what Ashtavakra says. The master doesn't teach anything. He comes and sits. If he is in the mood, he says something. If it happens, it happens.

Once an emperor invited a Zen master to his palace. The master came and mounted the dais. The emperor had been very eagerly awaiting him. He sat before him like a disciple.

After sitting a short time on the dais, the master looked left and right, pounded the table with his fist, stood up and left!

The emperor was surprised, and wondered what had happened. He asked his chief minister. The minister said, 'I know him—he has never given a more significant commentary than this. But if you get it you get it, it you don't get it you don't get it.'

The emperor said, 'This is a commentary? Beating three times on the table with his fist and leaving—this is it?'

The minister said, 'He tried to wake us up and then left, so we would wake up if it was possible. He just sounded the alarm and left.'

Rajababu, get up, morning has come.

The minister said, 'I have heard other discourses of this master, but I have never heard him give a more potent, a more wakefulness-provoking discourse than this one. But don't worry, I have listened to him many times, and I have not awakened yet. You have only heard your first discourse. Keep listening, perhaps it will happen.'

It is an instantaneous event, it is not related to cause and effect. It is completely fresh, it has no connection with your past—if it happens, it happens. This is not a scientific experiment, like when you heat water up to one hundred degrees and it becomes steam. This event is as if steam is happening without heating the water. It has no scientific explanation.

Ashtavakra is beyond science. If you have a scientific mind and you say, 'How can it happen that way? It can only happen by doing something,' then follow your scientific mind. Then ask Buddha about the eightfold path. Then ask Patanjali about his yoga. Then there are methods. This is not yoga, this the pure expression of what Indian philosophy calls sankhya.

It is not that Ashtavakra can awaken many. If a Janak or two can awaken it is miracle enough. That Janak was able to awaken was more than enough. And there is no mention anywhere of Ashtavakra awakening anyone else.

Buddha awakened many. Even now Patanjali goes on awakening people. Ashtavakra only awakened one person—and it is hard to say if he awakened even this one. Janak was ready to be awakened, Ashtavakra was only an instrument. Not a cause—a catalyst.

With the devices of sudden enlightenment, the master is only a catalyst. He will try—if it happens, it happens. It is not a science. If it doesn't happen, don't become disheartened. A master cannot have any conviction that it will happen to you. It will happen to some, and whomsoever it doesn't happen to this way will at least have their thirst aroused. They will then search for a method, and they will move along this path.

The general rule is that it can only happen with methods. If it happens without methods it is the exception, it is unusual.

So listen attentively here. If it happens, be blessed—if it doesn't, don't be disheartened.

Hari-om-tat-sat!

10

Beyond Cause and Effect

> Osho,
> Yesterday you said that sudden enlightenment is
> not bound by the law of cause and effect. But if nothing
> is haphazard in existence—that nothing happens
> accidentally—then how can the highest experience like
> enlightenment happen this way?

It is true that in existence nothing happens without cause,
but existence itself is uncaused. Existence has no cause—
enlightenment means existence. Everything else happens,
existence does not happen—it is. There has never been a
moment when it was not, there will never be a moment
when it will not be. Everything else happens: man happens,
trees happen, birds and animals happen. Existence is not a
happening, existence is. Enlightenment is not a happening;
if it were so and it happened uncaused, then it would be
an accident. Enlightenment does not happen, because
enlightenment is your nature; you are enlightenment. This
is why it can happen suddenly, and it happens without
cause.

You have asked, 'How can the highest experience like enlightenment happen this way?' Because it is the highest. Everything lower occurs by causation. If samadhi occurs by causation like other things, then it becomes lower and ordinary. Heat water to one hundred degrees and it becomes steam; similarly, if you do one hundred degrees of ascetic practice and samadhi occurs, then it would be captured in a scientific laboratory and very soon there would not be any way to save religion . . . because whatever happens with a cause comes into the grasp of science. Whatever has a cause will fall within the limits of science.

Religion remains religion because enlightenment is uncaused. Science will never be able to contain it. Whatever is caused will eventually become science. Only one thing will remain that can never become science, that is existence itself, because existence is uncaused, it simply is. Science has no explanation for it. How can there be a cause for this vastness, for the whole? Because everything that is, is included in it, there is nothing outside of it.

This is why samadhi does not happen through the law of cause and effect—because it is not limited, it is vast.

You have asked, 'The highest experience like enlightenment . . .' It is the highest precisely because it does not depend on your limited law of cause and effect: do this many virtuous acts and samadhi will happen; give that much charity and samadhi will happen; renounce so much and samadhi will happen. Then samadhi would follow your calculations, would come into the account books; it would not keep its height. It happens uncaused.

This is why the devotees say it happens as grace. It does not happen through your making it happen. It showers on you—suddenly, as a gift, as grace.

Then what is the result of our struggle and efforts? If you can understand Ashtavakra, then any effort will be useless; then you are practising rites and rituals uselessly. There is no need to practise, understanding is enough. Just understand that only existence is, and let go of the search.

Understand this: what we are is joined with the source, hence running around doing things and making efforts to reunite must be dropped—and the union will happen. The union will happen not from making an effort but from dropping the effort.

Efforts to reunite increase the gap—the more you long for union, the more the distance grows. The more you seek, the more you are lost because what you go on seeking is not to be sought. It happens by waking up and looking. It is present, it is standing at the door. It is manifest within the temple, manifest within you. It has never abandoned you for a moment, it has never been separate for a moment. You remain lost by searching for what is not separate, what you have never been parted from, from which you cannot be separated.

Only one result is possible from your practices: you will become tired, your whole effort will reach a place one day where you are fed up with effort. In that moment of weariness you let go, and immediately you see how mad you have been.

Yesterday I was reading someone's autobiography. He has written that he had travelled to a foreign city and became lost. He did not understand the language and he became very nervous. In his nervousness he forgot the name of his hotel, and forgot the phone number too. Then his panic increased: now how would he make inquiries? He was looking with great anxiety as he walked along the road, looking for someone who could understand his language. It was an Eastern country, in the Far East, and this American . . . He kept looking to see if any white-skinned person was appearing who would understand his speech, or if he could find a store with an English signboard so he could go and ask there.

He was walking along looking with such intensity, sweating, that he did not hear a police car that was coming behind him sounding the horn again and again. The police had begun to suspect that the man was lost. But he only heard the horn after two minutes; then he stopped in shock. The police got out and said, 'Are you in your senses or not? We have been sounding the horn for two minutes! We suspected you might be lost—come, ride in the car.'

He said, 'This is strange! I was searching ahead for someone who could guide me, and the guide was behind me. But I was so absorbed in my search that I didn't hear the horn sounding behind me. I didn't even look back.'

What you are seeking is following you. Of course existence does not blow a horn nor call out to you, because calling out will be a violation of your freedom. It whispers, it secretly says something in your ear. But you are so preoccupied, when do you listen to this whispering? You are so full of noise, the mind is reflecting so much, for and against; you are so involved in seeking.

Ramateertha has told a small story . . .

A lover went away to a far land and did not return. His beloved kept watching the road until she became tired, waiting and waiting. He wrote letters, saying again and again, 'I am coming now', 'I am coming soon—this month, next month . . .' Years passed and finally the beloved got upset. There is a limit to waiting. She travelled to the distant city where her beloved was. She asked where he could be found and finally arrived at his house.

The door was open. It was evening, the sun had set. She stopped at the door and looked inside. For many days she had not seen her lover. He was sitting before her, but he was absorbed in deep concentration, he was writing something. He was so absorbed that the beloved felt to wait a little, not to interfere with him: who knows what threads of thought might be lost? He was so overwhelmed with emotion that tears were flowing from his eyes. He was writing something.

Then he lifted his eyes and saw: he couldn't believe it, he was shocked. He had been writing a letter to his beloved. He was writing a letter to this one who had sat two hours in front of him! And she was waiting for him to lift his eyes.

He couldn't believe it, he thought, 'It must be a hallucination, it is an illusion, perhaps a sort of autohypnosis. I had such abundance of feeling for the beloved, perhaps that is why she is appearing like a dream. It must be an illusion.' He rubbed his eyes.

His beloved began to laugh. She said, 'What are you thinking? Do you think I'm a mirage?'

He started trembling. He said, 'But how did you come? I was writing a letter to you. Mad one—why didn't you stop me? You were in front of me while I was writing you a letter!'

Existence is here in front of us and we are praying to become one with it—'Oh lord, where art thou?' Tears are pouring from our eyes, but because of our wall of tears we don't see what is in front of us. We are searching for it. We miss only because of our search.

Ashtavakra's words are very clear. He says, 'Stop this letter writing. Stop this practising.'

Samadhi doesn't happen. Yes, if samadhi were also a happening then it would happen by cause and effect. If it happened by cause and effect it would become an item in the market. Samadhi is virgin, untouched—it is not sold in the market.

Have you ever noticed that your market-oriented mind also brings enlightenment into the market? You think that if you do this much you will be enlightened . . . as if it is a business deal. If you do good deeds you will attain the divine itself. Your so-called religious people go on telling you this: do good deeds if you want to attain the divine. As if to attain the divine one has to do something . . . as if the divine will never be attained without doing something. As if one must pay the price to buy the divine—do this many good deeds, this much ascetic practice, this much meditation, this much reciting of prayers—only then you will attain it.

You have brought it to the market. You have made it an item for sale. Customers will buy it. Those who have virtue will buy, those without virtue will be denied it. One needs the coin of virtue. If you show the coins of virtue you will attain it.

Ashtavakra is saying that what you are suggesting is madness! The divine will be attained by virtue? Then it has become a business transaction. You will attain the divine through prayer? Then you have bought it. What happened to its grace? And if something is received through a cause, when the cause disappears it will also disappear. That which is attained through a cause will be lost when the cause is destroyed.

You have accumulated wealth; you worked hard, you competed well in the market and you earned money. But do you think this money you earned will last? Thieves can steal it. A thief means one who is more ready to stake his life than you. A businessman makes effort, but the thief stakes his very life. He thinks, 'I am ready to die and kill, but I will take it.' So he steals it.

What is attained through a cause can be lost. Enlightenment is attained without cause, but our ego does not believe it. Our ego says, 'Does receiving it without cause mean that those that didn't do anything will also attain?' It is very difficult to swallow that those that didn't do anything will also receive.

Arup is sitting here in front laughing. Yesterday he told me he has no feeling to do anything. I said okay, dissolve into non-doing. Is there any need to do anything for enlightenment? Although I say it, it is hard to believe, because our mind says, 'Without doing?' One cannot get ordinary things without doing—you won't get a house, a car, a business, wealth, power, you won't get fame; enlightenment happens without doing anything? You don't believe it. 'One has to do something. There must be some trick to it. This non-doing will also have to be done.' This is why we make up such expressions as 'non-action in action', 'action in non-action'—but we insist on doing. 'Doing in non-doing'—do things in this way, but keep on doing. 'Has anyone attained without doing anything?'

Ashtavakra is saying the same thing that I am telling you: it is already attained. The very language of 'attainment' is wrong. Distance is part of the very language of attaining—as if existence is separate from you. If it is separate, could you live for a single moment? How could you live separate from existence? Separate from existence your condition would be like a fish out of water . . . Yet a fish can be separated from the ocean because there are places other than the ocean, but how can you be separated from existence? It is and only it is; everywhere it is this, every place is in this. Where can you be separated? Where will you go? Does existence have any shore? It is an unending ocean. There is no way to move outside it.

Ashtavakra is saying you have never gone away from enlightenment, hence it can happen uncaused. If it is not lost then it can be attained uncaused.

Enlightenment is not an event—it is your nature. But does it ever happen that grace showers without doing anything?

We have become very poor, poor through our experience of life. Here nothing is attained without doing, so we have become very narrow-minded. We cannot think that enlightenment could be attained without doing. Our poverty cannot even imagine it.

But we are not poor. This is why Janak says, 'Oh! I am amazed! I bow down to myself.' 'I bow down to myself,' means both the devotee and the divine are within me. To say 'both' is not right; there is only one within me, and mistakenly I think he is a devotee. When I realize this error, I know him as the divine.

Think of it this way: you have two chairs and you put them in a room, then you put two more chairs in the room and count them, mistakenly getting five. But in the room there are only four. If you mistakenly count five, or six, or fifty, the number of chairs in the room does not become five or six or fifty. There are four chairs, whether you count three or you count five. Only you know about your three or five; it doesn't make any difference to the chairs, they are still exactly four.

Your thinking to seek the divine is your three or five. The divine is already attained, the chairs are exactly four! Whenever you find out the right calculation will you think, 'Oh, but before there were five chairs, now they have become four'—will you think this way? No, you will think, 'I was mistaken: there were always four, I had counted five. The error was only in addition.'

The error is not existential, the error is only in memory. The error is not existential, the error is only in your arithmetic. This error is in your understanding.

This is why Ashtavakra says there is no question of doing. To make these five chairs into four one doesn't have to take one out. Or if you counted three, you don't need to bring one in from outside to make four—there are four chairs already. It is only an error of addition. Add it correctly. When the addition is correct, then would you think that it was without cause that the three chairs became four? Without cause five chairs became four? No, you would laugh. You would think, 'It was not a question of becoming, they already were, the error was only in thinking. The error was only mental, not existential.'

If you take yourself to be a devotee it is an error in addition. This is why Janak can say, 'Oh! I bow down to myself! What an idiot I have been! How amazing that I had gone astray in my own illusions. I did not know what always was, but knew what has never been. I saw a snake in a rope. I saw silver in mother-of-pearl. I saw an illusion of an oasis in the play of light. I saw what was not! "What is" was hidden in this hallucination, in this maya, and I did not see it.'

Enlightenment is the highest experience, because it does not happen. Enlightenment is the highest experience because it is beyond cause and effect. Enlightenment has already happened. The moment you become ready, the moment you take courage and are ready to drop your poverty of mind, the moment you are ready to drop your ego—that very moment it will happen.

It is not dependent on your asceticism, it is not dependent on your prayer—don't remain lost in asceticism and prayer.

Once I was a guest in a house. The whole of the house was full of books. I said, 'This is a big library!'

My host said, 'It is not a library. I have been writing the name of God, Rama, in all these books. This is what I have been doing my whole life. I buy books and write 'Rama, Rama, Rama, Rama' all day long. I must have written it many millions of times. Perhaps you can tell me how much virtue have I gained in doing that?'

'What virtue is there in it? It may well be a sin. So many notebooks could have been used by school children, you have ruined them. You are asking about virtue? Has your brain stopped functioning from writing 'Rama, Rama' in notebooks . . . ?'

He was very shocked, because other religious people had visited him and they had said, 'You are very virtuous. You have written "Rama" so many times, you have counted the beads of your rosary so many times, you have remembered Rama so much—just by remembering once one reaches heaven, and you have done this so many times!' He was angry with me, he never invited me again: 'What use is this man who says it is sin?' He was very shocked. He said, 'You are hurting my religious feelings.'

I do not hurt your religious feelings, I am only asking, what madness is this? What is the meaning of writing 'Rama, Rama'? Let the one who is writing know himself: he is Rama. How did he get involved in writing 'Rama, Rama'? Tell me: if the historical Rama is captured, sat down, and told to now drop his bow and arrow and to take up a pen and write 'Rama, Rama', instead of going off in search of his beloved, Sita, will it be sin or virtue? And the historical Rama, who is a gentleman, would agree, thinking, 'This man is after me. If I don't write he will feel hurt,' so Rama sits writing 'Rama, Rama' . . . Then you have destroyed his life.

When you are writing, it is also Rama writing. Who is it who is writing? Come to know that one. Who is it that is repeating 'Rama, Rama'? Where is this repeating of God's name arising from? Descend to that depth. Ashtavakra says you will find Rama there.

The second question:

Osho,
      Yesterday, you said, 'Don't let your intellect control the feelings of your heart.' But Osho, I find your

discourses absolutely logical. So is the mind nourished by the satisfaction of reasoning? Is it not a danger for me that the argument-nurtured mind will take control of the heart and suppress the experience of feelings? Please show me the path.

What I am saying is certainly logical, but not just logical—something more too. I speak logically for you, and something more is for me. If I do not speak logically you won't be able to understand. And if I do not say *that*, which is beyond logic, then I would not speak at all: what would be the use of speaking?

When I am talking, speaking to you, two are present: you and I. There is both a speaker and a listener.

If it was up to me I would speak in transcendence of logic, I would drop arguments completely, but then you would think I am insane. Then you wouldn't understand anything; you would feel it is just noise with no meaning.

I speak logically to fit with your pattern of logical thinking. But if this is all you understand, then your visit here has been useless.

It is like filling a spoon with medicine and pouring it in your mouth—we don't pour the spoon. With the spoon of logic I go on pouring what is beyond logic. Don't swallow the spoon, otherwise you will be in trouble. Use the spoon. Drink the liquid that is on the spoon.

Logic is a spoon, logic is an aid, because right now you don't have enough courage to listen to that which is beyond logic. If you want to hear what is beyond logic, then listening to the songs of birds will be the same as listening to the song of Ashtavakra. They are beyond logic.

The whispering noise of wind passing through the trees, the rustling of dry leaves blowing on the path, the sound of running water, the thundering of clouds—they are all beyond logic. Ashtavakra is speaking to you from all eight directions, from all sides! But you will not understand anything. How long can you listen to this chirping of birds? You will say it is nonsense. To listen a little is okay but there is no meaning in this chirping.

That which is beyond logic is like the chirping of birds. I make a bridge of logic so it can reach to you. If you hold on to the bridge and forget the destination, if you catch the words and forget that which was delivered by the words, then you are collecting pebbles where you could have filled your bag with diamonds and jewels.

The friend has asked, 'You said . . . not to let your intellect control the feelings of the heart.'

Certainly. Understand with the intellect but let the heart be the master. Make the intellect a slave and mount the heart on the throne of the master. The servant has sat on the throne too long. You are not living for the intellect, you live for the heart. This is why fulfilment never comes from the mind. No matter how great a mathematician you become, will the heart ever become peaceful? And no matter how great a logical thinker you become, will fulfilment ever arise? And no matter how many scriptures you gather, will this become samadhi? The heart asks for love, the heart asks for prayer. The final demand of the heart is for samadhi: bring samadhi, bring samadhi! At the most, intellect can bring logical arguments for samadhi, can bring theories about samadhi. But what can theories do?

Someone is sitting there hungry and you give him a cookbook, saying, 'Everything is written here, read it and enjoy!' And he reads it because he is so hungry he hopes it can help. Discussions of the finest tasting foods—recipes of how to fix, how to prepare them—but what can this do? He asks, 'What help is a cookbook? I need food.' The hungry need food. The thirsty need water.

You can write and give a thirsty man . . . he is thirsty and you write down H_2O, the formula for water. He will sit down with the paper, but what will happen? It is just the same as people sitting reciting 'Rama, Rama'. All mantras are like H_2O. Certainly water is made by a combination of oxygen and hydrogen, but thirst is not quenched by writing H_2O on paper.

Understand with logic, but drink with the heart. Use logic, but understand it is only useful; don't think it is all. Let the heart be the master. And remember, don't let the intellect interfere in love and prayer, in worship and offerings, in meditation and samadhi. The more helpful it can be, the better. This is why I speak to you using logic, so I can persuade and convince your intellect, convince you to come two steps towards the heart. If you get just a little taste you will be engrossed in its joy. Then you yourself will drop worrying about the intellect. When the real taste comes, who cares about the words?

'But Osho, I find your discourses absolutely logical.' They are logical. My whole effort is to make what I say to you logical so that you are ready to walk with me. Once you are convinced then you have fallen into the trap, then there is no way out. Once you are convinced, once our hands come together, then there is no worry. Once your hand has come into my hand you will not remain out of my hands for long. First I grab the wrist, then the forearm, then . . . you are just lost!

So I make the first contact with logic because that is where you live. Contact can be made there—that's where you are. This is why atheists also come to me. Atheists can accept me too. Atheists have no arguments with me because I speak the language of atheists. But it is a trap, the language is a snare. It is like going fishing and putting bait on the hook. It is bait. If one wants to avoid the hook, he has to avoid the bait, because once the bait is in the mouth one finds out it is a hook.

Logic is bait, the beyond is the hook. I persuade you: to give you bitter medicine I sugar-coat the pill. Man's state is like that of very small children. Enjoying sugar he swallows bitter medicine—you can even swallow poison. But if what is beyond logic is put directly before you, you will start running away: 'No, my mind does not believe this.' So I want to convince your intellect. But if you stop there and think that the intellect is convinced, you can go home now—then you missed the point. Then it is as if you have taken the sugar coating off the medicine, eaten it, and thrown away the medicine.

'Is the mind nourished by the enjoyment of argument?' It all depends on you. If you hear nothing but logic, then the mind will be nourished. But between arguments, if you allow in a little of the illogical, the irrefutable, just a drop at a time, then that drop in your brain will create the revolution of the heart. It depends on you.

There are some people who hear nothing but logical arguments. Whatever is outside logic they push aside. Then they have not come close to me—then coming here and not coming here are equal. They return exactly as they came—they go strengthened in their beliefs. They have chosen what fits with their thinking, chosen by their own understanding. They have chosen what fits with their understanding. What doesn't fit they drop. What doesn't fit with your understanding becomes a spark of transformation inside of you. What fits with your understanding will strengthen you as you are: your illness, your worry, your anxiety will become stronger—your ego will be strengthened.

So be a little skilful. This is why Janak says to Ashtavakra: 'What skill, that I saw in an instant! What dexterity I have, what ability!' Remember that skilfulness, remember that ability.

It depends on you. When I am speaking here, the speaking is my responsibility, but the listening depends on you. After speaking, I have no control over what I have said. As soon as I speak it is out of my hands—a released arrow. Then it is up to you where it will land, where it will strike home. Will you let it strike you or will you save yourself? Will it land in the intellect? Then you will go back a bigger scholar, strengthened in your debating skill, more skilful in argument. But you missed. If you let it strike the heart you will be more blissful, you will be filled with gratefulness. Then the door of blessedness opens. Then the possibility of grace increases. Then you have come towards the immortal a little. You have taken two steps towards the final destination.

Don't return as a scholar. Return as a lover. Kabir says:

Two letters and a half constitute the word *prem*, love, one who learns this is wise.

Don't forget these letters of love.

Listen to my arguments, be persuaded by my arguments— but as a means. The end is that one day you will gather courage and take the jump into that which is beyond logic. By means of logic, I will take you as far as your intellect can go. Then a frontier will come, then a border is reached; then the responsibility is yours. You can stand at the border and take a look—both at your past and at your future. Then you will see—backwards into the intellect you have come through, and ahead towards the potential that is opening. The future is of the heart.

No one has ever attained the real wealth of life by thinking. But one can attain through meditation, through witnessing, through love, through prayer, through the juice of devotion. Then it is in your hands if you want to remain a barren desert, it is up to you, you are your own master. But once I have brought you to the edge where you begin to see beautiful forests, greenery, valleys and passes and mountains, snow-capped peaks—let me show this to you once, then it is up to you. Then if you want to go back, go back. But then you will know that you are returning of your own choice. Then the responsibility is yours.

So I take your logic up to the point where you get your first glimpse of the golden peaks, where you see the open sky for the first time; then that glimpse will start following you. Then it will hover around inside you. Then the call will become louder and louder. Then slowly, slowly the drip-drip-drip that was falling will begin pouring as a great current. You will not be able to save yourself, because once you get even a small glimpse of the heart, the intellect is just rubbish. Before the glimpse, this rubbish seems to be diamonds and jewels.

'Is it not a danger for me that the argument-nurtured mind will take control of the heart and suppress the experience of feelings?'

It is a danger. Be alert. If we want it to, a stone lying on the path can be a block and we can stop right there. And if we wish, the stone can be made into a step to climb and go beyond. It depends on you whether you make the logic-nurtured mind a block or a step. Those that have made it a step have embarked on a great journey. Those who have made it a barrier have remained small ponds.

An atheist is a pond. One who trusts is a river flowing to the ocean. An atheist stagnates. As soon as water is stopped from flowing it starts stagnating. Water stays clean when it is flowing. But to flow the ocean is needed; otherwise, why would the water flow? For flowing, the divine is needed—

otherwise there is nothing more to be attained, nothing more to become, whatever has already happened is enough.

Remember, there are two kinds of people in the world— the world can be divided into two types. One type is of those who are never satisfied with outside things: we have this house, we need another one; we have this much money, more is needed; he has a woman friend or a wife, another kind of woman is needed. He is never satisfied with outer things, but he has no dissatisfaction with the inner: one who has no inner dissatisfaction, just outer dissatisfactions—this is the worldly man.

Then there is the second type of person. He is satisfied with whatsoever is outside, but is not satisfied within. There is a fire blazing inside him—a divine discontent. He lives in continuous process, in continuous change, in continuous transformation.

Let skill with reasoning be helpful in your inner revolution, in your transformation—remember this. Where logic becomes a rock and a barrier to your transformation, drop logic; don't drop the transformation. I am saying that ultimately the choice is in your hands.

> One is supposed to rise higher than the intellect,
> Love is supposed to go beyond the obsession with destination,
> Yet where I was starting from was unknown, O friend,
> What to say of the direction.

The intellect doesn't know anything about where it has to go. This is why intellect never goes anywhere. It goes around in circles like a bullock grinding grain. You have seen a bullock with blinkers over his eyes, going around and around. With these blinkers over his eyes he feels as if he is moving, that he is going somewhere, that something is happening.

Have you observed how you go around and around? The same morning, the same activities, the same day's work, the same evening, the same night, again the same morning, again the same evening. Life goes on passing away like this and you go on circling around and around like a bullock grinding grain.

When you rise a little above the level of intellect you rise into the sky, leaving the earth behind. Limits drop, the infinite begins. Bondage drops—one has a small glimpse of liberation.

Then a moment also comes—first you move from the intellect towards the heart, then a moment comes when you go deeper than the heart. Then love is freed from the object of love. Then the devotee is liberated from the love of God as the object. Then the worshipper is liberated from worship.

So first move with logic towards love and then move with love towards silence. That great silence is our home.

You are in the mind; you are to be in the heart. I begin with intellect to bring you towards the heart. But I also don't allow one who has arrived in the heart to sit still. I tell him: Keep moving, keep moving.

> Each new moment like the previous one,
> a familiar love song
> echoing in your bosom—
> go on planting them note by note.
> Belonging to each note in such a way
> that the departing melody never ceases.

A new step has to be taken into the unknown, the unfamiliar. Don't remain stuck with the familiar.

Have you ever thought what intellect means? It is the collection of what you know. What does it mean? Just the accumulation of your past. In the intellect is accumulated whatever you have heard, read, studied or experienced. Whatever has already happened is accumulated. The intellect has no idea of what is about to happen. The intellect is of the past—finished, dead! The intellect is dead ashes. If you are stuck in intellect you go on wandering the byways of the past; moving in the known.

Any movement is into the unknown. There is no movement in the known, it is just going round and round like the bullock grinding grain.

To be in the heart means: the unknown, the unfamiliar, an adventure. Who knows what will happen? It is not certain because it has never been known, so how can it be certain? The map is not in your hands, it is an unknown journey. There are no mileposts or police on the path to tell you the way. But a person who makes a journey towards the unknown makes a journey towards enlightenment.

Enlightenment is the most unknown happening in this world. Even when we know it, we still don't know it; it always remains unknown. Go on knowing, go on knowing: still it remains unknown. The more you know, the more it feels there is more left to know. The challenge becomes greater and greater. Peak after peak goes on emerging. While ascending one peak it seems the goal is reached; when you arrive at the top more peaks appear ahead. One doorway is entered and new doors appear in front of us.

This is why we call enlightenment an unending mystery. Mystery means that which we know but still are unable to know. This is why we say enlightenment is never attained by intellect—because intellect can only know that which it has finished knowing; enlightenment is never finished.

So don't miss with the mind, don't remain bound with the dead past. If you tie a dead body to yourself, you will understand what the mind is. Tie a corpse to you and you will be unable to move around. That corpse is rotting, decaying, and has become a burden. Intellect is a corpse, the heart is a new sprout—life's new sprout. And one has to go even beyond the heart. Move afresh with each new step, and keep the heart open for every available possibility— welcoming!

Keep the heart ready. Don't hold back when the unknown calls. Don't hesitate when the unfamiliar beckons. When the unknowable is knocking on the door don't be frightened, move with it. This is the characteristic of a religious person.

The third question:

> Osho,
> I bow down to you! In a thousand lives I could not have achieved as much as you have effortlessly given me. Please accept me as your disciple!

If you have taken, then you have become a disciple. Becoming a disciple is not dependent on my acceptance. Becoming a disciple is dependent on your acceptance. A disciple means one who is ready to learn. A disciple means one who is ready to bow down, to fill his begging bowl. A disciple means one who is eager to listen in humility, eager to contemplate deeply and quietly, eager to meditate.

You have become a disciple. If you took it, then by your very taking you have become a disciple. Being a disciple is not dependent on my agreement. What can I do if I accept you but you don't take it? What can I do if I don't accept you but you go ahead and take it anyway? Discipleship is your freedom. It cannot be anyone's charity. Discipleship is your privilege, your dignity. There is no need for any certificates to prove it.

This is why Eklavya, in the Mahabharata, could sit alone in the forest without worrying about the master Dronacharya's refusing him. The master simply refused, but the disciple was ready, insisting on becoming a disciple. So what could the master do? One day the master discovered that the disciple had defeated him. Eklavya had made a clay image of the master and was practising archery in its presence. He was obeying it and touching its feet.

When Dronacharya heard that Eklavya had become very adept at archery, he went to see. He was surprised . . . not just surprised, he became frightened. He was upset because Eklavya had become so well-practised that Arjuna paled in comparison.

Dronacharya may not have been much of a master, but Eklavya was a very great disciple. Dronacharya must have been an ordinary master—most common, not worthy of being called a master. He must have been skilled, well-versed, but he had nothing at all of the quality of a master. First he had refused because Eklavya was a Sudra, an untouchable.

Is this something a master would do? Does a master still see any distinction between a Brahmin and a Sudra? No, he must have been a businessman, with his mind on the market. How can a master of Kshatriya warriors accept a Sudra? He must have been very afraid of society. He must have been a pillar of this society and lived therefore within its restraints. He must have been narrow-minded. The day that Dronacharya refused Eklavya, saying he was a Sudra, was the day Dronacharya himself became a Sudra! Such foolishness!

But Eklavya was wonderful. He didn't bother that the master had refused. In his heart he had accepted him as his master—it was finished. Even the refusal of the master did not destroy his respect for him. He must have been a rare disciple!

And then the ultimate dishonesty: when Eklavya's skill was known he became famous. Dronacharya was shaken because he wanted his disciple Arjuna to be known to the world. Eklavya was also his own disciple, but without his assent. The master felt at a loss. The one he had taught with heart and soul, had put all his efforts into, had paled before this man who had only made a crude clay statue of Dronacharya with his own hands and had attained great skill practising in front of it. As it was a customary practice for the disciple to offer a gift to the master, Dronacharya said that he wanted Eklavya to cut off his thumb and present it to him.

It is very strange—Dronacharya was not ready to give instruction to Eklavya, but he had come to ask for a gift for being his master! But Eklavya must have been an amazing disciple: he did not refuse to give the gift to the man who had refused to initiate him. A disciple like Eklavya is a real disciple. He immediately cut off his thumb and gave it to Dronacharya. Dronacharya had asked for the thumb of the right hand—it was cunning politics to have him cut off his thumb: then Eklavya's archery would be useless.

This Dronacharya certainly must have been a cruel, evil-natured person. Far from him being a master, it is not easy to call him human. What a low trick he played! And played it on such a simple-hearted disciple. And still Hindus consider Dronacharya a master, they go on calling him a guru. One does not become a real Brahmin just by being born a Brahmin.

Eklavya was a real Brahmin and Dronacharya just a Sudra. His mentality is low. This Brahmin Eklavya cut off his thumb; he didn't hesitate a bit. He didn't even say, 'What are you asking? When I asked for instruction you refused to give it. I have not learned anything from you.' No, although the whole affair was wrong, it never even occurred to him.

He said, 'I have learned from you. What difference does it make that you refused me? I have learned this art from you. You went on refusing, but still I learned from you. Look, I have made your statue, so I am indebted to you. You ask for a thumb; even if you ask for my life I would give it.' He gave him his thumb.

To be a disciple depends on you. It is not a question of anyone's agreement or disagreement.

If you feel that you have received much, then it has happened. Let this feeling go on deepening. Don't lose the feeling of being a disciple and your growth will be tremendous. You will go on and on receiving. Discipleship is nothing but the art of learning.

The fourth question:

> Osho,
>   I had heard that wine is bitter and burns in the chest;
> but the taste of your wine is something else.

Then the wine you are familiar with is not real wine, because wine is neither bitter nor burns in the chest. And what burns in the chest and is bitter is fake wine, not real wine. This is the first time you have come to know the taste of wine. Don't bother with false wine anymore. You have entered the tavern for the first time. Now make your heart a vessel and drink to your heart's content, because this drinking will bring transformation. This wine will not bring forgetfulness, this wine will bring remembrance.

Is it really wine that makes you unconscious? This wine is that which brings you consciousness. This wine will wake you up. This wine will acquaint you with the one who sits hidden inside of you. This wine will make you 'you'.

Outwardly you may seem to others to be a drunkard—don't worry. Perhaps people outside will misunderstand your ecstasy and think it is insanity or unconsciousness. You needn't bother about them: the real test is within you. If your consciousness is growing you needn't bother; let the world understand whatever it wants to.

Listen to these lines of Mazaz:

There is messiahhood in my words,
People say I'm sick.
Recognize well, I am a secret,
I am an admirer of the crop of love.
Love and only love is my world,
I have turned my face away from the bother of the intellect.
The evil that was in Hafiz and in Omar Khayyam,
yes, I am guilty of that too to some extent.
What is life? Adam's sin?
If life is this then I am a sinner.
There is messiahhood in my words,
people say I am sick.

People said that Jesus too was just sick, only with great reluctance did they call him messiah. People also called Socrates insane, and they poisoned him. People never thought Mansoor was intelligent, otherwise why did they execute him? And I have told you the story of Ashtavakra: his very father got so angry that he cursed him, saying that his body would be deformed in eight places.

Jesus was on the earth for thirty-three years before he was crucified. Socrates was already old when he was poisoned. Stones were thrown at Mahavira and Buddha, it is true. But consider Ashtavakra: he was not even born and he was already cursed. He was still in the womb and he was deformed for life. And if someone else had done it, it would be forgivable—but his very father did it. The one who was the cause of his life got angry.

The message of enlightenment does not fit with people. The truth troubles people. An ecstatic person fills people with uneasiness. If you are unhappy no one is disturbed—just enjoy being unhappy. People say, suffer to your heart's content, there's no harm—this is exactly how it should be. If you laugh, people become restless. Laughing is not acceptable. People suspect that you are mad. Does a sensible person ever laugh? Do you ever see a wise man laughing? Do you see intelligent people dancing or singing a song? An intelligent person is serious, his face is long, his mood is sad. We call them great saints, great mahatmas: the more sick a person is the greater a saint he becomes. If someone sits like a corpse, sick, poverty-stricken, people say, what asceticism, what renunciation!

I once went to a village and some people brought a saint to meet me. They said, 'He is very miraculous: he only rarely eats, he rarely sleeps. He is very quiet, he speaks very little. And his asceticism is so powerful that his face has become like pure gold.'

When they brought him I said, 'Why have you tortured this man? He is sick. His face is not like gold, he is merely starving and thirsty—his face has become yellow because he is anaemic. You think he is religious? And how can he speak? He doesn't have energy to speak. This man seems to be a little idiotic. There is no fire in his eyes, no individuality, no joy. How can there be? He doesn't sleep properly, nor does he eat and drink properly. And you are worshipping him? He is only interested in your worshipping him for what he is doing. He does it for your worship.'

Stop worshipping them for a while and you will find that ninety-nine out of one hundred of your mahatmas disappear—disappear the very night you stop worshipping. They do all kinds of idiotic things because of your worship. They do whatever you want them to do. If you say, 'Pull out your hairs one by one,' they pull out their hair. If you say, 'Be naked,' they stand naked. If you say, 'Starve yourself,' they starve themselves. In return you have to do only one thing: respect them, give strength to their egos.

The real religion is always a laughing religion. The real religion is always healthy, fulfilled and life affirming. The real religion is just like flowers—there is no sadness there. People understand sadness as peace! Sadness is not peace. Peace sings joyously. Peace is very vibrant. Peace is a great drunkard. Your feet become unsteady, ecstasy surrounds you. You walk on the earth, yet you are not walking on the earth, you are moving in the sky . . . as if you are spreading your wings, just ready to fly off.

It is good—if you have tasted my wine, you have tasted the real wine—now there will be no need of going to any other tavern.

Just feel only one thirst—for love; desire only one thing—love. Let your whole world and your whole being be filled with love, it is enough. And be finished with the disturbances of the mind; descend into the protection of love.

Omar Khayyam has not been understood. A great injustice has been done to him. One day in Bombay I saw the sign for a bar, it read: 'Omar Khayyam'. A great injustice has been done to him. Fitzgerald was very mistaken when he translated his poetry into English. He did not understand Omar Khayyam. Fitzgerald could not understand, because to understand Omar Khayyam one needs to experience the ecstasy of the Sufis, the samadhi of the Sufis.

Omar Khayyam was a Sufi mystic. He is one of those rare people who have attained: he is in the same category as Buddha and Ashtavakra, Krishna and Zarathustra. The wine he speaks of is divine wine. The beauty he speaks of is divine beauty. But Fitzgerald did not understand. With his Western mind he understood wine to be literally wine.

He translated Omar Khayyam's words and this translation became very famous. The translation is very beautiful, its poetry is very beautiful; certainly Fitzgerald is a great poet. But he could not understand. The special character of the Sufis was lost in his poetry. And Omar Khayyam became known through Fitzgerald.

So everything known about Omar Khayyam is mistaken. Omar Khayyam never drank wine, never went to any tavern. But he certainly drank that wine which makes all other wines pale. He went into that tavern which we call the temple, which we call the temple of the divine.

'The evil that was in Hafiz and in Omar Khayyam, yes, I am guilty of that too to some extent.' Mazaz, who wrote these lines, also misunderstood Omar Khayyam; he too thought Omar Khayyam was a drunkard. Mazaz died of excessive drinking. The wine that you have mentioned as being bitter and that which burns in the chest, Mazaz died in his youth because of drinking it. He died an unfortunate death.

Don't misunderstand the wine that I am talking about to be something else. Don't make the same mistake with me that was made with Omar Khayyam. It is possible.

I say unto you: enjoy life with the witnessing consciousness. But you want to drop 'the witness'. You catch only the 'enjoy'. Enjoy life, but if you enjoy it without remaining the witness you won't enjoy it. Real enjoyment is only when you remain a witness. Drink wine, but if you lose consciousness this is not right drinking. You are drinking the real wine only if your consciousness grows as you drink it. There is no wine other than samadhi.

As I see it, the attraction for alcohol will continue in man until the attraction for samadhi grows. People will go on drinking fake wine until the real wine is available to them. False coins will circulate until the real coin is available. Governments throughout the world try to stop the consumption of wine, but it doesn't happen. They have always been trying to do it. Religious people have been advising governments to enact prohibition. They fast, and do this and that: 'Alcohol consumption must be stopped.' But no one has succeeded with prohibition. Under various names and by differing means man goes on seeking intoxicating substances.

As I see it, it is beyond the power of any government to enforce prohibition. But if the wine of samadhi begins to spread, if the real wine appears on the earth, the false will stop. If we make temples into taverns and there starts to be joy and songs and bliss and celebration, and if we live by healthy principles instead of the wrong ones and let life become a blessing—then alcohol will disappear on its own.

Man drinks wine because of misery. If misery decreases, wine will decrease. Man drinks alcohol to forget himself, because there are so many worries, so many problems, so much misery—if we don't forget them then what will we do? If worry, unhappiness, and misery are decreased, alcohol consumption will decrease.

And I have seen a rare thing happen: many times drunkards have come and taken sannyas from me. They got caught by mistake. They came to me, thinking 'This man does not prohibit anything: drinking or not drinking, eating or not eating this or that—there's no harm in trying. They were very happy.

They say, 'We totally agree with what you say, no one has ever said it before.' But as their meditation deepens, as the colour of sannyas deepens, their feet stop taking them to the tavern, another tavern begins to call them.

After meditating for six months one drinker told me, 'Previously I drank because I was unhappy, then I would forget the unhappiness. Now I am a little happy, and if I drink, happiness is forgotten. Now it has become a problem—no one wants to forget happiness. What have you done?'

I said, 'Now you choose.'

He said, 'Now if I drink, my meditation goes bad. Otherwise the slow gentle current of meditation flows inside, a faint cool breeze goes on flowing. If I drink wine then the flow of meditation is disturbed for two to four days. Then I can bring it back only with difficulty. Now it has become a problem.'

I told him, 'Now you will have to decide, now the choices are before you. If you want to drop meditation, drop meditation. If you want to drop alcohol, drop alcohol. They don't go together, but if you want to have both, then try both.'

He said, 'Now it is difficult because the juice of meditation that is flowing is so sacred and it is taking me to such heights—I had never imagined that a sinner like me could ever have such experiences! I don't talk about this to anyone except you because if I say it to anyone else they think I am a drunkard, I must have drunk too much. They tell me to sober up, speak soberly. If I tell them of my inner experience they think that I have drunk too much. They don't believe it. Even my wife won't believe it. She says, "Stop talking nonsense. This is not a question of spirituality . . . you have drunk too much." I tell her I have not touched a drop for a whole month.'

'So you are the only one I can tell,' the drunkard said, 'Only you understand. And now it is difficult to drop meditation.'

See life from a positive viewpoint. If you start being happy, then the things that you grabbed on to because of your misery will drop by themselves. If meditation comes, then wine will drop. If meditation comes, then meat-eating will drop. If meditation comes, then slowly, slowly sex energy begins to be transformed into brahmacharya. Just let meditation come.

I say unto you, drink the wine of meditation. I say unto you, enter the tavern of samadhi and join the assembly of wine drinkers.

Let me live this one moment of happiness.
Let me sew the torn blanket of dreams—
such a raincloud can never cast its shadow again.
Let me drink, if not from a cup, then from thy eyes.

Drink this satsang, 'if not from a cup, then from thy eyes'. Drink this satsang, return drunk from this satsang. But in this drunkenness don't let your awareness be lost. Be ecstatic, but burn the inner lamp of awareness.

Such a raincloud can never cast its shadow again,
let me drink, if not from a cup, then from thy eyes.

The fifth question:

Osho,
Are belief and autosuggestion one and the same thing? What is the difference between belief and inner nature, or awareness?
Was the Mother Kali of Ramakrishna Paramahansa purely his belief, his projection, or does she have her own reality?
Is dialogue not possible with the supernatural or God?

Belief and autosuggestion are the same thing. Autosuggestion is the scientific name for belief. There is no difference between them.

However, inner nature and belief are very different. Inner nature is that which becomes manifest when all beliefs have been dropped. When all thoughts and all beliefs have disappeared from your mind, you experience your inner nature. Inner nature is not to be made a belief.

Once a sannyasin was a guest at my house. He would sit morning and evening chanting 'Aham Brahmasmi—I am the ultimate reality. I am not the body, not the mind, I am the ultimate.'

I listened to this for two or three days. I said, 'If you are, you are. So why repeat it again and again? If you are not, then what will repeating it do?'

It is possible to create an illusion by repeating it over and over. By repeating, 'I am the ultimate' the illusion can happen that one has become the ultimate—but this illusion is not the inner experience of one's nature. If you know that you are the ultimate, then why do you repeat it? If a man is on the road repeating, 'I am a man, I am a man', then everyone will suspect that something is not right. People will say, 'Stop, is something wrong with you! Why are you repeating this? If it is true, then the matter is finished. Do you have some doubt about it?'

Is 'I am the ultimate reality' something to be repeated? It is a declaration made once and for all. It is a declaration of realization that arises only once. After that, the matter is finished. It is not a mantra. A mantra is only a suggestion; the meaning of the word 'mantra' is 'suggestion'. This is why we call people who give advice, who give suggestions, mantri—minister. A mantra is the repetition of a suggestion again and again. From repeating it again and again an impression is made in the mind, and because of that impression we begin to project illusions.

'Was the Mother Kali of Ramakrishna Paramahansa purely his belief, his projection, or does she have her own reality?'

It was pure projection—it was just his belief. There is no Kali anywhere, nor any Virgin Mary: they are all projections of the mind, and all projections have to drop. This is why, when Ramakrishna's projection of Kali dropped, he said the last barrier had fallen. It was his own projection. And when Ramakrishna raised a sword to behead his projection of Kali, do you think blood came out? Nothing came out. The projection was false, the sword was also false: two false things crashing into each other and nothing else.

'Is dialogue not possible with the supernatural or God?'

No! Whatever dialogue you have will be your imagination, because as long as you exist there is no God, and when God is you are not—how can there be any dialogue? Two are needed for dialogue. If you and God stand face-to-face then dialogue is possible. As long as you are, where is God? And when God is, where are you?

Kabir says:

The path of love is very narrow.
There, two cannot walk.

Two cannot walk on that path, two cannot fit, only one remains; so how can there be a dialogue? Two are required for a dialogue, a minimum of two.

So whoever you are talking to is in your imagination, it is not the real godliness. When godliness happens, dialogue does not happen: a roar happens; a declaration, not a dialogue . . . what the seers of the East have called 'the unstruck sound' happens—a sound of humming. But that vibration happens only in oneness, with no exchange of words with any other. It is the arising of the sound of aum. But it is not talking to any other, the other no longer remains.

No devotee has ever seen God. As long as God is seen, the devotee is also present. Then it is still an imaginary vision. This is why a Christian meets Jesus, a Jaina meets Mahavira, a Hindu meets Rama. Have you ever heard of a Hindu meeting Jesus? Somehow accidentally meeting Jesus on the road? They never meet him. It is not their projection, so how can they meet him? Have you ever heard of a Christian sitting in meditation and Buddha appears to him? It never happens. How can it happen? How can a seed that has not been planted by belief enter the imagination? Whatever your belief is, it will be developed by your imagination.

Ashtavakra's sutra is this: Be free of all projections, all beliefs, all imagination, all interpretations, all practices and rituals.

Practices and rituals are always bondage. When no one remains within you—no devotee, no God—then a silence manifests. In that silence a shower of bliss falls, day and night. In that moment how can there be dialogue, how can there be debate? No, all dialogue is only of the imagination.

A poet says:

Sometimes night surrounds me,
sometimes I summon the day.
Sometimes a radiance seeks me,
sometimes I radiate light.
How do I know when it is the voice of my being
and when it is the mind?

I tell you, the recognition is simple: as long as something is spoken, it is the mind speaking. As long as something is visible, the mind is visible. When nothing is seen, when nothing speaks—then what remains is no-mind, is samadhi.

As long as there is experience, there is mind. This is why the expression 'The experience of God' is not correct, because experience is always of the mind. Experience is always of duality, of two. How can there be experience when only non-duality remains? This is why the expression 'spiritual experience' is not correct. Spirituality is where all experience has ended.

Or you can go on playing games. It is a game of hide-and-seek, of sunlight and shadow. If you want to play, play. It is a delightful play of imagination, very lovely, very juicy—but it is the play of imagination. Do not pretend it is truth. Truth is when there is no I, no thou. Truth is when the two are gone, the duality is gone. Then only one remains: *Ek Omkar Satnam*—the sound of aum is the truth.

The last question:

> Osho,
>
> Trillions of bows to you! On sacred Mount Abu, I was blessed to come to the protection of your blessed hand. Since then there is no calculating how much I have lost, how much I have gained. My life has become a gratefulness, a benediction. No question comes, so I am making one up.
>
> Today, on the closing day of the meditation camp, my heart is restless to hear a couple of words from you. Please, just drop two flowers into my beggar's bowl today.

Why two. Let it be more.
Hari-om-tat-sat!

Osho International Meditation Resort

Each year the Meditation Resort welcomes thousands of people from more than 100 countries. The unique campus provides an opportunity for a direct personal experience of a new way of living—with more awareness, relaxation, celebration and creativity. A great variety of around-the-clock and around-the-year programme options are available. Doing nothing and just relaxing is one of them!

All of the programmes are based on Osho's vision of 'Zorba the Buddha'—a qualitatively new kind of human being who is able to *both* participate creatively in everyday life *and* relax into silence and meditation.

Location
Located 100 miles south-east of Mumbai in the thriving modern city of Pune, India, the OSHO International Meditation Resort is a holiday destination with a difference. The Meditation Resort is spread over 28 acres of spectacular gardens in a beautiful tree-lined residential area.

OSHO Meditations
A full daily schedule of meditations for every type of person includes both traditional and revolutionary methods, and particularly the OSHO Active Meditations™. The daily meditation programme takes place in what must be the world's largest meditation hall, the OSHO Auditorium.

OSHO Multiversity

Individual sessions, courses and workshops cover everything from creative arts to holistic health, personal transformation, relationship and life transition, transforming meditation into a lifestyle for life and work, esoteric sciences, and the 'Zen' approach to sports and recreation. The secret of the OSHO Multiversity's success lies in the fact that all its programmes are combined with meditation, supporting the understanding that as human beings we are far more than the sum of our parts.

OSHO Basho Spa

The luxurious Basho Spa provides for leisurely open-air swimming surrounded by trees and tropical green. The uniquely styled spacious Jacuzzi, the saunas, gym, tennis courts . . . all these are enhanced by their stunningly beautiful setting.

Cuisine

A variety of different eating areas serve delicious Western, Asian and Indian vegetarian food—most of it organically grown especially for the Meditation Resort. Breads and cakes are baked in the resort's own bakery.

Nightlife

There are many evening events to choose from—dancing being at the top of the list! Other activities include full-moon meditations beneath the stars, variety shows, music performances and meditations for daily life.

Facilities

You can buy all of your basic necessities and toiletries in the Galleria. The Multimedia Gallery sells a large range of OSHO media products. There is also a bank, a travel agency and a Cyber Café on campus. For those who enjoy shopping, Pune provides all the options, ranging from traditional and ethnic Indian products to all of the global brand-name stores.

Accommodation

You can choose to stay in the elegant rooms of the OSHO Guesthouse, or for longer stays on campus you can select one of the OSHO Living-In programmes. Additionally there is a plentiful variety of nearby hotels and serviced apartments.

www.osho.com/meditationresort
www.osho.com/guesthouse
www.osho.com/livingin

For more information

For a full selection of OSHO multilingual online destinations, see www.osho.com/allaboutosho.

The official and comprehensive website of OSHO International is www.osho.com.

For more OSHO unique content and formats see:

— OSHO Active Meditations: www.osho.com/meditate.
— iOsho, a bouquet of digital OSHO experiences featuring OSHO Zen Tarot, TV, Library, Horoscope, eGreetings and Radio. Please take a moment to do a one-time registration which will allow you a universal login. Registration is free and open to anyone with a valid email address: www. osho.com/iosho.
— The OSHO online shop: www.osho.com/shop.

- Visit the OSHO International Meditation Resort: www.osho.com/visit.
- Contribute to the OSHO Translation Project: www.oshotalks.com.
- Read the OSHO Newsletters: http://www.osho.com/read/newsletter.
- Watch OSHO on YouTube: www.youtube.com/user/OSHOInternational.
- Follow OSHO on Facebook: www.facebook.com/osho.international.meditation.resort.
- Follow OSHO on Twitter: www.twitter.com/OSHO.

Thank you for buying this OSHO book.